Inhabitants

of

Baltimore County
Maryland

1763-1774

Henry C. Peden, Jr.

HERITAGE BOOKS
2007

HERITAGE BOOKS

AN IMPRINT OF HERITAGE BOOKS, INC.

Books, CDs, and more—Worldwide

For our listing of thousands of titles see our website
at
www.HeritageBooks.com

Published 2007 by
HERITAGE BOOKS, INC.
Publishing Division
65 East Main Street
Westminster, Maryland 21157-5026

Copyright © 1989 Henry C. Peden, Jr.

International Standard Book Number: 978-1-58549-144-5

INTRODUCTION

The United States in modern times has been described as a mobile society. The same description could be applied to the Colony of Maryland. Individuals did move - from Europe to Maryland, from one colony to another, and even from one county to another. Unmarried and unpropertied individuals such as younger sons of landed families, newly freed servants, and recently arrrived artisans who wanted to seek their fortune elsewhere found it quite easy to pull up stakes, since they often had few, if any, stakes to pull up. Books like the present volume help to place an individual in a given geographic location at a specific time. Such placement can assist researchers in finding clues to that individual's origins in the colony or elsewhere.

Inhabitants of Baltimore County, Maryland, 1763-1774, is a welcome companion and sequel to Wright's Inhabitants of Baltimore County, 1692-1763. the present volume, compiled by Henry Peden contains lists of inhabitants for the period 1763-1774, and thus forms a vital link between the earlier volume and Peden's own two books of Revolutionary Patriots of Baltimore and Harford Counties, 1775-1783. Researchers now have a series of volumes containing the extant lists of inhabitants in Baltimore and its offspring counties, Harford and Carroll (eastern portion), stretching from the end of the 17th century through the Revolutionary period.

The lists are drawn from a variety of sources. Tax lists for the entire county (1773) and for St. Thomas' and St. Paul's Parish (1763 and 1774 respectively) represent official attempts to list the tithables -- all free males 16 years and over, plus in some cases the slaves. A second category of lists are the membership rosters of various groups such as the Mechanical Company (1763-1774), The Sons of Liberty (1766), Baltimore Mason(ic) Lodge No. 16 (1773), and the Baltimore Town and County Committee of Observation (1774). A third type of list is made up of several petitions and addresses (1763-1768). A final major grouping is that of lists found in some unusal places - the creditors of Samuel Hyde, prisoners in the county jail, and letters remaining in the post office.

The compiler has included an appendix made up of some lists from the 1692-1763 period that were found after the publication of the earlier volume.

Researchers using any of these "books of lists" will be able not only place an individual in the county at a given time, but in many cases will have some idea of the activities and associations of the inhabitants of early Baltimore County. Finding the name in one list may give clues to other sources to check. Someone in the Sons of Liberty may later have joined the Revolutionary effort, 1775-1783. A prisoner in the county jail may have come into the colony as a convict as listed in Peter Wilson Coldham's Complete Book of Emigrants in Bondage, 1614-1775 (Baltimore: The Genealogical Publishing Company, Inc., 1988).

The compiler is earning a well deserved reputation for helpful source materials. This volume will add to that reputation.

/s/ Robert Barnes

iii

In 1987, two important genealogical source books were published by Family Line Publications, both with respect to early Baltimore County, Maryland.

One book was compiled by F. Edward Wright and entitled Inhabitants of Baltimore County, 1692-1763 and the other was researched by this compiler and entitled Revolutionary Patriots of Baltimore Town and Baltimore County, Maryland 1775-1783.

As can be seen, the two books covered the period from 1692 through 1783 with the exception of 1764 to 1774. Thus, in order to fill in this gap and to publish some information that had been inadvertently left out of Mr. Wright's book, I prepared this book, Inhabitants of Baltimore County, 1763-1774.

Now researchers have available to them three Baltimore County genealogical source books containing "finding lists" ("unofficial censuses," if you will) for the colonial period spanning the 90 years between 1692 and 1783. Among other things, this book contains tax lists for 1763, 1773, 1774, and the Joppa Petition of 1768. Since Harford County was not carved out of Baltimore County until 1774, many of those named herein as residents of Baltimore County soon became inhabitants of Harford County (without physically moving) when the official change took place in March, 1774. Likewise, the eastern portion of now Carroll County was a part of Baltimore County until that county was established in 1837. Carroll County was formed from that portion of Baltimore County which contained North Hundred, Pipe Creek Hundred, Delaware Upper Hundred and and Delaware Lower Hundred – and a large section of Frederick County.

The sources for each list are contained within the text and I wish to express my appreciation for the help of the staff at the Maryland Historical Society Library Manuscript Division, and the assistance of the following people during the research of this book: F. Edward Wright, Martha Reamy, Marlene Bates, and Robert W. Barnes (who also prepared the Introduction).

I trust that this book will be a useful genealogical tool for those who research in early Baltimore County, including the areas covered by the present-day counties of Harford and eastern Carroll.

Henry C. Peden, Jr.

TABLE OF CONTENTS

INHABITANTS OF BALTIMORE COUNTY, MARYLAND, 1763-1774

A LIST OF TAXABLES IN ST. THOMAS PARISH IN THE YEAR 1763

The Tax List of 1763 for St. Thomas Parish was found by William N. Wilkins in 1959 in the Harford County Historical records on loan at the Maryland Historical Society. (Harford County was part of Baltimore County until 1773.) It contains entries for the four Hundreds of Soldiers Delight, Pipe Creek, Back River Upper, and Delaware. This 1763 tax ledger shows the names of the various parties against whom charges were made for apparent church and county support and other sundry charges. There were a few items in this tax ledger for years other than 1763 and they have been so identified. The following names are listed according to the arrangement given in the tax list; therefore, strict alphabetical conformity is not observed. The notation "run" meant that the person named had left before paying his full charges.

SOLDIERS DELIGHT HUNDRED, 1763

Ashman, George
Ashman, George Jr.
Ansell, Henry
Bond, Samuel
Bond, Benjamin
Bailey, John
Bailey, William
Bailey, George
Brooks, Humphrey
Baseman, William
Butler, Amon
Brothers, Nathaniel
Brothers, Thomas (run)
Branwell, George
Barber, Robert
Baker, Morris
Baseman, Joseph
Baker, Michael
Belt, Benenoni
Butler, John
Bardell, Joseph
Bowers, James
Bowers, Nicholas
Bosley, Jacob John
Baker, Isaac
Blazzard, William
Baker, Ketturah
Barney, Moses
Basey, John
Boocock, John
Bowers, Daniel
Bowers, Daniel
Boyer, Malachy
Baker, Joseph
Burk, Darby
Chapman, Nathan
Carter, John
Clarke, Henry
Choate, Solomon

Clarke, Clara
Cross, Robert
Clark, John
Clarke, Charles
Collyday, Jacob
Chynoth, Arthur, Jr.
Chinoth, Arthur
Chapman, John
Crosswell, James
Connoway, Aquilla
Craddock, Rev. Thomas
Cook, John
Croxall, John
Davis, Richard
Davis, Robert
Davis, Nathaniel
Day, Stephen
Dunkin, Patrick
Demmitt, Sophia
Demmitt, William
Dorsey, Francis
Dailey, Toole
Dayer, Henry
Dunkin, Patrick
Demmitt, William
Dorsey, Francis
Dailey, Toole
Dayer, Henry
England, John
Frizzell, Jacob
Frizzell, John
Gist, John
Griffith, James
Griffith, Jonathan
Griffith, Benjamin
Goose, Adam
Griffith, John
Gosnell, William
Gosnell, John

Gosnell, Mordecai
Gosnell, Zebediah
Gosnell, Yaunal
Gosnell, Peter Jr.
Gosnell, Peter Sr.
Gilreath, Robert
Greewalt, George
Gallahoth, Peter
Gladman, Michael Jr.
Gladman, Michael Sr.
Gervis, Mead
Gibbins, John
Gallohorn, Francis
Gest, William Sr.
Goins, Jason
Goodwin, George
Gest, Joseph
Green, Joseph
Hambleton, Rachael
Hammond, Isaac
Hodge, John
Hammond, Mordecai
Hurd, John
Hanes, Michael
Howard, Richard
Hambleton, Sarah
Hambleton, John (He ran
  away last spring; owes
  500 lbs.)
Howard, Charles
Harwood, James (He ran
  away a long time ago.)
Hazer, Casper
Howard, Cornelius
Harvy, Thomas
Hall, Elisha (His
  Quarters)
Holder, Charles

1

Harvy, William Sr.
Harvy, William Jr.
Hambleton, William
Hammond, Lawrence
Frush, Francis
Isgrigg, William Sr.
Igoe, William
Igoe, William
Israel, Gilbert
Igoe, Daniel
Jacks, Richard Sr.
Jacks, Thomas
Jacks, Richard Jr.
Jones, Evan (dead)
Jones, John (His
  Quarters)
Jones, Nicholas (His
  Quarters)
Jones, John
Kelley, William
Knight, Benjamin
Lane, Dutton Sr.
Lane, Dutton Jr.
Lane, William
Lane, Thomas
Longworth, Peter
Lett, Zachariah
Lee, Edward
Lewis, John
Lett, Robert
Lett, Samuel
Leavens, Thomas
Lyons, John (His
  Quarters)
Lyons, William (His
  Quarters)
Lant, John (William
  Isgriggs, Security)
Mathews, George
Mannell, Samuel
Murrick, Thomas
McLane, Alexander
McCoile, Philip
Murrey, James
Mash, Richard
Marsh, William
Murphey, William
Mason, William
McLane, William
McLane, John
Munk, Reneldo
Moales, John (His
  Quarters)
Mash, Josias
Mash, John

Orick, Nicholas
Oysler, Edward
Oysler, Ele (Edward
  Oysler was his
  security) Odle, John
Odle, Walter
Owings, Thomas
Owings, Joshua
Owings, Joshua Jr.
Owings, Stephen
Owings, Henry
Porter, Thomas Jr.
Porter, Richard
Parrish, Richard Sr.
Parrish, Edward (of
  John)
Parrish, John
Puntney, Edward
Piper, Henry
Punbarton, Henry
Petticoat, William Jr.
  Petticoat, William
  Sr. Petticoat, Nathan
Parrish, Edward Sr.
Parrish, Richard Jr.
  (His Security: Edward
  Parrish)
Parker, James
Parker, Thomas
Pickaw, Joseph
Penny, Henry (His
  Security was Henry
  Warrell)
Robinson, Absolom (His
  Security was N.
  Brothers)
Richards, Isaac
Richards, Richard
Rystow, John
Rogers, Benjamin (His
  Qtrs.)
Randall, Christian
Robinson, John Sr.
Rowles, John (His
  Security was William
  Murphy)
Randall, Roger
Randall, Christian Jr.
  Randall, John (not in
  county)
Reasteau, George
Rowles, Jacob
Rutter, Thomas (His
  Security was John
  Jones)

Rucas, Henry
Rawlings, Aaron
Stodgsdale, Solomon
Stodgsdale, Thomas Sr.
Stodgsdale, Edward
Spring, James
Slyder, Christian
Sandey, John
Stinchcomb, John
Stinchcomb, Nathaniel
Spike, Joseph (Wm.
  Petticoat, Security)
Shalmedine, John or
  Shamedine, John
Sunkins, John
Simson, Samuel (N.
  Orrick, Security)
Saint, John
Stocksdale, John (His
  Security was Charles
  Howard)
Solomon, Robert
Sollers, Francis
Seabrooks, William
Sanders, Benjamin
Saysor, Felix
Thomas, Edward
Treakle, Stephen (His
  Security was Stephen
  Wilkinson)
Treakle, William (His
  Security was John
  Hambleton)
Tayler, Samuel (His
  Security was Thomas
  Yarman)
Tryal, George
Wattling, John
Walker, Henry
Worrell, Henry
Wells, Thomas
Willson, John (His
  Security was William
  Willson)
Wason, Thomas
Wells, John
Winters, Martin
Wells, Benjamin
Wells, Charles
White, Charles (in Anne
  Arundel Co.)
Wetherington, Thomas
Willson, William
Wright, William
Weaver, Lodowick
Yarman, Thomas
Zimmerman, Mathew

SOLDIERS DELIGHT HUNDRED, 1763

The following persons were in arrears for last year's taxes:

Colleral, Henry
Carter, Robert (can't find)
Cox, Samuel
Cresswell, Robert
Gladman, John
Glover, Thomas (run a long time)
Horn, Ludwick (run)
Hawkins, Elizabeth (can't find)
Hollwell, Sarah (can't find)
Jordon, Robert (tho't in Delaware)

McQuery, William (run)
Nash, John at John Parrishes (run)
Peer, Malair (can't find)
Smith, John
Stockdale, Samuel (can't find)
Smith, James
Shoat, Solomon
Seuville, Comfort
Wallen, John
Williams, William

PIPE CREEK HUNDRED, 1763

Alken, Jacob
Aclar, Jacob
Aclar, Volmck
Brown, John
Beekle, Henry
Baxter, Greenbury
Brown, William
Belt, Richard
Belt, Nathan
Belt, Jemiah
Belt, John
Booker, Henry
Burns, Michael
Borin, Ezekiel
Burns, John
Burns, Adam
Brothers, Tobias
Belt, Leonard
Brock, William
Brown, William (of
A.A.County At South
River Ferry)
Bell, John (run)
Brost, Conrod (in North
Hundred)
Crease, Philip
Carter, Thomas
Cummill, Martin
Crady, John
Creag, Hugh
Comely, James
Christholm, John (A. A.
County)
Deal, Philip
Deane, John Jr.
Dunbo, Conrod
Decker, Ruda
Dean, John Sr.
Decker, Frederick
Decker, Stohl

Driscal, David (In
Baltimore Town, goes by
water)
Epaw, Jacob
Estub, John
Earb, Peter
Everhart, George
Fisher, John
Fisher, Michael
Fisher, George
Grimer, Peter
Giles, William (Sec:
Robert Story)
Grose, Francis
Hooker, Samuel
Hooker, Richard
Hooker, Thomas
Hennestophel, Henry
Helms, John
Hoke, Peter
Havaner, Michael
Hendrick, James
Hudson, Rober
Hall, William
(Elkridge)
John, James
Johnson, Jeremiah
Kiddinger, John
Klink, William
Laine, Daniel
Louderslagle, Philip
Louderman, George
Loveall, Tebton
Loveall, Henry
Loveall, Ethan
Loveall, Luthan
Laine, Samuel Jr.
Lusby, Peter
Lingfelty, Daniel
(Security: Peter Euler)

Lippy, Conrod
Little, John
McQueen, Thomas
McQueen, William
Murrah, Josephas
McHard, John
Morrow, William
Mesar, Richard
McQuane, Samuel
Magers, John
Mollton, Ester
(Security: Jeremeah
Johnson)
Mane, Margaret
Nearover, John
Osborn, Joseph (Spelt
Osbirn)
Osborn, Daniel (Spelt
Osbirn)
Osborn, John(Spelt
Osbirn)
Oats, Jacob
Oats, Henry
Piler, Ledwick
Pilar, Conrod
Parrish, William Jr.
Plowman, John
Plowman, Jonathan
Peace, Nicholas
Plowman, John Sr.
Patrick, Charles
Rivel, John
Rease, Adam
Rinehart, Ludwick
Ritter, Ludwick
Richards, Richard
Reese, Milken
Reese, Henry
Roberts, William

3

Ridgely, Henry
  (Elkridge)
Stapleton, Francis
Story, Thomas
Story, Robert
Snap, Peter
Shake, Adam
Stiles, William
Shuster, Francis
Scott, Thomas

Stropel, Zachariah
  (Sec: Peter Earb)
Shepherd, Nathan (Sec:
  Robert Story)
Sence, Christopher
Sence, Peter
Shower, John
Salbecker, Henry
Smith, Mary (not in
  county)

Smith, Henry (can't
  find; abt 5 miles from
  Deer Park, 7-5-1761)
Trash, Jacob
Vaughn, Christian
Upperco, Jacob
Williams, Luke
Welty, Andrew (or
  Andran)
Woyes, Adam
Wright, Isaac
Winchester, William

The following persons were shown as being in arrears for last year:

Cairey, John
Collinger, Henry
Carbolt, Thomas (dead)
Dean, Joshua
Gorden, Robert (tho't in
  Delaware)
Hooper, Richard (tho't
  in Delaware)
Kelley, Charles
Kelley, William
Lowry, Godfrey (dead)
Magis, Peter (run)

McGee, Peter (run)
Organ, William (run)
Parrish, Robert (Sec:
  John Helms)
Palmer, John (dead)
Rind, John (In Calvert)
Shrimplen, John (run -
  lives in Frederick)
Scott, Fred (can't
  find)
Tomes, Christian (lives
  in Frederick)

Tumbolt, Conrod (lives
  in Frederick)
Taylor, Benjamin (can't
  find)
Trush, Martin (run -
  dead)
Utz, Peter
Wout, George
Way, John (can't find)
Willson, William

ACCOUNT OF JEREMIAH JOHNSON, DEPUTY SHERIFF, 1764-1771

Various items of debit and credit found in the account of JEREMIAH JOHNSON, DEPUTY SHERIFF UNDER A. HALL. ITEMS, NOT VERY MANY, RUN FROM THE YEAR 1764 TO 1771. Among names shown in these items are:

YEAR 1764: Edward Corbin, Reese Bowers, William Parrish, William Barneys, John Dean, and Robinson Chilicoate.

YEAR 1765: S. Owings, Jr., John Belt, Samuel Owings, John Evans, Zebediah Baker, John Gosnell, Joseph Gosnell, George Smith, William Scarf, Margarett Shipley, Adam Shipley, Sull Young, Vashall Young, Edward Hewitt, Mordecai Gosnell, Martin Snyder, Thomas Staines, Jeremiah Belt, William Brock, John Kittinger, Ester Motter, Conrod Pilar, Charles Patrick, Peter Gallohoth, Isaac Richards, Richard Richards, William Marsh, Samuel Cox, Moses Black, Richard Gornet, William Patterson, Nicholas Smith, James Simms, Samuel Buchanan, Jeremiah Lary, John Morrison, Edward Butler, Benjamin Barney, Conrod Brost, Benjamin Cross, Solomon Cross, James Demmitt (or Demitt), John Gruir (or Gruin), Jr., Stophal Killyear, George Killyear, Mordecai Cross, and Corbin Lane.

YEAR 1767: John Plowman, John Tipton, William Murry, Elias Harrage (?), John Silman, Mordecai Gosnell, and James Simms.

Ambrose, William
Ancil, Henry
Abbott, Oliver
Asquith, Thomas
Asherton, Joshua
Annice, John
Bramwell, George
Bond, Susannah
Banks, John
Bond, Nichodemus
Bosley, John Sr.
Bowen, Benjamin
Bowen, Solomon
Bowen, Rees
Bowen, Joseph Jr.
Barram, Joseph
Britton, Nicholas
Burham, John
Burnby, Thomas
Bowen, Nathan
Barney, William Jr.
Bond, John
Buchanan, Archibald,
  Qtrs.
Beard, George Adam
Buchanan, Andrew, Qtrs.
Boan, Edward (At Andrew
  Buchanan Qtrs.)
Baisey, John
Baltemore, John
Bowen, John
Bosley, Walter
Bellows, Elizabeth
Brown, Edward
Cockey, Edward
Craddock, Thomas, Qtrs.
Carroll, Charles, Qtrs.
Clapton, Joseph
Cromwell, Nathan
Cromwell, Joseph Jr.
Cumley, Joseph
  (Security:
  Mordecai Price)
Cross, Richard
Carnan, Christopher
Cockey, Thomas
Constancy, Patrick
Chambers, James
Cole, William (Britton
  Ridge)
Cole, Samuel
Cockey, John
Cockey, Joshua
Curtis, Daniel
Colegate, John

Cole, Celathael
Cole, Dennis Garrett
Cole, Henry (Security:
  Dennis G. Cole)
Cromwell, John
Cox, John
Cole, William
Colegate, Cassandra
Cole, Thomas Sr.
Chenworth, Richard
Cole, George Jr.
Cockey, William
Deaver, Stephen (Spelt
  Dever)
Daughertery, John
Daughertery, Richard
Deye, Penelope
Deye, Thomas Cockey
Deer, John
Deaver, Benjamin
Deaver, Henry
Dumbald, Frederick
Ensor, John, Qtrs.
Ford, John
Ford, Thomas
Ford, Benjamin
French, Robert
Ferrell, James
Ford, Mordecai
Fishpaw, John
Fancut, William
Fogal, Ludwick
Francis, Samuel
  (Sec: John White)
Fryer, George (taken
  also by name Tryal)
Gorsuch, Charles
Gorsuch, William
Goodwin, George
Gott, Richard
Green, Henry (taken in
  Middle River Hundred,
  folio 6 [sic])
Gorsuch, Loveless
Gill, Stephen
Gill, John Sr.
Gill, John Jr.
Gill, William
Gott, Samuel
Gott, Anthony
Govans, William
Green, Thomas (Sec:
  John Lowers)
Goodwin, John
Gooden, Henry

Hair, John
Hammond, Benjamin
Howard, John (son of
  Phil)
Howard, Benjamin (Sec:
  John Howard)
Hooks, Joseph
Hooks, Jacob
Hall, James
Hail, Nicholas
Hopkins, Richard
Hail, George Sr.
Hail, George Jr.
Hopkins, Samuel
Howland, John (run)
Haile, Neal
Hooker, Thomas
Hudgell, Joseph (Sec:
  Dalee Hudgell)
Harbott, William (Sec:
  James Hammond)
Hawkins, Joseph (for
  Ford, Stephen the
  second time)
Huttson, Thomas
Hisor, Godfrey
Halloway, Thomas (Sec:
  William Nethercliff)
Hawkins, John Jr.
Hawkins, Joseph (Sec:
  John Hawkins
Hammond, James
Hurd, James
Jones, Thomas (Security:
  Christopher Carnan)
Isor, John
Jones, John (Security:
  Mordecai Price)
Jones, Benjamin
Isor, Samuel
Johnson, Richard (Sec:
  Joshua White)
Jackson, George
Jetter, John (run)
King, William
Kelley, James Sr.
Kelley, Nathan
King, Henry
Keepaut, Matthias
Legree, Jeremiah
Leekings, James
Lane, John
Motherby, Charles
Matthews, Thomas (Sec:
  Sam Worthington)

5

Moals, John
Miller, John
Matthews, Oliver
Males, John (has run)
Maples, John
Nethercliff, William
Nailor, John
Owings, Samuel
Owings, Beal
Owings, Bazil
Pindell, John
Philpot, Brian, Qtrs.
Price, Mordecai
Price, Aquilla
Price, William Sr.
Powell, Benjamin
Pring, James
Pasor, George
Price, John
Parks, William
Parrish, William Sr.
  (William Parrish
  himself is levy free)
Parrish, Edward (son of
  William)
Price, Stephen
Pearce, William
Ristau, George, Qtrs.
Ridgley, Charles Sr.
Ridgley, Charles Jr.
Risteau, Isaac, Qtrs.
Randall, William (Spelt
  Randell)
Randell, William (Second
  time)
Raven, Abraham
Rhodes, Showl Thomas
Sayter, George
Sowers, John
Stevenson, Henry Jr.
Stansbury, John
Stevenson, Henry Sr.
Swan, James
Sparks, David
Stansbury, Thomas Jr.
Stansbury, Thomas Jr.
  (son of Thomas Jr.)

Sollers, John
Tipton, Thomas Jr.
Towson, William
Towson, Ezekiel
Tipton, William
Tye, George
Talbot, Edward
Tee, John
Turnbull, Frederick
Talley, William Towson
Tully, Edward
Taylor, Thomas
Taylor, John (Sec:
  Thomas Towson)
Tiffin, Mary
Van Sant, Isaac (also
  shown as Isaiah)
Wells, Francis
Worthington, Samuel
Worthington, Vachel
West, Jonathan
Willmott, Robert
Willmott, John
Wheeler, Wason
Wheeler, William Jr.
Wheeler, Solomon
Whoolf, Michael
Willson, Peter
Wing, Valentine
Young, Jacob
Yaun, Yowm (?)

The following persons
  were in arrears for
  last year's tax:
Carr, Elizabeth (can't
  find)
Deaver, Samuel (can't
  find)
Deaver, Ann (can't
  find)
Drake, Francis (in Pat.
  Upper)
Davis, James (can't
  find)

Falchin, Phillip (in
  Pat. Upper)
Ford, Lloyd (in Patapsco
  Lower)
Ford, Leah (can't find)
Fowler, John (in
  Frederick)
Ford, Benjamin
Green, Joseph
Gudgeon, Mary
Huddleston, Robert
  (can't find)
Hawen, Joseph (can't
  find)
(Joseph Wells, Security)
Harwood, James (run)
Musgrove, Ant. (run)
McCubbins, Joshua
McGumney, David
Nicholas, John Williams
Pinkham, Richard (in
  Patapsco Upper)
Paus, Nicholas (run)
Price, William Jr.
  (can't find)
Roach, Samuel (can't
  find)
Richards, Abraham (run)
Rawlings, Richard
Right, John (run)
Scarf, Joseph (can't get
  him in North Hundred)
Shauld, Joseph
Seals, William (Sec: Jo.
  Clapton)
Stevenson, James
Tipton, Mary
Tipton, Thomas
Towry, Thomas (run)
West, Thomas
Waller, Christopher
Whey, Richard
Walker, John
Wheeler, Benjamin (dead)

Anderson, William
Arnel, William
Askren, Thomas
Brown, Abel Sr.
Brown, Abel Jr.
Brown, David
Brown, Jacob
Brown, John
Brothers, Francis
Bennett, Thomas Jr.
Boren, William
Buchenham, John
Buchenham, Benjamin
Bennett, Thomas Sr.
Brunts, John
Barnes, John
Baker, Absol
Benion, Peter
Baker, Dimion
Barnes, Richard
Baker, Silvester
Baker, Charles
Baker, John
Baker, Zebediah
Baker, Greensberry
Bly, Robert
Burkett, Israel
Boring, Elizabeth
Brown, Mary
Brown, George Jr.
Beatty, Thomas
Baker, Abner
Baker, Bazil
Baker, Nathan
Bennett, Joseph
Boring, William (son of Thomas)
Chapman, Robert
Crage, John
Coals, William Qtrs
Chapman, Robert Sr.
Carr, Daniel Sr.
Chaney, Benj. Burgess
Corvel, Frederick
Cindle, William
Chapman, Luke
Chapman, Robert Jr.
Chapman, James (Sec: Robert Chaney)
Cille, Charles
Cille, James
Criswell, Richard
Crage, William
Cook, Thomas
Clary, Benjamin

Condon, David
Cook, Robert
Dorsey, Nicholas Sr.
Dorsey, Nicholas Jr.
Dahaven, Isaac
Doughaday, James
Deaver, Philip
Dillen, James
Dorsey, Charles
Dorsey, Lanslot
Dorsey, Andrew
Dorsey, Edward
Dorsey, John, Qtrs.
Davison, William
Davis, Francis
Dorsey, Vachael
Diggs, Exrs (?)
Esteps, John
Edwards, John
Evens, Job
Evens, John (He has John Hooker, but says one taxable)
Fowler, John
Franklin, Thomas
Franklin, Charles
Frizzel, Jason
Greathouse, Harmon
Gosage, Loveless, Qtrs.
Gladman, John
Glover, John
Gardner, Christopher
Gosnell, Peter
Gosnell, Charles
Gosnell, Joseph
Gillis, John
Hooker, Richard
Hawkins, Abraham
Hawkins, Benjamin
Howard, Jos., Qtrs.
Hudson, Mathew
Harris, Benjamin
Holebrook, John
Hooker, Barney
Huet, Edward
Hammond, Reason, Qtrs.
Holden, John
Hewitt, Edward
Henry, Howard
Jurden, Robert
Lindsey, Anthony
Lane, Corbin
Logstone, Laurance
(Sec: Wm. Logstone)

Lane, Samuel Sr.
Lane, Samuel Jr. (In Pipe Creek)
Lowry, James
Lynther, Martin
Marsh, John
Messer, Luke
Mattox, William
Mattox, Benjamin
Mecollester, Robert
Macklefish, David
Neph, Henry
Ogg, George Jr.
Ogg, Dunken
Ogg, William
Ogg, George Sr.
Overy, Brian
Owens, Richard
Pool, Richard
Petticoat, Nicholas
Shipley, Peter
Smith, George
Smith, Richard
Stevens, James
Suel, Christopher
Selmon, Thomas
Shipley, James
Shipley, Samuel
Suel, Samuel (also spelt Sewel)
Shipley, Adam
Selmon, John (J. Johnson must pay)
Scarfe, William
Shipley, Greenbery
Shipley, Margaret
Shipley, Absolom
Stevens, Thomas
Stocksdale, William
Stocksdale, Thomas
Shivers, John
Shepard, Charles
Stevens, Abraham
Shipley, Richard
Stocksdale, Thomas
Swoope, Benjamin
Snyder, Martin
Stump, Peter
Shaver, Christian
Strauble, Zachariah
Shipley, Ezekiel
Staines, Thomas
Tevis, Robert
Tevis, Peter
Tevis, Nathaniel

DELAWARE HUNDRED, 1763

Taylor, Francis
Wagers, Benjamin
Whips, Susannah
Wells, Valentine
Williams, Shadrick
Wagers, William
Wilson, William

Wright, John
Williams, Mary
Wilson, William
Whips, John
Wright, Joshua
Williams, Owen

Young, Henry
Young, Sewell
Young, Joshua
Young, Vachel
Young, James
Yeo, William

Note by William N. Wilkins: The last six pages of Delaware Hundred are missing. Last page of this Hundred is marked as #22. The names on these missing pages, however, can be determined from the index; thus, all of the names are shown.

Historical Notes on St. Thomas Parish, Baltimore County: In a deed, bearing date July 4, 1743, Christopher Gist of Baltimore County, Gentleman, conveyed to William Hamilton, Samuel Owings, Christopher Randall and Nicholas Haile, two acres of ground, part of "Adventure." According to this deed, the parties of the second part had been empowered by the Act of Assembly dated September 21, 1742 to purchase land "and thereupon erect a chapell of ease for the forest inhabitants of St. Paul's Parish," and by the same Act of Assembly, it was provided that on the death of the then incumbent of St. Paul's Parish the hundreds of Soldiers Delight and Back River Neck were to be separated from St. Paul's Parish and erected into a new parish called St. Thomas Parish. (Maryland Historical Magazine, 15:352) In the Proceedings of the Baltimore County Court for November, 1755 (Liber BB, No. B, ff. 390-391) will be found an order for dividing Soldiers Delight into three hundreds: "The lowest (still called Soldiers Delight).....a new Hundred called Delaware hundred.....and another new hundred called Pipe Creek Hundred....." (Maryland Historical Magazine, 15:351). The early church register and vestry proceedings of St. Thomas Parish Church (1732-1850) are on file at the Maryland Historical Society in Baltimore, MD. They were published by Bill and Martha Reamy in 1987 and the book is available from Family Line Publications, Rear 63 E. Main Street, Westminster, MD 21157. (Ed. Note)

PETITION FOR ORGANIST FOR ST. PAUL'S PARISH, CIRCA 1763

This undated petition appears to have been presented circa 1763 by sundry inhabitants of St. Paul's Parish who sought legislative authority to impose a tax not exceeding three pounds of tobacco on the taxable inhabitants of the parish to hire an organist to play "the very good organ" at Saint Paul's Church. (Archives of Maryland, Vol. 61, p.499-500, and, Calendar of MD State Papers, The Black Books, p. 189)

Thomas Chase
N. Ruxton Gay
John Moale

William Rogers
J. Ridgely
Andrew Buchanan

Mayberry Helms, Jr.
Richard Moale
William Sanders

8

PETITION FOR ORGANIST FOR ST. PAUL'S PARISH, CIRCA 1763

Mayberry Helms
William Lock
Christopher Carnan
F. Jones
Thomas Dick
Brian Philpot, Jr.
Alexander Stenhouse
Jonathan Plowman
Henry Stevenson
W. Wilkinson
Richard King Stevenson
Thomas Johnson
William Lux
William Lyon
John Orrick
Daniel Donovan
William Hacket
Jacob Mayer
John Stark
Conrad Schmidt
Samuel Messerschmidt
Friedrich Meyer
Phillip Baker
Conrad Conrath (?)
------ Schaub (?)

Samuel Hooke
Michel Dieffenbach (?)
Jacob Hook
Jacob Richbortz
William Hansman
Rudolf Galkmann, or
  Rudolf Gallimann (?)
Carl Schiel
Jonathan Hanson
William Carter
John McLure
William Mackubin
Elisha Hall
John Reddin
David Gorsuch
Valentine Larsch
Alexander Stewart
James Cary
John Carnan
John Pibbrasch
Martin Hinner, or
  Martin Schmidt (?)
Henry Tar
Philip Fisher
Job Garrison

John Shepheard, or John
  Physhard (?)
Edmund Talbott
Joseph Bankson
John Merryman, Jr.
Edward Fell
James Cole
John Stansbury, Jr.
Daniel Bernitz, or Daner
  Berwitz (?)
John Moller, or John
  Haller (?)
Caspar Grasmick
Heinrich Hofsteter
Heinrich Huber
Racherd ---aith (?)
Jacob Reichert, or Jacob
  Wichert (?)
Johannes Schrimm
Johannes Paull (?)
Georg Fredich Baum
Peter Littig
Vitus Hartweg
Andrew Steiger, or
  Andreas Steiger (?)

MECHANICAL COMPANY OF BALTIMORE, 1763-1774

On September 22, 1763, a number of settlers in the town of Baltimore met at the store of Melchior Keener on the corner of Charles and Pratt Streets and organized an association of men for the protection of themselves and all under their charge. Known as the Mechanical Company of Baltimore (a name proposed by Mark Alexander in deference to the large number of tradesmen enrolled), the Company soon took an important role in the conduct of the town's affairs. While the act of joining was purely voluntary, dues were required of each member, and fines imposed without mercy for absence, neglect of duty and non-payment of dues. Muster was held at regular intervals. In his book The Ancient and Honorable Mechanical Company of Baltimore, George McCreary wrote, in 1901, that "from 1763 to 1820 there was not a protest, not a proclamation, not a subscription for any purpose whatsoever, in which Mechanical members were not prominent, and in many cases, formed the major part." Names of the early members of the Company were given as follows:

1763: Gerard Hopkins, Thomas Burgess, Edward Sanders, Isaac Grist, David McClellan, David Rusk, John Dever, Aaron Mattison, Alex. Leith, John Cannon, William Richardson, Elisha Hall, Paul Pennington, Benjamin Dugan, Hugh Burgess, Basil Stiles, Richard Mason, Elias Barnaby, John Shule, David Shields, William Laverly, Christopher Nice, Melchior Keener, Frederic Myers, John Wilkerson, John Lee, Philip Graw, Philip Grace, George Presstman, Thomas Worthington, James Holliday, Jacob Myers, Levanal Barry, William Lobel, Jacob Brown, Thomas Constable, John Gorden, Robert Moore, Jacob Welsh, Frederic Cole, Richard Lemmon, William Wesley, John Clements, William Duncan, William

MECHANICAL COMPANY OF BALTIMORE, 1763-1774

Clem, Andrew Davidson, Cornelius Garrison, James Edwards, Henry Lorah and, as mentioned in the same book, probably John Flemming.

1764-1765: Nicholas Rittenhouse, Michael Patten, David Evens, William Spear, David Poe, Jacob Rhume, Lewis Philip Hopkins, Peter Frick, Michael Diffendaffer, Philip Yeiser, Erasmus Uhler, William Wilson, William Forepaugh, Michael Shrigley, William Rodgers, Christopher Raborg, Joseph Slater, George Keeport, Daniel Grant, James Calhoun, Richard Lawson, David Emmit, Jesse Hollingsworth, Edward Johnson, Throughgood Smith, and Philip Graybill.

1766-1768: Joshua Bosley, William Adams, John Chambers, Thomas Croxall, Isaac Burnetson, Archee Campbell, Cyprian Wells, James Cox, Emanuel Kent, Robinson James, George Nace, William Askew, Elisha Winters, William Goddard, Cumberland Dugan, Anthony Pontier, William Lusby, Adam Fonerden, John Dukehart, Isaac Hill, Mark Alexander, Benjamin Griffith, Michael Allen, Daniel Bowley, Hercules Courtney, George Lindenberger, and William Aisquith.

1769-1770: John Sterns, William Lyon, David McMechen, Robey Adair, John McClure, Paul Bentalou, Francis Sanderson, David Strother, William Nelson, Francis Dawes, Mordecai Amos, John Jeffers, Thomas Morgan, Robert Sinclair, David Geddes, James Wainwright, William Merryman, John Norris, Benjamin Dutton, Peter Perine, John Barrow, Ignatius Jenkins, George Duvall, William Lux, Oliver Cromwell and Zebulon Hollingsworth.

1770-1774: John Hawkins, William Cook, Isaac Taylor, David Yearks, Sol Morgan, George Franciscus, John S. Martin, Henry Didier, Thomas W. Chiplane, Francis Curtis, Francis Hager, Abram Ensor, Frederic Shaffer, George Dutro, James Dorsey, John Hillen, John Hays, Nathaniel Peck, Henry Payson, James McCullough, James Fleming, John Brice, Baltzel Shafer, William Sharpe, Frederic D. Seidenstricker, Obediah Starr.

SONS OF LIBERTY IN BALTIMORE, 1766

In February, 1766, a number of Baltimore citizens met in the "Lodge Room" of the Mechanical Company of Baltimore and organized what was afterwards known as the "Sons of Liberty." The membership increased rapidly and they took upon themselves the duties of maintaining order and protecting property. Subsequently, the order was extended into the counties, and the members enrolled for the defense of the colonies during the Revolutionary War. The following members of the Mechanical Company of Baltimore were members of the Sons of Liberty. (McCreary, George W. The Ancient and Honorable Mechanical Company of Baltimore, pp. 18-19)

Aaron Levington, William Baker, Samuel Hollingsworth William Willson, John McLane (McLure?), Daniel Bowley, Caleb Hall, Elisha Winters, Michael Allen, George Leverly, John Dever, James Cox, David Shields, Gerard Hopkins, George Lindenberger, Erasmus Uhler, Richard Moale, William Clemm, Hercules Courtney John Sterrett, Robey Adair, Benjamin Griffith, William Aisquith, Melchior Keener, William Spear, James Sterrett, Archibald Buchanan, William Lyon, Isaac Grist, George Patton, William Lux, George Duvall, George Wells, James Calhoun, David Rusk, Cyprian Wells

LIST OF CREDITORS OF SAMUEL HYDE, 1764

The following notice appeared in The Maryland Gazette on September 13, 1764: "Pursuant to a letter, which I received lately from John Hyde, Esq., of London, I hereby give notice to those persons who were creditors of his brother Samuel Hyde, of London, Merchant, for the sums affixed to their respective names mentioned in the following list, or to their representatives, that the subscriber will attend at the house of Mrs. Orrick, in Baltimore-Town, the sixth day of November, to pay the said sums to the persons, on their applying to him at that time and place; but if any whose names are inserted, did proceed by way of attachment against the effects of the said Samuel Hyde, so as to run him or his estate to any costs, they need not apply; for payments are only intended for those who did not proceed to recover their debts, or those who may have proceeded and did not recover without burdening him or his effects with costs. Signed: Charles Ridgely, Jr."

The list contains 186 names of persons residing in Anne Arundel, Baltimore, Patowmack, Patuxent, Herring Bay and the Clifts. The highest amount owed to one creditor was seven pounds, sixteen shillings (7.16), with the average being around two pounds. The fifty creditors who lived in Anne Arundel and Baltimore were grouped together and separated from the rest, as shown on the following list:

Atkinson, John 3.14
Baynard, Hester 1.10
Bond, Thomas 2.3
Burle, John 1.7
Clarke, Robert 1.7
Chocke, John 2.2
Colegate, Benjamin 0.18
Day, Edward 5.2
Dyer, Penelope 1.5
Frisby, Peregrine 2.14
Gay, Nicholas Ruxton 1.7
Giles, John 0.6
Hanson, Samuel 2.2
Hanson, John 2.2
Hammond, Col. Charles 2.10
Hall, William 0.17
Hammond, Philip 0.12
Hughes, Thomas 0.13
Hughes, Mary 0.14
Italian John Poteet 1.6
Lloyd, John 0.7
Lusby, Jacob 0.14
Lusby, Robert 0.13
Hughes, John 0.3

Maccomas, William 0.12
Maccomas, Daniel 3.14
Matthews, Elizabeth 2.3
Marshal, Mary 1.14
Mead, Edward 0.4
Middlemore, F. Edward 1.5
Owings, Samuel 0.5
Orsler, Edward 0.17
Pribell, John 0.12
Pumphrey, Ebenezer Jr 1.13
Puttee, Lewis 3.12
Preston, James 3.2
Pike, William 4.8
Rigby, James 3.2
Risteau, Talbott 0.11
Rhode, Richard 0.14
Roberts, John 0.18
Shay, Thomas 0.4
Tolly, Walter 0.5
Thomas, David 2.14
Wheeler, Benjamin 4.19
Brown, George 5.16
Day, John Jr. 7.14
Macgill, James 5.14

This portion of the debt book, most of which is missing, is held in the Manuscript Division (MS.1711) of the Maryland Historical Society, Baltimore. Only pages 103 to 109 of the original ledger remain. It shows the residents' names, their land tracts and the quit rent owed [not included here].

John Shelmerdine - part of Mt. Organ and Simkin's Addition; Ising Glass Glade; and, part of Ashman's Delight.
Samuel Gott - part of Gunner's Range.
Catherine North - Phillip's Addition.
Edward Cockey - Cockey's Delight.
William Nelson - Hamford and part of Tricks and Things.
William Cox - part of New Westwood and West's Beginning Improved; Coxes Farm.
Benjamin Osborne - part of St. Margaret's Ludgate, Bradley Resurveyed, and Scotman's Generosity. Also mentions a "Wids. Osborne."
Edward Mattingley - Bond's Beginning; part of Bond's Fortune and Good Neighbourhood; France's Delight; Bond's Choice.
Ephraim Andrews - part of New Westwood.
Antell Deaver's heirs - part of Sedgly and Best Endeavour.
Michael Webster's heirs - part of Best Endeavour and Webster's Enlargement; Second Venture; Webster's Oblong; Webster's Double Oblong. Also mentions a John Lynch.
John Talbott - part of Molly's and Sally's Delight. Also mentions a B. Philphot.
Samuel Webster - part of Webster's Enlargement and Howard's Forrest; Webster's Forrest.
James Nicholson - Coxes Prospect ("sold William Hopkins").
Col. Thomas Sheredine - part of Cubb Hills, Celsed, and Carrick Fergus; Sheredine's Range; Mary's Desire.
John Cross - Crosses Park and Crosses Chance.
Thomas Hooker - Bathell, Hooker's Meadow, Come By Chance, and Hooker's Liberty.
William Amos' heirs - Planter's Purchase.
Col. William Hammond - part of Buck Ridge.
John Kimble - part of Expectation (mentions a Jas. Kimball).
Reneldo Munk - Turkey Cock Hall, Munk's Discovery, and Cook's Adventure.
John Porter - Ashman's Retirement and Meadow Land (mentions a William Crooks).
John Allender - part of Ogg King of Bashan; Pearson's Outlet and Wetherell's Addition.
Stephen Roberts - part of Ogg King of Bashan; Pearson's Outlet and Wetherall's Addition.
Simon Boom - Jacoborough.
Michael and George Fisher - Tiperara.
Jacob Cox - Coxes Range; Coxes Pleasant Meadows; part of Barney's Timber Ridge Resurveyed.
Jacob Shilling - Germain Church; Cole Chester (mentions a Peter Fowble).
Christopher Carnan - Brother's Choice; a lott in Baltimore Town; part of Shawhan Hunting Ground; Hooker's Chance; part of Sheridine's Grove; part of Chevy Chase; part of Addition to Sheridine's Grove; part of Calf Pasture; part of Brown's Chance; half of Green Spring Forrest; part of Nicholson's Mannor; part of Cole's Harbour and Tod's Range (also mentions a Richard Croxall).
Benjamin Cross - Sawrange.
John Wooden, Jr. - part of Parishes Range; Wooden's Venture.
Soloman Wooden - part of Parishes Range.

BALTIMORE COUNTY DEBT BOOK, 1765-1766

John and Thomas Gorsuch, Jr. - Loveless Addition and Ensor's Choice Resurveyed.

Nicholas Tempest Rogers (son of William) - part of Addition to Batchellors Neck (also mentions a Benjamin Rogers).

John Rigdon - part of Jenkins' Range.

James Billingsley - part of Jenkins' Range.

Peter Myer - part of Broad's Improvement.

William Anderson - part of Buck's Park.

Joseph Lusby - part of Drew's Enlargement and part of Drew's Enlargement Improved.

Mary Ruff - part of Ruff's Chance and Howard's Harbour.

Henry Ruff - part of Ruff's Chance.

David Rowles - part of Jones' Adventure; Rowle's Care.

Samuel Forwood - Maiden's Meadow; part of Contrivance to Cole's Chance; part of St. Omer (Ames?); Colegate's Addition; Henry's Pleasure; Forward's Purchase.

Nathan Nicholson - Limerick; part of Midsummer Hills.

John Craton - part of Uncle's Goodwill; Craton's Plains.

Soloman Bowen - part of Samuel's Hope.

Thomas Watson - Barnes' Levell; Addition to Barne's Levell (also mentions a Robert Gilvreash?).

Soloman Stoxdale - part of The Reserve; Stoxdale's Content; pt of McClain's Hills; Buckingham;s Prevention; Addition to McClain's Hills (also mentions T. Stoxdale).

Charles Howard - Howard's Adventure; Howard's Fancy (also mentions a Eli Owings).

Jemima Robinson or Jackson - part of Hall's Ridge (mentions a Jas. or Jos. Maxwell).

James Whitacre - part of Birr.

Buckln. Partridge - part of Thomas's Adventure, part of Good Luck, part of Thomas' Range, and part of Balleston.

Robert Morgan - part of Paradise.

Edward Corbin - part of Cumberland.

William Govane - Drumquhasle and Benjamin's Lott.

William Denton - James' Beginning and part of Colling's Choice.

AN INDEX OF SOME BALTIMORE RESIDENTS IN 1765

The following index was found in the Maryland Historical Society Library's Manuscript Division (MS.1711) and, even though there is nothing to indicate what the purpose of the index, it was determined that those listed were Baltimore residents circa 1765. This determination was made from the compiler's familiarity with Baltimore families prior to the Revolution and also because this index was found with the remnants of a Baltimore Debt Book for 1765 and 1766. This is not an index to the debt book because the highest page number in the book is 109 while the highest page number in the index is 58. The index is, nonetheless, a "finding list" for early Baltimore.

James Anderson, Fran. Acworth, George Ashman, Nich. Andrews, Richard Anderson, Jacob Anthony, Lawrence Ash, Christian Apple, William Armstrong, Robert Alexander, Conrod Appleman.

AN INDEX OF SOME BALTIMORE RESIDENTS IN 1765

Ferdinand Battee, George Bramwell Exrs., Edmund Baxter, Jr., Daniel Bowers, Elijah Baily, John Brown (Milliner), James Bonniday, Michael Barn, Anthony Barriere, Dixon Brown, John Brown (son George), Benjamin Barny, Samuel Bond, Elias Barnaby, Kerenhappuck Baily, Nathaniel Bradley, Henry Blyhart, John Bond, Jr., Nathaniel Brothers, Linn & Bond, Samuel Bell, William and Ann Bond, Elias Boyer, Francis Baker, Thomas Blany, Solomon Boston, William Barney, Peter Baker, Robert Burrage, James Baily, Jervase Biddison, Thomas Biddison, Hugh Brown, Richard Bassett, Francus Brothers, Henry Brown, William Buckingham, Vandle Bright, Samuel Bailiss, Edward Blany, Caspar Balsar, Jacob Brown, Thomas Brereton, Francis Bruisbanks, John Beaver, Abraham Britton, John Burk.

John Cannon, Ellis (Elln?) and Robert Cunliffe, Nicholas Clagett, John Clarkson, John Curtis; Chew, Clayton & Chew; Richard Clark, Thomas Cook, Nathan Corbin, Joseph Chester, John Clements, William Corbin, John Cross, Hugh Carson, Alexander Crawford, John Clark, James Curry, Caspar Carver, William Collins, Mordecai Cole.

Rachel Demmitt, Brittingham Dickinson, Robert Davis, Mary Davis, Christian Davis, John Daughaday, Jacqery DeSal, Thomas Dicas, Francis Daws, John Dodge, George Doubenhover, William Davis, Charles Dukes, James Daughaday, Nathan Dorsey, Charles Dunn, William Davis (Sadler), William Dicks, Anthony Durant, Leakin Dorsey, Magdalen Devine, Charles Daffin.

Abraham Enloes, Brown & Ewing, Abraham Eaglestone, John Ewing, John Earman, Barnet Eichelberger, Thomas Eaglestone, Jon. Eaglestone, James Elkins, Hugh Eagon, Delilah Elder, Jacob Eichelberger, James Edwards.

Alexander Frow, Henry Fetter, Cumberland Ferguson, Patrick Fowler, Michael Foy, Jacob Frissell, Stephen Ford, William Fish, Ann Flannagan, Hugh Frazier, Peter Fowble, Samuel Fisher, Andrew Ferguson, Samuel Fowler, George Fletcher, Adam Fonerdon, Ruth Frazier.

Abraham Green, John Gregory, Charles Gorsuch, Sr., Acquila Goswick, Peter Gosnell, Abraham Gorman, John Gordon, William Gill, Warnall Gosnell, William Glowman, Zachariah Gray, Thomas Graves, Philip Gover, Mordecai Gist, Richard Graham, Jacob Glatz, Richard Graves, Philip Graybill, Charles Gartz, Charles Gilbert.

Henry Hostiter, Joseph Hoke, Andrew Hoke, John Howlett, George Houfnagel, William Hardigan, James Hamilton, Aaron Harkins, Thomas Hunter, Jacob Houser, Isaac Hall, Ludowick Hannervelt, L. J. Elizabeth Hyde, Edward How, William Hunt, John Hart, George T. Howard, Elisha Hall, John Hawn, Joseph Hayward, George Hooper, William Harris, John Hobbs, Lawrence Half(?), Randall Hulse, Charles Hissey, Lambert Hyland, George Holtzinger, Jacob Hewett, Jonathan Hanson, Jr., John Peter Hiser, Philip Hall, Mordecai Hammond, Edward Hanson, Edward Harris, Jacob Hoke, Andrew Hoofman (Hoopman).

Robert Irvin, Daniel Igon, Cornelius Jewell, Nicholas Jones, John Jones (forrest), Richard Jones, Joseph Jacobs, Richard James, Roger Jones, Wimbert Judah, William Jones, Jonathan Jones, William Jacob, Martin Judah.

Sylvester Kick, Nathan Kelly, James Kelly, Margaret Kelly, Charles Aug. Keys, John Kemp, Jacob Keepotz, John Kean.

AN INDEX OF SOME BALTIMORE RESIDENTS IN 1765

Alexander Leith, John Lees, George Lindenberger, Peter Litzinger, Simon Lowdigger, John Little, Joshua Lynch, Peter Lauderman, William Lynch, Philip Lydick, Patrick Lanahan, Margaret Long, Thomas Lancaster Lansdale, Joshua Legate.

John Merryman, William Moron (Morow?), Thomas Miller, Jacob Myers (Carpenter), Jacob Myers (Sadler), Jacob Madeira, Oliver Matthews, Richard McCollister, Daniel Merrick, David McClure, James McCubbin, John Megay, Robert Megay, Thomas Marshall, William Megrath, William Miller, Hugh McKinnie, John Malonee, Mordecai Mordecai, Alexander McLure (McClure), William Marsh, Joseph Merryman, Roberts & Mildred, Joseph Miller (Carpenter), George McKendless, William Murphy, John McNabb, Samuel Merryman, Andrew Meek, Nicholas Miller, John Miller (at Caton), Samuel Mannen, John McKirdy, Aaron Mattison, Enoch Mitchell, Joseph McGraw.

Joshua Newman, Benjamin Nelson, Edward Neal, William Neal, Thomas Nott.

Jacob Oister, James Orrick, Nicholas Orrick, William O'Bryan, Joseph Osborn, John C. Owings.

James Postlewait, John Pitts, William Peckard, Richard Pritchard, Edward Preston, John Perrigo, William Parks, John Penn, Daniel Pennington, Archibald Perkins, Reuben Perkins, Joseph Pennell, Henry Pintz, David Pensly, Edward Parker, Elizabeth Parker (adm. of Richard), Samuel Pritchard, Daniel Pritchard, Richard William Perkins, John Parrish, Martin Parker, Capt. John Parker, Clark & Pearce.

James Richard, Lettis Raven, Charles Rogers, William Rowles, Christopher Randall & Bond, Sophia Robinson, Thomas Rutter, Francis Richardson, Thomas Rogers, John Rick & Aikenhead, Morris Ragan, Thomas Reeves, John Rupert, William Roundtree, Andrew Rider, Adam Reigart, John Read, Jacob Raybolt, Henry Reese, Larkin Randall, William Reese, John Rick, Christopher Rodes, Browning & Rogers, Vorhees & Rhea.

Joseph Smith, Thomas Savage, Joseph Scott's adms., William Share, Smith & Sterrett, John Shaver, Daniel Sapp, William Spear, William Spencer, William Scott, John Stedham, James Sage, Elizabeth Smith, Tobias Stansbury, Jacob Sapp, Edward Stevens, Holtzinger & Swope, George Shack, George Stansbury, Ezekiel Shiply, John Shrim, Andrew Stigar, Thomas Stoxsdale, John Shly, Adam Shiply, Amos Sinclair, John Stover, Jacob Scott, Benedict Swope, Jacob Sindall, Edward Stoxsdale, Thomas Stout, John Starr, Joseph Smith, Archibald Steel, William Scarf, John Stevenson, Joseph Sollars, Jacob Short, David Sheilds, Rowland Spencer, John Shepherd, John Shee, Solomon Stoxsdale, Francis Sanderson, John Summer.

Ecan Thomas, Luke Trotten, Frederick Thomas, Ezekiel Towson, Stephen Treacle, Emmanuel Teal, Edward Talbott, Joshua Tull, Peter Turnpower (?), John Thompson, Richard Taylor, Samuel Thompson, William Thornton, John Todd, Robert Thompson.

Gist Vaughan, Simon Vanhorn, John Vansant, Cornelius Vangiff, Thomas Vysher (?) & Co.

John Worthington, Thomas Worthington (Baltimore Town), John Webster, George Wells, Robert Woods, Moses Wheeler, John Wells, Henry Warrell, Nathaniel West, Peter Warking, William Wheeler, Joseph Wells, William Whitney, William

AN INDEX OF SOME BALTIMORE RESIDENTS IN 1765

Wilson, John Wild, Elizabeth Webster, William Worthington, Richard Welsh, John Woodward, Josiah Wheeler, Solomon Wooden, Abraham Weaver, William Lock. Weems, Greenbury Wilson, Michael Wolf, Christopher Wonder, Charles Worthington, James Walker, Thomas Wells, Taylor & Willing.

William Young, Jacob Young, Englehard Yeizer, Yocum Yawn.

PRISONERS IN BALTIMORE COUNTY JAIL, 1765-1773

The following persons are referred to as "the prisoners languishing in Baltimore County goal" (jail) from 1765 to 1773, and their petitions for relief were presented before the Lower House of Assembly. These Baltimore County lists (and other county jail lists) may be found in the Archives of Maryland (Vol. 59, pp.47-48, Vol. 61, p. 296, Vol. 62, p. 179, and, Vol. 63, pp. 10, 17, 25, 272, 319, 320, 376).

November 12, 1765: John Greeniff Howard, John Denning, Joseph Barham, James Agar, John Condron, Nathan Shaw, Thomas West, Solomon Wheyland, John Lemmons, and John Jones.

November 13, 1765: John Hughes.

June 7, 1768: John Bain, Francis Harris, William Conhold, Thomas Day, Joseph Hayward, William Andrews, George Green, William Jones, John Clay, James Oliver, Richard Treadwell.

October 10, 1770: James Guffey, James Henderson, William Potters, Thomas Treadway, Levi Pottle, Francis Casey, Basil Francis, Joshua Allender, and William Walsh.

October 15, 1771: Alexander Monroe, John Rourke, Hugh Woods, Edward Robinson, Richard Crutchedly, Aquila Gostnick, Thomas Rountree, George Wells, John Serjeant, John Gordon Thompson, William James, George Griffin, Owen Dunn, and Basil Dunn.

October 29, 1771: Nathaniel SMith and George Baxter.

November 7, 1771: Charles Lyn (Lin). Subsequently noted that Charles Lin, Basil Lucas and Nathaniel Smith were set free.

June 23, 1773: Gotlip Neeth, Robert Elder, John Leeds, Andrew Williams, Edward Preston, Patrick Quigley, John Keeting, Owen Keef, George Baxter, Joseph Finley, Joseph Robess Rogers, Jane Johnson, Charles Kees, Thomas Tomkins, James Fitzsimmons, Samuel Gosnell, Patrick Henesey, Philip Barnethouse, James Woodward, Jacob Stoy, Thomas Smyth, Mark McLoughlin, John Curtiss (Curtis), Daniel Harkins, John Taylor, Vachel Worthington, John Hobbs, and John Linney.

INDEX TO AQUILA HALL'S ASSESSMENT LEDGER, 1762-1765

Aquila Hall was High Sheriff of Baltimore County and after Harford County separated from Baltimore County in 1773 he was appointed Colonel of Militia and one of the Lord Justices of the new county of Harford from 1774 to 1779. While serving as Sheriff of Baltimore County he compiled a tax assessment ledger of 145 pages which named 1,380 persons, their land tracts, and their assessments. The original ledger is in the Maryland Historical Society Library's Manuscript Division. The book (MS.1565) was prepared during the years 1762 and 1765. Its index contains the following names.

16

INDEX TO AQUILA HALL'S ASSESSMENT LEDGER, 1762-1765

Anthony Asher, William Andrews, Ann Acton, Robert Adair, Thomas Ashram, Thomas Arnold, Nathaniel Ayres, Walter Ashmore, Henry Adams, John Allen, Joseph Arnold, Thomas Archer, William Arnold, Philip Adkinson, Thomas Allender, George Ashman, Joshua Allender, Dr. Ephraim Andrews, William Amos, Jr., William Amos' heirs, John Allender, William Anderson, William Askew, William Arnett, Jacob Ansbow, James Armstrong, Benjamin Arnold, Andrew Appenhymer, Thomas Amos, James Amos, Benjamin Amos, Joshua Amos, Jacob Alguire, Mordecai Amos, Anthony Arnold, Philip Adleman, William Asquith, John Adlesborough, Charles Anderson, Charles Angel.

Jacob Bull's heirs, Andrew Buchanan, Dr. George Buchanan, John Buck, Esq., Edward Baxter, William Bosley, Benjamin Bond's heirs, Thomas Bond's heirs, Richard Bond, Jr., John Bosley, Joseph Bosley, Reese Bowen, John Bond (son of Peter) Charles Bailey's heirs, John Basey, James Billingsley, Thomas Bond (son of Peter), Charles Bosley, John Bull, Robert Brierly, Thomas Brown, John Bowen, Roger Bishop, Thomas Bailey, Morris Baker (Patapsco), Morris Baker (Gunpowder), Ann Burk, Benjamin Bowen, Absolom Butler, Charles Baker, Nathan Brothers or Thomas Brothers, Mick Buck, Ford Barnes' heirs, John Boring, Peter Bingham, Thomas Broad, William Banks, David Bissett's heirs, George Botts, William Burton, James Bonfield, Walter Billingsley, Benjamin Bordillons heirs, Thomas Bradley, Sarah Bond, Absolom Brown, William Bradford, William Bond's heirs, Sarah Boreing, William Beaver, John Brierly's widow, John Bond, William Baseman, James Brice, Daniel Barrett, Charles Bolton, Samuel Borven (Borden), Edward Borven (Borden), Henry Beach, Joseph Bowen's heirs, Robert Banaker, Thomas Bond, Joseph Bardell, John Baxter, Bush River Company, Thomas Bentley, William Barney, Amon Butler, Capt. William Bond, Samuel Barry, Alexander Baker, Roger Bishop, John Boring, Rhuebin Boring, William Boring, Michael Barns, Thomas Biddison, William Bennett, Abell Brown, Absolom Barney, John Brown, Dixon Brown, Jabis Bailey, William Banister, Joshua Bond, Moses Byfoot, Josias Bowen, James Boring (?), George Browne, James Browne, Samuel Barkell, Elizabeth Burgess, Thomas Ball, Joseph Barrett, James Boston, Benjamin Barnes, Abner Baker, Edward Bull, Charles Baker (son of John), Edward Bull, John Baker (son of Abm.), George Bradford, Thomas Birchfield, Joseph Barkley, William Browne, Jr., Baptist Barber (or Barker), James Barton or Martin Barton, Benjamin Barney, Francis Brucebanks, Thomas Bladen, Esq., Roger Boyce, Roger Brookes, Simon Boom, Thomas Boring, James Billingsley, Jr., Soloman Bowen, James Briant, Elizabeth Body, Isaac Butterworth, Robert Boom, Elizabeth Bankson, Jacob Bond, Loyd Buchanan, Esq., John Buck (or Burk), Greenberry Baxter, Beale Bordley, Esq., John Brown (son of Thomas), Arraana (?) Bankson, John Baker (son of John), Joseph Bosley, Jr., Zachariah Barlow, Benjamin Buckingham, Thomas Bond, Jr., Chaney Benjamin Burgess, Tobias Brothers, George Browne, Jr., John Biggerton, Arthur Brownlow, George Bramwell, John Barnes, William Barnes, Joseph Barnes, John Buckingham, John Bruents(?), James Bissett, Esq., Adam Barnes, Lodowick Brierly (Bierly), Conrod Brierly (Bierly), Thomas Bennett, Nathan Bowen, Richard Barnes, John Bristoll, Joseph Bankson, Jarvis Biddison, Absolom Baker, William Blissard, John Black, Samuel Budd(?), Paul Barns(?), Enoch Bailey, Indimeon(?) Baker, Conrode Brost, Samuel Bond, John Brown, Shradrach Bush, William Baxter.

Robert Clark's widow, Luke Chapman, Thomas Cawdrick, Thomas Carr, William Crabtree, William Crabtree, Jr., Thomas Crabtree, John Condron, Garrett Dennis Cole, Robert Chapman, Thomas Cole (Patapsco), Richard Cole, Christopher Cole, Robert Clarke (Winters Run), William Carter, James Crosswell, Arthur Chinoworth, John Cowen, Jr., Henry Charlton, Benjamin

INDEX TO AQUILA HALL'S ASSESSMENT LEDGER, 1762-1765

Colegate, John Clarke (Swan Town), John Carter, George Chancey, John Cooper, William Carr, Aquila Carr, David Carlisle, James Crafford, John Colegate, Oliver Crumwell (Cromwell), Joseph Crumwell (Cromwell), James Carroll, Robert Cammell (Campbell), John Cammell (Campbell), Robert Cross, Jacob Cord, William Coine, William Cole (Deer Creek), John Chalk, Thomas Colegate, Peter Carroll, Clara Clarke, Thomas Cook, John Carroll (Carwell?), George Cole, Jeremiah Coney, Esther Camrone (?), Skipwith Cole's heirs, John Clarke (Patapsco), Thomas Casebolt, Valentine Carbach, Jacob Combess, Benjamin Culver, John Copeland, William Cross, William Cowin, Nathan Chapman, Charles Croxall, Robert Collins, The Reverend Thomas Craddock, John Chilcoat, John Crumwell or Cromwell (son of John), Richard Croxall, John Crabtree, Richard Chinoth, William Cockey, Lawrence Clarke, John Cryder, Frederick Cryder, Joshua Cockey, John Courts, Nicholas Carver's widow, Edward Corbin, William Cromwell's heirs, Richard Carter, Capt. James Cawley (in England), Thomas Cole, Jr., Thomas Cockey, Charles Carroll, Jr. (son of Daniel), Charles Carroll's heirs, William Cole, Samuel Chew's heirs, Charles Carroll and Company, Daniel Clarey, Cumberland Company, Edward Cockey, William Cox, John Cross, Jacob Cox, Benjamin Cross, John Craton, Edward Cook, Edward Corbin, Jr., Samuel Cole, William Cole, Jr., Charles Carroll, Esq. (son of Daniel), James Connoway, Charles Carroll, Esq., Abell Chanley, Mathew Coulter, John Cross, John Cook, William Craton, Charles Christie's heirs, Hugh Creagh, Benjamin Burgess Chaney, Philip Crease, James Cole, John Carnan, Daniel Chamior(?), Richard Cresswell, William Cresswell, Robert Clarke, David Clarke, William Clarke, John Carey, George Clarke, John Cradey, James Carey, Robert Cook, Samuel Clark, Martin Cammell, Nathaniel Chapman, John Carter (up the Bay), Henry Collinger, Franck (French?) Croose, John Carnan, Ascah Carnan, Christopher Carnan, Michael Coulz(?).

Richard Dimmitt, Staley Durham, Thomas Denbowe, Thomas Downey, Anthony Drew, Thomas Dimmitt, William Debruler, William Dallam, Rober Donahue's heirs, Penelope Dye (Deye), the widow Darby, Daniel Durbin, James Death, Nathanial Davice, Richard Dallam, John Dunn, Robert Dutton, John Hammond Dorsey, Thomas Durbin, The Reverend Hugh Deans, William Daugherty, Thomasa Donovin, Walter Dallas' heirs, William Davice, Christopher Dukes (Dukas?), Thomas Durbin, Samuel Durham, Rudolph Decker, Thomas Davis' heirs, John Day (son of Edward), Samuel Durbin, Simon Denny, Vincent Dorsey heirs, Thomas Downes, Charles Dorsey, John Dean, Andrew Dorsey, Edward Day, John Dean(?), son of Walter(?), Samuel Durbin, Jr., Benjamin Deaver, Henry Darnall, Daniel Dulany, Phillip Darnall, Joshua Dorsey, Walter Dulany, Caleb Dorsey, Bazil Dorsey, Edward Dorsey, Thomas Davice, Antell Deaver, William Denton, Caleb Dorsey, James Dougherty, John Daugherty, Richard Dorsey, John Dilley, Christopher Dawes, Samuel Day, Isaac Daws, Richard Daugherty, Vachell Dorsey, Hugh Doran, Thomas Dick, George Daugherty, John Dorsey, John Deaver (son of Antell), Robert Davice, John Daugherty, John Dawley, Richard Deaver, Patrick Dunkin, Rudolph Dukes.

John Ensor, John Edwards, James Elliott, George Eager's heirs, Anthony Enlowes' heirs, Abraham Eaglestone, Job Evans, John Everitt's heirs, Michael Eastwood, William Elliott, Edward Evans' heirs, George Ensor, John Elder, Thomas Ensor, John Ensor, Jr., Joseph Ensor, John Evans, William Peale's executors, Jacob Elagh(?), Ulrick Elkin(?), Abraham Ensor, James Eagon.

Edward Fell's heirs, John Fuller, Thomas Fowler, Thomas Ford, Jr., William Fell's heirs, Capt. Peregrine Frisbey, Thomas Ford, Jr., William Few, John Ford, Major Thomas Franklin, Thomas Farmer, William Fitch, Edward Flanagan,

Charles Flanagan, John Frazier, Thomas Finly, Edward Foothell's heirs,
Lancaster Forge, William Frisbie, Jacob French, John Fishpaw, George Fisher,
Michael Fisher, Samuel Forwood, William Fell, Stephen Ford, Jason Frizzell,
Loueves(?) Forney, Francis Frask (Frank?), William Forehead, John Fisher,
William Fisher, Edward Fell, Daniel Fisher, John Foster, Michael Fisher,
Stephen Fisher, John Fowler, John Fowle, Thomas Forster, Peter Fowble,
Charles Franklin, Henry Fetter.

William Green, Ann Grant, John Gorsuch, William Goslin, Conjuice Gash, John
Garrison, William Grafton, John Giles, James Gallion, Charles Gilbert, George
Garrison, John Gray, Zachariah Gray, Thomas Green, John Gill, Thomas Gilbert,
Jacob Giles, Michael Gilbert, Richard Gott, Peter Goslin, William Greenfield,
Mark Gushard, James Gardiner, Thomas Gorsuch, John Green, Charles Green,
Robert Green, Michael Gladman, Jarvis Gilbert, Luke Griffith, Samuel
Griffith, Ephraim Gover, Soloman Gallion, James Griffith, Thomas Gibbon, John
Gregory, James Garrison, Abraham Green, Nicholas Ruxton Gay, Thomas
Gittinger's heirs, Robert Gilchrist, Joseph Green, Loyd Goodwin, Stephen
Gill, Thomas Gist, Amos Garrett, Philip Gover, Ambrose Gougagan(?), Moses
Galloway, William Gosnell, Jr., Richard Garrison, John Gardner, James
Gallion, Jr., John Galle, George Galle, Ann Greenall, James Greenfield,
Edward Garritson, Peter Goslin, Jr., Nicholas Gash, Samuel Galloway, Amos
Garrett's heirs (in England), Samuel Gist, Ann Greenfield, Samuel Gott,
Christopher Gardiner, John Gorsuch, Thomas Gorsuch, Jr., William Govane,
Joseph Galloway's heirs, Capt. Nicholas Gassaway, Charles Green (son of
Charles), Thomas Gassaway, George Green, Patrick Gray, Peter Gramore, George
Geese, Loveless Gorsuch, Mordecai Gosnell, John Giles (son of Jacob),
Jonathan Griffith, Dinah Gosnell, Harman Greathouse, William Gain, Henry
Green, Garrett Garretson, Job Garretson, John Gill, Jr., John Griffith, John
Gillis, Adam Gah.

John Hopkins, Neale Haile, Samuel Hooker, William Hughes, William Harvey,
Isaac Harding, Thomas Horner, John Hall (Cranberry), Thomas Hawkins, Lemuel
Howard, Parker Hall's heirs, Colonel John Hall, Jacob Hanson, John Hanson,
Jane Hughes, William Hollis, Robert Hawkins, William Hamilton, Richard
Hendon, John Hurd, George Harryman, Solomon Hillon's heirs, Joseph Harryman,
Charles Harryman, Oliver Harriott's heirs, Jonathan Hanson, Thomas Henry,
Nehemiah Hicks, John Hawkins, Cornelius Howard, William Hill, Samuel
Harryman, Mary Hanson, Adam Hendrixon, Samuel Howell, Mayberry Helms, John
Hall (Spesutia), Joseph Hopkins, Thomas Harris' heirs, Michael Hodskins,
Charles Hessey, Thomas Harrison, Jonathan Hartson (in England), George Haile,
Thomas Hutson, George Hase, John Holt's heirs, William Hammond, Doctor
Hollidays heirs, William Hutchins, Joshua Hall, Aquila Hall, John Hyde (of
London), Benjamin Hammond, Michael Huff, John Hendrixon, John Hays, Adam
Hubbard, John Greeniff Howard, William Hall, Jacob Hook, Christian Hersey,
Thomas Harrison, Hyde Horton's heirs (England), Storndort Hollidays, Nathan
Horner, Mathew Hawkins, Richard Hooker, Thomas Holland's heirs, William
Holland's heirs, Harman Husbands, John Hatton, Joseph Hill, Nathan Hammond,
Captain John Howard, Paul Heath Jr.'s heirs, John Hood, John Hall (son of
Jos.), William Hopkins, Samuel Harris, William Holmes, Thomas Hooker, Colonel
William Hammond, Charles Howard, Samuel Hopkins, Richard Hopkins, Edward
Howard, Michael Hannah, Thomas Hooker (son of Samuel), Cornelius Howard,
Peter Harman, Thomas Harley, Michael Haune, Samuel Hughes, Thomas Husbands,
Mordecai Hammond, William Horton, James Hammond, Henrietta Holland, Joel
Higginbottom, William Husband, John Hughes, Samuel Higgerson, Capt.Thomas
Hammond, William Hammond (son of Ben), Philip Harrin, Mayberry Helms, Jr.,

Martin, James Murrey, Peter Major (or Majors), Stephen Mattors (Mattox?),
Peter Minkey, George Mathews, William McCanley, George Myers, David
McCullock, Levin Mathews, Nicholas Merryman, George Merryman, William Martin
(son of John), John Meharge, Basil McGruder (Magruder?), Nicholas Merriman,
Charles Milldews, John Miller, Thomas McQueen, Oliver Mathews, Robert
Marshall, Thomas Miller, James McComas, William Morrow, William McClane,
James McCances(?).

Benjamin Osborne, George Ogg, Samuel Owings, Stephen Onion's heirs, John
Owings, Joshua Owings, Laban Ogg, Sarah Owings, Stephen Owings, Edward
Oursler, William Odle's heirs, Copper Oram, William Oldham, Samuel Owings,
Jr., Jacob Oats, James Osborne, William Osborne, Robert Owings, Joseph
Osborne, George Ogg, Jr., Nicholas Orrick, Elijah Owings, William Ottey,
Henry Owings, Jacob Opercock, John Osborne, Daniel Sullivan Osborne.

Thomas Pycraft, Robert Patterson, John Price (of Gunpowder), William Parish,
Lewis Potee, John Pennington, Mordecai Price, William Petticoate, William
Parish, Jr., James Preston, Rebecca Potee, Samuel Pritchard, George Presbury,
William Presbury, Col. Benjamin Pearce, Thomas Presbury, Nicholas Power,
James Pritchard, John Poteet, Heathcoat Pickett, Edward Peregoy, Thomas
Porter, Thomas Philips (or Phelps), Edward Parish, William Perkins, Moses
Parris, John Price (Garrison), John Penn, Capt. James Phillips, Daniel
Preston, Richard Parish, Robert Patterson, William Parlett, John Pribble,
Principio Company, Capt. John Paca, Christian Peglar, Ralph Peale, John
Pendall, Jonathan Plowman, John Plowman, Henry Peregoy, Jr., John Paca, Jr.,
William Parks, Richard Pinkham, Nicholas Petticoate, Stephen Price, Joseph
Presbury, Jane Partridge, St. Paul's Church, Parish of Saint Thomas, James
Powers, Barnett Preston, Charles Pierpoint, Brian Philpott, William Pike,
John Porter, John Price, Jr., Dr. Buck Partridge, Henry Pemberton, John
Pollard, Richard Poole, Paul Plenstone(?), John Phillips, Bevis Paine, Simon
Person, Henry Peglar, Absolom Price, Conrod Prost, William Ponteny, Dorsey
Pettycoat, Thomas Pribble, Edward Puntney, Phillip Peller, Robert Patterson,
John Puket, Henry Paper.

John Quarterman, George Rigdon, Isaac Raven, William Reaves, Charle Robinson,
Daniel Rawlins, Jr., Richard Robinson, Richard Rhodes, Lawrence Richardson,
Capt. Charles Ridgley, Capt. William Rogers, Edwards Richard, William
Robinson, John Randell, Luke Raven, Richard Ruff's heirs, Christopher
Randell, Thomas Rutter, Abraham Raven, Solomon Rowles, Joseph Renshaw, George
Rock (England), Thomas Richardson, Col. Nathan Rigbie, John Roberts (Joppa),
Francis Rider, Jacob Rowles, Francis Russell's heirs, Richard Rutter, Talbott
Risteau's heirs, James Rigbie, Nathan Rigbie, Jr., Moses Ruth, John Robinson,
James Rowland, William Rigdon, Thomas Renshaw, Abraham Renshaw, Benjamin
Ricketts, John Robinson, Nathan Richardson's heirs, James Richard, Joseph
Rogers, William Roberts, Henry Rutter, William Ramsay, John Renshaw, Isaac
Risteau, William Roberts (Pipe Creek), Peter Robinson, John Riston, Patrick
Rewark (Rouark?), Richard Richards, Michael Rawlins, John Ridgley, Jonathan
Rawlins, Hugh Ross, Thomas Reynold (Calvert County), Stephen Roberts,
Nicholas Tempest Rogers (son of William), John Rigdon, Mary Ruff, Henry Ruff,
David Rowles, Jemima Robinson or Jackson, John Rhodes, Thomas Randell,
William Ray, John Rivell, Hannah Rucker, Derrick Rhinehart, Thomas Rigdon,
John Rister, Leven Roberts, Stephen Rigdon, George Risteau, Solomon Rutter,
Jacob Rowles, Jr., Adam Reese, John Rind, Charles Ridgley, Jr., William
Ramsay, Aaron Rawlins.

Edward Sanders, Thomas Smithson, Samuel Smith, Richard King Stevenson, Daniel Stansbury, Major Sabrett Sollers, John Sargant, Henry Sayter, Tobias Stansbury, Edward Stoxdale, James Sinclair, Mary Scott, Richard Sampson, William Stiles, Edward Stapenton, Thomas Stansbury, William Savory, Jonathan Starkey, Christopher Sheppard, John Sumner, Jacob Sindall, Edward Stevenson, Capt. Tobias Stansbury, Thomas Sligh, John Swinyard, Edward Sweeting, Henry Stevenson, Thomas Shidd, Joshua Sewell, Capt. John Stinchcombe, Skelton Standiford, Winston Smith's heirs, William Standiford, John Standiford's heirs, John Stoxdale, Samuel Smith (Gunpowder), Nathan Stinchcombe, High Sollers, Robert Scott, Richard Shedwicks, Bevis Spain, Nicholas Smith, John Stansbury, Nathan Smith, Thomas Stoxdale, Robert Sanders, James Scott, Robert Stokes' heirs, Samuel Stansbury, Samuel Sandell, Christopher Sewell, Dixon Stansbury, Elizabeth Scott, Daniel Scott's heirs, Aquila Scott's heirs, Joseph Sollers, Samuel Smith (Deer Creek), William Shaw, John Simkins, William Smith, William Seabrooks, Richardson Stansbury, Jacob Scott, Conrod Smith, Phillip Smith's heirs (in England), John Smith (Millwn.?), James Stewart, Andrew Shriver, Ludwick Shiver (Shriver?), Mathew Smiser, Burrage Scott, Jacob Stroup, Jonathan Scarfe, John Steel's widow, George Shipley, Christopher Sutton, Peter Shultz, Joseph Sutton, Amon Shipley, Thomas Sheredine, Rebecca Speier, Thomas Sprigg, Walter Smith, Samuel Sewell, George Simmonds, Edward Stansbury, John Shelmoredine, Capt. Thomas Sheredine's heirs, Jacob Shilling, Solomon Stoxdale, Charles Shipley, Samuel Shipley, William Shirter (Shirten?), John Summers, Thomas Storey, Jacob Shilling, Jr., Greenberry Shipley, Adam Shipley, Peter Shipley, Henry Stump, Nicholas Slutover(?), James Spring, Thomas Stephens, Henry Salbecker, Christopher Senee, Peter Senee, Charles Smith, Philip Lauden Stigher (or Philip Laudenstigher?), Alexander Stewart, Mrs. Alexander Stewart, Thomas Sanders, Robert Stevenson, John Peter Snapp, John Shly, Christopher Shaffer, Andrew Stigar, Hickman Henry Stoffell, Sebastian Settlemin, Henry Slagell, Robert Storey, John Sappington, Christopher Shilling, Thomas Speier, Francis Shuster, John Shovar, Benjamin Swope, Casper Starr, Jacob Spindler, Frederick Shacklin, Martin Shacklin, Mathias Skilman, Henry Sower, James Smith, Henry Smith, John Stapleton, Comfort Sewell, Thomas Stapleton, John Solomon, Adam Shack, George Smaltz, John Shrimplin, Alexander Stenhouse, Dr. Henry Stevenson, Thomas Stocksdale.

Edmund Talbott, Thomas Talbott, Edward Thorpe, David Thomas' heirs, Abraham Taylor, Edward Tulley, James Taylor, Emanuel Teile, Luke Trotten, John Timmons, William Towson, Thomas Tipton, Jr., John Taylor, Charles Taylor, Joseph Taylor, William Talbott's heirs, John Tipton, Alexander Thompson, Capt. Walter Tolley, William Tipton, John Thomas, Thomas Thompson, Andrew Thompson, Christopher Topham, Robert Tevis, Benjamin Taylor's heirs, Col. John Taylor (Tayloe?), John Thompson, Thomas Towson, Edmund Talbott, Philip Thomas, John Taylor's heirs, Benjamin Tasker, Esq., Lawrence Todd, John Tye, John Talbott, Christopher Thornback, Martin Trist, Thomas Tredway, Jacob Thrush, Edward Talbott, Luke Tipton, Christian Tomer, Edward Tipton, Philip Teile, Henry Thomas.

Samuel Underwood, Valentine Vance, Christopher Vaughan, Thomas Vaughan, and "Visitors of Baltimore County."

Dr. Edward Wakeman, Isaac Webster's heirs, John Wilson (Deer Creek), Robert Willmott, John Wooden, Peter Whitaker (son of Abram), George Withs' heirs, Thomas West, William Wheeler, Thomas Wright's heirs, Thomas Wheeler, Charles Worthington, Benjamin Wheeler, Leonard Wheeler's heirs, William Williams,

John West, Robert Wilkinson, William Wood's heirs, Benjamin Wells, Samuel Wallace, Isaac Wood, James Wells, Col. Thomas White, Thomas Wells, Jr., William Wright's heirs, Joseph Wilson, Richard Wells, Capt. John White, Soloman Wheeler, Edward Ward, Jonathan White, Abraham Wright, William Wilson (Pipe Creek), Stephen Wilkinson, Wason Wheeler, Ignatius Wheeler, Francis Watkins, Henry Wetherell, William Wells, James Wells, Jr., Jonathan West, James Whitaker, John Welsh, James Welsh, Thomas Waltham, John Woody, John Whyatt, Robert West, William Wilson (Soldiers Delight), Benjamin Whips, Samuel Whips, John Whips, William Winchester, John Watts, William Wilson, Henry Wilson, Benjamin Kid Wilson, John Willmott, Samuel Wheeler, Joshua Wood's heirs, John Wicks' heirs, Thomas Watson, Woolwrick Whistler, Henry Warrell, John Waters, Mary Wate, Thomas Ward, John Watkins, Peter Welthy, Michael Webster, Samuel Webster, John Wooden, Jr., Solomon Wooden, Thomas Watson, James Whitaker, Edward Wann, William Wheeler (the youngest), Brice Worthington, Nicholas Worthington, John Worthington, Richard Willmott, Charles Wells, Hugh Whiteford, Benjamin Wager, William Wooden, William Wright, Nathaniel West, Richard Winn, Martin Winter, Michael Whebright, Robert Ward, Adam Wise, Thomas Ward, George Williams, John Woodward, John Worthington, Jr., Richard Williams, Jethro Lynch Wilkinson, Benjamin Wheeler, Owen Williams, William Wages, Samuel Webb, James Waters, Elex Wells, Andrew Welty, Samuel Wilson, East Walker, William Wilson, Vachell Worthington, Peter Wollerick(?), William Wright (Patapsco), Isaac Wright.

Jacob Young, Henry Youston or Auston, James Yew, Alexander Young, Col. William Young, Samuel Young's heirs, William Yates, William York, Edward York, John York, Sewell Young.

LIST OF LETTERS IN THE BALTIMORE POST OFFICE, 1766

The following is a list of letters remaining in the Post Office in Baltimore Town on July 18, 1766 as published in the Maryland Gazette on August 7, 1766.

James Anderson, Robert Adair, Mr. All, James Boyd, Robert Bryce, Matthias Bush, William Banks, John Barret, James Burns (Blockmaker), John Bayley, Thomas Bayley, William Boyce, Daniel Chamier, William Coleman, Abraham Cuzier, John Casy, Benjamin Corne, Abraham Cole, Joseph Cromwell, David Cobb, Dennis Croghan (to the care of Bar. Hughes), William Chitham, Messrs.Caleb Dorsey and John Howard, Jose DeVerges, William Dervil, Francis Davis, Patrick Dinnis (Elkridge), Thomas Dirkson (to be left at Andrew Buchanan's), William Elgar (to be left at Jacob Myer's), Lettice Fleming (sold to John Beal), John Frazer, William Fowler (Lancashire Furnace) Benjamin Grymes, Job Garrison, Thomas Gordon, John Gardner (to the care of Mr. Simple), Leonard Gale, Barnabas Hughes, William Hircom (to the care of F. Chisholm), Sarah Horrod, Joseph Higgins (at A. Stiger's), Samuel Hopkins, Edward Hiley (Sailmaker), Nich. Hoffelbauch, Mr. Hick (Lancashire Furnace), Derick Jones (care of N. Crews), Benjamin Jinkins, Acquilla Johns, Robert Kay, Melchior Keener, William   Kneller, William Lee (Elkridge), John Leea (at F. Wilmot's), Michael Little (Fork of Gunpowder), Thomas Lorain, Elizabeth Lee (at John Wilmot's), John Lawson (at Mrs. Orrick's), Capt. Cuthbert Lindsey, John Merryman, Jr. and Company, William Miller (Cooper at West Ogle Mill), Edward Mills, William McKubbin, Henry Morgan, John Maddocks (North Point), William Mullineer, Anthony Magawon (Black Church), Andrew McInteer (care of Joseph Miller), William McCamish, Captain Aaron Martin, William Matthews, Widow

LIST OF LETTERS IN THE BALTIMORE POST OFFICE, 1766

Orrick, Alexander Offut, Capt. John Parsons (care of W. Lux), Thomas Philips, Hance Rudolph, Messrs. Roberts and Chamier, Daniel Rodagh (at James Smith's), Richard Rolls, Blaze Robertson, Clara Rhodes, John Rowe, John Robinson, John Scoolfield, Dr. Henry Shnebely (care of Mr. Keener), Ephraim Stevens, Charles Stracban, John Smith (Ship Carpenter), Durham Sharp, Francis Simpson (Elkridge), Richard Smith (at Mrs. Orrick's), The Executors of John Shute, James Thompson (Master of the ship Nancy), Robert Tovel (at William Harvy's), Margaret Tupeoner, Thomas Vaughan (at Caleb Dorsey's), George White (Painter), Richard Wagstaff, Robert Wagstaff, Messrs. Wagner and Adams, William Williams (Lancashire Furnace), Richard White (Mariner), Capt. John Walker (of the ship Friendship), George Walker, Martha Young.

ADDRESS FROM SUNDRY INHABITANTS OF BALTIMORE TOWN, 1767

The following address from sundry inhabitants of Baltimore Town to his Excellency Horatio Sharpe, Esquire, Governor and Commander in Chief in and over the Province of Maryland, was presented on April 2, 1767 (Archives of Maryland, 32:187):

"We the Inhabitants of Baltimore Town, ever desirous of shewing our Loyalty to the best of Kings; beg leave to Address your Excellency on an Affair which we deem Important and if not attended to in time may interrupt the future Welfare of many of his Majesty's faithful Subjects. About Eight Months past a Number of French Neutrals from this Place and other parts Embarked as we always understood on a Voyage to Pensacola, but since learnt they have Landed at New Orleans and are become Subjects of the French King; another Body of these People near 300 in Number are now preparing to embark from hence in Order to go to the same Place. When we consider how well these People are acquainted with the Navigation of our Bay That of Delaware and of Fundy that many have Piloted Vessels into the Harbour of Boston and New York, We have too much Reason to apprehend that in Case of a future Rupture with France or Spain they must do inconceivable prejudice to the Commerce of this Continent. When we reflect on the inveterate Hatred they retain against this Nation on Account of their having been Supplanted from their Lands in Acadia, we think it highly impolitic (not to say imprudent) to suffer them to settle among our Avow'd Enemies on the back of a new Colony where they may possibly Foment a Misunderstanding between us and the Indians to the great Detriment of his Majesty's faithful Subjects. With the Strictest Truth we can assure your Excellency that no Public Animosity or Private Pique to these People have induced us to Address your Excellency on this Subject but merely Duty to our King and Justice to our Country. We flatter Ourselves therefore that your Excellency will take the Premises into Consideration, And as to Northward his Majesty has Territory enough to accommodate them & Millions more, That your Excellency will not permit them to depart for New Orleans or any other French Settlement, notwithstanding other Governments have permitted it. Permit us Sir this Occasion to express our sincere Regard for you and our hearty wishes for your Health and Prosperity and that your Excellency may long continue to Preside over Us." The Council's remarks were that "it is the Advice and Opinion of this Board that his Excellency ought not in Consequence of the Address to take any Measures to prevent the Departure of these People."

ADDRESS FROM SUNDRY INHABITANTS OF BALTIMORE TOWN, 1767

Thomas Chase
John Ridgely
Ruxton Gay
Andrew Buchanan
William Lux
Darby Lux
John Smith
Samuel Brown
William Aisquith

John Moale
William Spear
James Sterrett
Daniel Chamier
Benjamin Rogers
Alexander Lawson
Alexander Steuart
Thos. Worthington
John McLure

David McLure
Charles Ridgely, Jr.
Benjamin Griffith
John Moore
Melchor Keener
John Hart
Valentine Lerrick
William Moore, Jr.
William Moore, Sr.

PETITION OF SOME GERMAN INHABITANTS OF BALTIMORE, 1767

On April 15, 1767, several German inhabitants of Baltimore petitioned the Governor of Maryland and complained that they were being charged exorbitant fees when having business with any of his Lordship's Justices in Baltimore County, simply because they were at a loss in understanding the English language. The Justices named in the petition were Nicholas Ruxton Gay, Benjamin Rogers, William Aisquith, Samuel Owings, and Richard Richards. The German inhabitants "being all naturalized agreeable to the Act of Parliamant" request relief from the Governor in this matter. (<u>Archives of Maryland</u>, 32:194-195)

Morice Werster
William Lobley
William Hackle (Silversmith)
Samuel Messersmith
Melchor Keener
William Caaws
Christopher Henneberger
Philip Heitshuh
Andrew Stigar
John Schligh
Conradt Smith
Jacob Keeport
Jacob Fowl
Virtus Hartway
Andrew Garing
John Srink
Philip Grace
Frederick Meyer
Peter Kinner
Henry Hossteter
Peter Streihback
Christian Waskey

Michael Shriak
John Pauer
Adam Shak
Abraham Gribolet
William Hoffman
Daniel Barnett
Christopher Neis
Anthony Hinckle
John Shrim
Christian Apeffel
Jacob Rock
Michael Engle
Moses League
George Loble
Simon Mathery
John Lewis
    Wittemberger
Mathias Bersheb
George Shack
Loenard Young
Adam Brandt
Balthazar Formeab.

PETITION OF SOME INHABITANTS OF MIDDLE RIVER UPPER AND LOWER HUNDREDS IN BALTIMORE COUNTY, 1767

On April 15, 1767 a petition by a few inhabitants of Middle River Upper and Lower Hundreds in Baltimore County was filed and presented to the Governor of Maryland. They complained that "owing to the want of Magistrates in their extensive neighborhood" they had to travel at much trouble and expense to Baltimore Town and pay Nicholas Ruxton Gay, Benjamin Rogers, and William Aisquith "such fees they are pleased to exact and extort from your petitioners." They requested the appointment of Justices in their area because they also have "gentlemen as well descended, as well educated, and as capable as any in the commission of the peace." (Archives of Maryland, 32:195-196)

James Richard
William Bond Whithead
Henry Oram
William Bond, Jr.
Joseph Crook
Richard Jones

Benjamin Mead
John Buck
John Murray
Chaney Hatten
Daniel Watkins

PETITION OF SOME ENGLISH INHABITANTS OF BALTIMORE TOWN IN SUPPORT OF THE GERMAN INHABITANTS, 1767

On May 16, 1767 a number of inhabitants of Baltimore Town presented a petition in support of the German inhabitants who had complained about the Justices who took advantage of their inability to understand English. The subscribers said they knew of such occurrences, but also expressed a belief that William Aisquith, one of the Justices, was not guilty of such charges. (Archives of Maryland, 32:203-204)

Thomas Chase
John Stevenson
Andrew Buchanan
Robert Alexander
Alexander Steuart
Joseph Burgess
Henry Stevenson
James Christie, Jr.
D. Chamier
R. Moale
Charles Rogers
James Cox
Samuel Bailey
Charles Ridgely, Jr.
John McLure
Mark Alexander
James Smith
Aaron Mattison
Nathan Griffith
Henry James
William Moore, Jr.
Alexander Leith
William Goodwin
Brian Philpot
John Ridgely
John Merryman, Jr.
Hercules Courtenay
Alexander McMechan

James Mayes
Robert Manley
James Kelley
Inones Dorling
John Wilkinson
David Humphrey
Robert Robison
George Williams
Jonathan Plowman
Robert Christie, Jr.
Alexander Stenhouse
Robert Adair
Thomas Harrison
William Smith
John Buchan
George Aston
David McClellan
Francis Thomas
John Cannon
John Lees
Nicholas Jones
William Spear
William Lock
James Boyd
John Moale
John Moore
Const. Bull
William Young, Jr.

26

PETITION OF ENGLISH INHABITANTS IN SUPPORT OF GERMAN INHABITANTS, 1767

William Adams
J. Worthington
Robert Mullan
Ewing and Brown
William Dunlop
John Deaver
William Wilson

John Marcery
William Lux
Robert Purviance
James Sterrett
Thomas Ewing
John Boyd
Samuel Thompson

JOPPA COURTHOUSE PETITION OF 1768

The petitions for and against the removal of the county seat of Baltimore County from Joppa to Baltimore Town in 1768 are discussed at length in the _Archives of Maryland_, Vol. 61 (Appendix). Notices were posted in January, 1768 at the door of the courthouse in Joppa, at the church door of St. Paul's Parish, at the church door of St. Thomas' Parish, at the church door of St. John's Parish, at the church door of St. George's Parish, at the door of the chapel of St. George's Parish, at the door of the chapel of St. John's Parish, and at the house called St. Thomas' Chapel in St. Thomas' Parish, by Absalom Butler and sworn to before the Honorable Benjamin Rogers. Notices were printed in English and German. Tabulations indicate that 2,271 voted for the removal of the courthouse, and 901 voted against it. (It should be noted that some signatures are missing due to the disintegration of the paper, and there also appears to be some who signed more than once.) Five years later, Harford County separated from Baltimore County and set up its court house at Bush (Harford Town) in 1774 and at Bel Air in 1782.

SIGNERS FOR THE REMOVAL OF THE COUNTY SEAT TO BALTIMORE TOWN (1768)

William Mackubin
Thomas Cockey
Nicholas Clagett
Thomas Davis
William Cromwell
George Ashman
Sabritt Sollers
John Worthington
Thomas Todd
William Randall
Edward Sweeting
Neale Haile
Phil. Rd. Francis Lee
Robert Willmott
Thomas Johnson
Edward Stevens
Joshua Owings
William Westbay
William Griffin
William Bond Whithead
William Towson
George Haile, Jr.
Charles Ridgely
Zekiel Towson

John Price, Jr.
David Moore (son John)
Josias Pennington
Jacob Osler
William Wood
Thomas Greenwood
John Cretine (Deer
    Creek)
Solomon Wooden
Samuel Harris
    (Susquehanna)
Thomas Johnson, Jr.
Edward Lewis, Sr.
Isaac Griest
William Moore
Christopher Carnan
Benjamin Nelson
Thomas Rutter, Jr.
Thomas Skinner
Benjamin Powell
Joseph Hamilton
James Morgan
James Bosel
William Edwards

Henry Stevenson (son
    Edward)
Thomas Jarreld
James Richardson
Lawrence Richardson
Lawr. Richardson Jr.
Alexander Long
Jacob Leafe
Henry Rutter
--- Sindle
Samuel Owings
John Cockey
Francis Turner
Robert Mitchell
Daniel Curtis
Solomon Wheeler
John Frederick
Nicholas Britton
John Edwards
Robert Long
Thomas Sollers
Septimus Noel
Elisha White
Thomas Gist, Jr.

SIGNERS FOR THE REMOVAL OF THE COUNTY SEAT TO BALTIMORE TOWN (1768)

Jo. Chenowith
Thomas Rutter
David McLure
John Ensor, Sr.
William Ball
Thomas Gladman
Jno. Daughaday
Henry Green
Joel Higginbottom
Thomas Worthington
John Buck
Benjamin Wells
Charles Wells
Samuel Worthington
Edward Norwood
William Young, Jr.
John Ross
Francis Thomas
Jonathan Hanson
John Odle
George Wells
Benjamin Powell
Charles Slagle
Charles Orrick
--- Howland
Thomas Constable
Michael Fowler
(Petition endorsed by
   Benjamin Rogers)

John Gill
Edward Gill
James Leakin
George Campbell
William Piper
John Howlett
Robard Sandarson
William Hodges
Warner Wood
Edward Mason
Conduces Gash
Jacob Myerer
--- Grey
John Mash, Jr.
Epham Gray
William Bosell(?)
Isaiah Vansant
Daniel Stansbury
Leonard Helm
John Mash, Sr.
Salathiel Cole
Caleb Warfield
Nathaniel Stinchcomb
James Buchanan
William Wheeler, Sr.

William Coale
Edward Bosman
John Slemanker
Thomas Gulliver
Robert Sanders, Jr.
William Pricheard
William Lynch
Thomas Downy
Mord ---(?) ---(?)
Luke Trotten
John Smith (Carpenter)
Edward Ware
Samuel Ward
Mordecai Price
Jacob Cromwell
Samuel Bowen
Edward Bowen
William Con
Leven Robert
Michael Kro---(?)
James Everitt, Sr.
John ---(?)
William Denton
---(?) Webster
Risen Gaines
Edmund Baxer, Jr.
Samuel Sollers
William Homes
Edward Radoston(?)
James Kelly (Deer
   Creek)
Nicholas Merryman (son
   Sam.)
Johannes ---(?)
John Ebert
Melkier Buyer
John Smith (Dutchman)
Samuel Norwood
John Motherby
James Barton, Jr.
Adam Buyer
George Adam Beard
Jacob Wileman
Daniel Lett
Edward Pontany
John Godert
Samuel Bernett
Gilbet Miland(?)
Henry Pemberton, Jr.
Emanuel Teal
Arthur Chenoweth, Jr.
George Green, Jr.
Ezekiel Bazill
Jno. Cornelius Gash
Thomas Jones (Planter)

William Jones
Son of Harmon Greathhouse
Edward Lewis
George Tuegail
William Watson
Benjamin Howard
John Welsh
Christopher Randall, Jr.
W. Isgrig, Sr.
Thomas Mills
John Taylor
Philip Barnethow (Philip
   Barnetharse)
Char. Peirepoint
John Prince
Edward Lowry
Richard Carter
Aquila Johns
John Bosley, Jr.
David Wake
Lawrence Hammnond
   (Baltimore)
Christian Aple
Johannes ---(?) (John
   Sower)
J. Cockey Owings
Samuel Stansbury, Jr.
Benjamin James
Alexander Vaughon
William Wells, Jr.
Joseph Murray
Amon Butler
John Roberts
Thomas Mash
Samuel Cookson
Benjamin Bowen, Jr.
Adams Shipley (son
   Charles)
Thomas Marshall, Jr.
Mathias Cannel
Michael Engel (Michel
   Angle)
Henrech ---(?) (Henry
   Pearkin)
Richard Williams
Thomas Alexander
Paul Pennington
Benjamin McMahon
Simon Reichart
William Shaw
Thomas Shaw
William Finn
Thomas Kitten
John Colegate
Benjamin Hood

SIGNERS FOR THE REMOVAL OF THE COUNTY SEAT TO BALTIMORE TOWN (1768)

Robert Ricks
Thomas Green
James Everett
Absalom Price
Absalom Butler
Edward Swan
John Malloonee
Elijah Bailey
Heinrich Lang
Henry Long
William Marnie(?)
Joseph McAllister
Jonas Mash
William Wallace
John Wallace
Pilib Peter (Peter
  Fotcher)
Stephen Wooden
George Robison
--- Straher (Jesper
  Starr)
William Miller
John Gardner(?)
John Smith
Charles Rogers
John Cook
Thomas Stevens
Morgan Mading
Peter ---(?)
William Brian
Henry Helm(?)
Nicholas Walker
John Hall
James Barton
Edward Edwards
James McRee
Valentine Hurd
William Pearce
Edmund Neal
William Boring
William Smith
Mich--- ---(?) (Michael
  Haines)
William Gosnell
John Clarke
George Buchanan
James Rodgers
Jehu Howell
Morriss Baker
John Patterson
Benjamin Crage
William Wodley
Robert Solomon
Andrew Hooke
Joseph Tea

Joseph Robinson
Richard Roles
Antoine Carrier
Samuel Simpson
James Dunn
William Black
William Winchester
Isaac Hicks
John Chapman
William Wells
John Simpson
James Bonnady
William Wright
William Burk
Bale Randall
John Penn
Daniel Miller
Henry Dunn
William Bell
William Wright
Robert Hall
J. Gardner
John Young
Stephen Haile
Samuel Coale
John Tibbon
Thomas Stansbury
Edward Hanson
William Ottey
Abraham England
William Phillips
Thomas Hunt
Joseph Perigo
Johannes ---(?) (John
  Stover)
John Stinchcome
John Condon
John White
Charles Frizell
Thomas Williamson
David Gorsuch
C. Bramwell
Denness Ryely
Abraham Walker
Isaac James
Jacob Young
Thomas Matthews
James Brown
Valentine Larsch
William Heath
William Lock
Robert Woods
David Richards
Joshua Sharpless
John Chalmers

William Gourlie
Henry Craymer
George Chiles
N. Alan(?)
Michael Reichart
Jarvis Biddison
John Sergeant
James Quinn
Jon Homer(?)
James Grayburn
John Morgan
James Wood
Joshua Lynch
Aaron Rawlings
(Petition endorsed by
  Benjamin Rogers)

John Taylor (late of
  Joppa)
John Willmott
John Taylor, Jr.
Richard Colegate
Benjamin Price
Joshua Hall, Jr.
Jasper Hall
Abraham Coles
Gist Vaughan
Charles Brooks
Samuel Brooks
William Marryman
Nathan Wheeler
Thomas Tudor
John Green (son Robert)
John Tipton
John Norton
Christopher Murray
Aquila Price
Charles Gorsuch (son
  Charles)
William Browne (son
  George)
Samuel Price
Joshua Hall
Henry Sater
Watkins James
Samuel Bond
T---(?) Hammond
Morde. Tipton
John Clairy
John Pearse
Benjamin Wheeler
Thomas Hickson
Benjamin Hookes
Thomas Stansbury
Thomas Cole, Jr.

Benjamin Long
John Tyler
John Green
Thomas Rowland
Robert Parker
Edward Edwards
Joseph H--(?)
William Brown
(Petition endorsed by
John Hall and John
Merryman, Sr.)

John Bardell
John Stocksdale
Thomas Evans
John Pitts
Tooley Dailey
James Spring
Job Hunt
Joshua Bond
William Parks
Henry Pemberton
James Kelley
John Banks
Christopher Thonback
James Comly, Jr.
Peter Igoe
Nathan Headington
William Tipton
Edward Talbott
Aquilla Conaway
Nathan Kelley
Stephen Wilkinson
Jacob Cox
Benjamin Banneker
John Stinchcomb
Edward Cockey
John Gosnell
Ethan Loveall
Benjamin Talbott
Henry Lewis
Peter Houk
Thomas Cole
Mycajah Merryman
Phinehas Hunt
Jonathan Plowman
Edward Mason, Jr.
John Murray
Thomas Gist
Francis Brothers
William Ambrose
Nicholas Murray
Thomas Js. Coats
William Trapnell
John Lane
(Petition endorsed by
Andrew Buchanan)

Jabez Bailey
Edward Owings
Oliver Cromwell
John Ford
Zachariah Gray
Nathan Joyce
Charles Ridgely (son
William)
George Ashman, Jr.
James Woodward
Thomas Wantland
Luke Johnson
Nathan Bowen
Nathan Corbin
Samuel Bailey
George Haile
Thomas Tucker
George Alger(?)
Henry Cross, Jr.
Henry Rock
(Petition endorsed by
Jonathan Plowman)

Elisha Dorsey
Samuel Price (son
Thomas)
Joseph Peregoy
Thomas Randall
Benjamin Gorsuch
Jacob Scott
William Hayward
John Gorsuch (son Jno.)
Nathan Johnson
Ephraim Rutledge
Daniel Powell
Alexius Lemmon, Jr.
Skilten Standfer, Jr.
Richard Deaver
Muck(?) Burk
Zabulon Hedington
Abel Hedington
William Parrish, Jr.
Jacob Swalsholder
Adam Slupnar(?)
Joseph Scarff
Walter Pirdew
William Ensor
Timothy Mahoney
George Harryman, Jr.
Charles Gorsuch (son
John)
Stephen Gorsuch
John Gorsuch, Sr.
William Nelson, Jr.
John Stewart

Richard Baskett
Thomas Eagle
T. Rogers
Francis Wilkins
William Hall
Jacob Johnson
William Sinkler
William Burton
Daniel Collett
William Corbin
Vinson Corbin
Thomas Price
Nicholas Corbin
Francis Hunn
Francis Miller
John North
Daniel Smith
Edward Corbin, Sr.
Joh John Syer
Joseph Syer
Jo. Chenoweth
Benjamin Corbin
(Petition endorsed by
Charles Rogers)

Samuel Mummey
Alexander Wells
Nathaniel Owings
William Marsh
Edward Wonn, Jr.
Stephen Hart Owings
William Bagford
Stephen Treacle
John Robinson
Abel Leatherbury
John Hurd
William Peddicoart
Jasper Peddicoart
William Gardner
Edward Hamilton
John Todd
Nathan Peddicoart
Thomas Simpkin
Isaiah Baker
William Murphey
Michael Gladman, Sr.
Michael Gladman, Jr.
Thomas Armes
Henry Leavins
Edward Ousler
Alexander Parker
Robert Marshall
John Hodge
William Willson
James Dinsmoor

SIGNERS FOR THE REMOVAL OF THE COUNTY SEAT TO BALTIMORE TOWN (1768)

James Homes
Willom Curlagh
James Wattson
William Wilson, Sr.
Bengeban Arnold
James Stens
Mikell Madeken
Richard Odle
John Lemans
Samuel Lane
Thomas Smith
Thomas Fowler
John Cornelius
Charles Kelley
Peter Gosnell
Thomas Stockdell
Thomas Leavins
Edward Wonn
(Petition endorsed by
  Alexander Wells)

Thomas Cradock (Rector of
  St. Thomas)
William Lyon
Abel Brown, Sr.
Nicholas Orrick
William Weecor(?)
Nathaniel Stinchcomb, Sr.
Thomas Wells
Henry Crooks
John Ward
Samuel Bell
John Bell
John Wood
Richard Wells
Patrick Mackinley
John Morrison
William Gaddis
John McIlwain
Arthur Cradock
John Cradock
Aaron Hawkins
Charles Walker
Jacob Madery
Johannes Heifer
John Low
Richard Howard
John McGee
(Petition endorsed by Dr.
  William Lyon)

Oliver Matthews
Nicholas Baker
Lott Owings
William Barney

Benjamin Bowen
Samuel Lett
Nathaniel Davis
Michael Dochterman
Anthony Arnold
Joseph Miller, Sr.
Andrew Hippinhammer
Jacob Greer
John Lewis
Joseph Partridge
John Wooding, Sr.
John Howard
David Mackelfresh
John Lant
Samuel How
John Lee
John Read
Nicholas Smith
John Calvert
(Petition endorsed by
  William Lux and
  Benjamin Rogers)

Joseph Cromwell
Benjamin Barney
John Jones
William Kelley
Nathan Cromwell
Richard Owings
John Pindell
William Jones
Stephen Cromwell
Thimey Ragan
Charles Gorsuch, Sr.
John Hall
Neal Lamont
Joshua Gist
Humphrey Brooks
John Griffith
James Griffith
Thomas Worrel
William New
Robert King
Philip Pindell
Richard Fortt
Thomas Bennett
Peter Bond
William Bell
James Welsh
John Boone
William Cockey
(Petition endorsed by
  Joseph Cromwell, Sr.)

Job Jacob Basler
Thomas Shettleworth
John Gilliss
Johannes Tschudi
Johannes Tschudi, Jr.
Matthew McKinnie
Elias Barnaby
John Hunter
John Lainy
Josias Shinton
George McLaughlin
A. Stenhouse
James Franklin
James Armstrong
Zachariah Mackubin, Jr.
Thomas Jones
John Read
Mark Brown Sappington
Philip Parks
John Wiesenthall
George Daffin
Worler Linschinker(?)
Samuel Smith
Nicholas Sinnett
William Nott
John Williamson
George Grim
Benjamin Jones
Hugh Dougherty
Thomas Lenthall
James Mayes
William Aisquith
Jacob Hart
Leonard Campbell
William Beavan
George Gentle
George Dacon
John Curtis
Joseph McVeagh
John Jones
Jno. Samuels
Thomas Marshall
George Leigh, Jr.
Hans Rudie Gallman
Davis Hamlind
Thomas McNimara
Richard Cromwell
Richard Goodman
John Sterett
John Clements
Lewis Weston
Thomas Towson
Sam Roddey
John Fitzgerald
Patrick Hensey

SIGNERS FOR THE REMOVAL OF THE COUNTY SEAT TO BALTIMORE TOWN (1768)

James Richardson
James Potter
Henry Rock
Jos. Gardner
Ulrich Brobeck
William Johnston
(Petition endorsed by
  John Merryman, Jr.)

Thomas Chase
John Smith
William Spear
N. Ruxton Gay
Alexander Stewart
John Talbott (son Edward)
Stephen Gill Wooden
William Denmitt
Thomas Ford (son John)
Abraham Green
Richard Hopkins
John Bond
John Foster
Job Evans, Jr.
Job Garrison
William Cromwell, Jr.
John Willson
Zebediah Gosnell
John Woodward
Jacob Frizell
John Frizell
Thomas Cook
Joseph Gist
David Brown
Samuel Merryman
George Ensor, Jr.
Stephen Ford
Robert Straffon
Nathan Hawkins
Elijah Bosly
William Worthington
Benjamin Tracey
Hill Tanay
John Oram
John Ensor (son George)
William Hunter
Abraham Ensor
Thomas Offout Rand
John Ensor (son Abraham)
Humphrey Chilcote
Roberson Chilcote
John Chilcote
Joshua Chilcote
William Whittington
Suttin Legit
Sater Stevenson

William Peddicoart, Jr.
Charles Haile
Richard Daughaday
Benjamin Burgess Cheney
Thomas Galloway
Edward Browne
Larkin Randall
John Roberts Campbell
John Frazier, Sr.
John Corbin
Abell Brown, Jr.
Francis Thornbury
Richardson Stansbury
William Noon
Thomas Cullings
John Keyth
Charles Phillips
Will Ball
Thomas Lane
Nehemiah Hicks
Alexander Maidwell
Edward Corbin, Jr.
Stopel Overgasht
Micle Hawn
Edward Oursler
Christopher Sence
Solomon Green
Peter Sence
Bale Owings
Benjamin Roberts
Nathan Perigo
John Cromwell
Will Fehaham
Valentine Spicer
Samuel Meridith
Brittingham Dickeson
Hugh Griffiss
Lawrence Oyster
John Tully Young
William Wright
Joshua Jones
Benjamin Price (son
  John)
Samuel Thompson, Jr.
John Sappington
Duncan Carmichael
Jacob Roberts
William Cox
William Bates
Samuel Bromadge
John Spellman
Philip Gover
  (Susquehannah)
Benjamin Ristone
John Wooden

Mathias Wasenor
Elexious Lemmon
Joseph Cromwell, Jr.
John Hopkins
Nicholas Hopkins
John Boyd
Clement Brooke
Mark Alexander
Robert Alexander
Job Evans
Benjamin Merryman
Joseph Merryman
Solomon Bowen
John Fishpaw
Isaac Rawlings
William Rawlings
William Pearce
William Johnson
William Wesson, Jr.
William Stansbury
William Hicks
Wheeler Murray
Heathcoat Pickett
Absalom Boreing
George Tye
Edward Clats
Nicholas Merryman
Solomon Cross
William Wilson
Samuel Fortt
Isaac Green
George Green
Samuel Tipton
Edward Young
Shadwell Green
Nicholas Gash
James Leggitt
Thomas Burk
William Kemp
John Lemmon
Jarvis Biddison
Richard Cole
John Bond
Martin Beard
Joseph Burton
John Cross
Martin Houck
Abraham Hicks
John Melone
John Tye
Nemiah Hicks
John Stansbury
John Carman
Thomas Wills, Jr.
John Parrish

Moses Colet
Shadrick Hicks
Josias Green
John Merryman
John Frazier, Jr.
William Harden
Alexander Walker
Robert Beridges
James Grimes
Adam Birns
William Hendingtone
Josephus Ashman
David McLure
Aquila Galloway
Peter Squiers
Richard Wheeler
Thomas Ward
William Kell
John Carlile
Richard Owings
John Spicer
Philip Sindal
Thomas Purgin
Samuell Sindall
Benjamin Johnson
Isaac Few
James Mockee
Joshua Chapman
Greenbury Baxter
Robert Green
Anthony Reader
Richard Rawlings
John Thompson, Jr.
Patrick Cretin
James Marsh, Jr.
Jacob Upperco
Samuel Martin
Samuel Martin, Jr.
Henrich Schneider
John Neal
(Petition endorsed by
    John Merryman, Jr. and
    John Leet)

Daniel Bond
Thomas Bond, Jr.
John Tracis
James Travis
John Barnethouse
William Patterson
John Barton, Sr.
Nathaniel Wilkes
Ezekiel Slade
John Ross
John Campbell, Jr.

Zachariah Strobell
James Anderson
Robert Humphrey
James Allen
John Speck
Robert Humphrey
John Smith
James Moore
John Ludwick
Frederick Luderitz
Bernhard Alberts
Stephen Sipson
Simon Rieger
John Woodman
Gittings Wilson
Willoughby Warren
Henry Jackson
William White
David Scott
Isaac Hall
John Caldwell
Adam Carehart
Peter Willmoth
James Jackson
William Slade
James Tibbitt
Robert Brown
Robert Cole
William Payne
John Anderson
Ignatius Davis
Henry Scarff
William Richison
John Hanby
William Goddard
John Philpot
William Andrews
John Phahey
Lawrence Conner
David Brown
George Seaton
John Herrington
John Daniel West
John Williams
Johns Hopkins
Arthur Owens
John Howlands
Edward Power
Robert Long
David Haize
Thomas Tucke

Samuel Lewis
Jon Owens
(Petition endorsed by William
    Smith, Elijah Merryman,
    John Merryman, Jr., Nicholas
    Rogers, and Robert Smith)

James Sterrett
W. Smith
Alexander Lawson
Alexander McMechan
Felix O'Neill
John Thompson
John Addison Smith
John Merryman, Jr.
George Reynolds
James Mayes
James Cox
Charles Croxall
Benjamin Griffith
Gerrard Hopkins
J. Worthington
John Wilkinson
William Young
Jonathan Plowman
Simon Ashon
John McLure
Moses Dorling
Welham Cloriss
Alexander Vaille
Samuel Purivance, Jr.
George Ross
Benjamin Dungan, Jr.
John Hadden
Adam Shore(?)
John Livingston
Samuel Thomas
Robert Skinner
Alexander Leith
Henry Hofsteter
William Moore
John Dodge
Thomas Cox Orrison
William Bell
Philip Chris Schuh
Joseph Duer
Thomas Ward
William Payne
James Fishwick
William Lux
Thomas Harrison
James Caldwell
Aquila Duvall
Edward How

SIGNERS FOR THE REMOVAL OF THE COUNTY SEAT TO BALTIMORE TOWN (1768)

Joseph Miller
David Peasley
James Hamilton
John Ward
David Rusk
Henry Veaser
Petro Drumbo
Henrich Schlegell
John McClellan
David Likn
William Hopem
John Depresfontaine
Benjamin Jervis
William Davis
William Richardson (Bush River)
John Evans
Aaron Mattison
John Robert Holliday
Abreaham Huelings
William Carter
William Murphey
George Lindenberger
Christian Diel
George Fletcher
Christian Waskey
William Thomas
John Cannon
Robert Lourey
John Loury
Josiah Lewie
Robert Purviance
John Purviance
George Baxter
Joseph Bounds
William King
Nathaniel Smith
Edward Allen
Edward Woods
John Gordon Thompson
Wheeler Denington
Thomas Rion
George Aston
O. Nc. Barney
John Stevenson
John Sollers
James Jackson
Hercules Courtenay
Samuel Roberts
Samuel Jaquery
Sebastian Madery
Joseph Stokes
Thomas Ewing
Samuel Brown
William Sadler

Hugh Burges
R. Moale
Charles Wiesenthal
James Boyd
Schon Schaun
John Lees
W. Barney
Jenkins Davis
Alexander McLure
Samuel Thompson
John Deaver
Nich. Jones
Benjamin Rogers
Hen. Brown
George Patten
David McClellan
William Goodwin
Daniel Bowly
Thomas Tees
George Williams
Carl Schiel
Vitus Hartweg
Conrath Conrath
William Hoffman
Jacob Brown
William Pontany
James Smith
Schan Schleich
Patrick Lynch
Adam Brant
Caspar Grasmick
William Hackle
Mathies Messersmith
William Askay
James Kelley, Jr.
George Aitkenhead
John Rick
Milkal Shriack
John Faul
William Miller
William Spencer
Nathan Griffith
David Fulton
George Monilaus
William Adams
Basil Francis
Hugh O'Neill
Robert Manley
Joseph Burgess
John Moore
Richard Tayler
Caleb Owings
John Price, Sr.
James Gaddes
David Shields

William Poole
Abraham Foster
Heighe Sollers
Abraham Inloes
Joseph Miller
Robeth Smith
Mabry Helm
Richard Rogers
David Peterkin
Hugh Carson
Daniel Grogram(?)
Francis Brookes
John Chew of (?)
William Scarff
William Cole
John Reily
Moses Bashford
James Boyd
William Reily
George Mackey
Eorge Sheke
John Armstrong
William Richardson
Charles Evans
Andreas Rohrung
Edward Harris
David Humphrey
Moses Faris
William Dunlop
(Petition endorsed in the Market Place by John Leets)

John Keys
James Roberts
James Ingrim
Lonn Connolly
Abraham Britten
Thomas Bedell
James Gittings
John Wilson
William Eede(?)
James Francis Moore
John Hiltin
George Rennolds
William Bosley
William Standiford, Sr.
Hew Grant
Henry McCaslin
Cornelius Lynch
John Standiford
Richardson Roberts
William Gad
Edward Rose
William Sinklair, Jr.

SIGNERS FOR THE REMOVAL OF THE COUNTY SEAT TO BALTIMORE TOWN (1768)

Henry Scarf
Thomas Nichols
Henry Proser
Thomas Boucher
John Green
William Standiford, Jr.
Thomas Buckingham
John McGonigal
James Campbell
Philip Chamberlain
Sammuel Chamberlain
Wilmer Maile
William Gulberert(?)
Patt Durham
William Fell
Cornelius McDonnald
Abraham Ditto
John Tomsin
George Hunter, Sr.
George Hunter, Jr.
John Donnely
James Doran
Thomas Barton
John Ward
James Baker
Rezin Moore
Thoomas Chenowith
George Cridginton
Francis Downing
Richard Perkins
Bloyce Wright
Clement Lewis
James Stewart
George McCandless
John James
Ignatius Jenkins
James Hunter
Peter Hunter
Jonathan Hunter
Thomas Ask
John Anerson
George Smith
William Allin
Dannal Wickes
Solomon Wright
John Inlows
Abraham Standiford
Samuel McNear
John Laremore
Thomas Chisholm
Hugh Eagon
Patrick Rion
Richard Green
James Dimmitt
Aquilla Dimmitt

John Hupper
Michael Little
Thomas Chamberlain
Henry Henden
George Councilman
Mike Gerhard
John Chamberlain
(Petition endorsed by
  James Gittings)

George Ogg
Samuel Merryman, Jr.
William Ogg
Edward Dorsey (of BC)
Nicholas Dorsey, Jr.
John Elder
Peter Leves (Tevis?)
Robert Teves (Tevis?)
Philip Teaver
Edward Talbot
Richard Hooker, Sr.
Vachel Dorsey
Jacob Hook
Henry Woolry
Richard Jacks
Thomas Phillips
John Baker
Benjamin Buckingham,
  Sr.
Benjamin Buckingham,
  Jr.
Christopher Owings
Richard Owings
Jacob Hooker
John Rite
William Walton
John Smith
William Arnold
Absalom Shipley
John Gladman
William Buckingham
John Whips, Jr.
John Delany
John Nickleson
Azariah MacClain
Adam Shipley (son
  Peter)
Edward Dorsey (son
  John)
John Baptist Snowden
John Mash, Jr.
Greenbury Willson
Richard Hooker (son
  Richard)
George Miller

James Brown
William Kindall
Richard Shipley
A. Geoghegan
Lancelott Dorsey
Charles Dorsey (son
  Nathan)
Ely Dorsey
Christopher Suell
Barney Hooker
Rezin Chapman
Indimum Baker
James Hamelton
Solomon Longsworth
John Cook
John Brunts
John Chressman
Edward Todd
Peter Longsworth
Henry Dorsey
Samuel Brown
Samuel Shipley
William Mackcullen
John Whips
John Grover
Charles Gorslin
Anthony Lindsay
Joseph Beasman
James Dorsey
L. Mercier, Sr.
Francis Mercier
Woldon Mercier
Moses Seirs
James Barnes
Charles Dorsey
James Conner
Joshua Ponten
Thomas Jacks
Jacob Gilburd
Charles Pickitt
Jacob Brown
Greenbury Wilson
William Madux
Aquila Hooker
Robert MacCollister
Nicholas Dorsey, Sr.
Amon Shipley
William Hauk
Jonathan Sellman
Wornell Gornnell
Nathaniel Neal, Sr.
John Scoles, Sr.
Charles Franklin
(Petition endorsed by
  George Ogg)

SIGNERS FOR THE REMOVAL OF THE COUNTY SEAT TO BALTIMORE TOWN (1768)

Jacob Myers
Francis Phillips
William Wilkinson
Cornelius Howard
Charles Duke
Edmund Talbott
William Lynch
Far. Battee
John Murray (Coler.?)
Thomas Cotterall
Thomas Miller
Lewis Wise
Benjamin Baxter
Robert Mathews
Edward Wigly
William Smith
James Wood
James Briant
Harry Carback
Henry Carback
Josias Bowen
John Gorsuch
Jacob Sindle
James Lennex
Christopher Rolles
William Rolles
Moses Green
John Cowper
Moses Mackubin
Peter Arnold
William Joyce
(Petition endorsed by
    Thomas Jones)

Richard Acton
Zachariah Mackubin
William Jessop
Benjamin Johnson
George Charge
Henry Wilson (Winters
    Run)
Samuel Owings (of Thomas)
Robert Freight
Jonas Jones
John Chapman
Mordecai Price
Benjamin Price
Abraham Handonson
William Williams
Edward Collet
Thomas Oram
Edward Teal
John Oram
John Shekell
Thomas Griffin

Obed Baker
Nathan Lewis
Elisha Hall
(Petition endorsed by
    Abraham Walker and
    Benjamin Rogers)

Christopher Duke
Frederick Gatch
Gideon Perveil
Thomas Graves
William Ravin
John Graves
Lemewell Hardisten
Robert Graves
John Lennex
Rolan Thornbury
Thomas Eaglestone
Benjamin Eaglestone
Abraham Durham
Thomas Green
Dixson Brown
Thomas Davis
Benjamin Curtis
Nathan Ireland
Richard Ireland, Jr.
William Aplebei
William Graves
John McConikee
Zaceriah Bays
John Sheals
Daniel Shaw
Phillip Sheals
John Rogers
James Busk
John Perigo
John Stansbury
John Grimbs
John Matax
James Taylor
John Taylor
John Ashman
Charles Stansbury
Francis Thornbury
Jorge Haramond, Sr.
John Marcer, Jr.
John Harryman
Charles Harryman
Vallentine Carback
Thomas Harryman
Samuel Clarke
Benjamin Buck
John Grigory
Edmund Stansbury
John Murrey

Joseph Skinner
Josias Dyer
(Petition endorsed by
    Christopher Dukes)

W. Govane
Samuel Gott
Richard Gott
Anthony Gott
Joshua Stevenson
John Adam Beard
John Deaver (planter)
Nicholas Haile
William Macquan
Daniel Fawlway
Stephen Deaver
James Swan
Larkin Hammond
Joseph Tayler
Peter Aston
(Petition endorsed by
    William Govane and
    Ezekiel Towson)

Nathaniel Martin
Thomas Dew
W. Galloway
Luke Raven
William Davis
James League
Samuel Smith (son of Wm.)
Moses League
Nathaniel Nicholson
William Jarman
Thomas Bond (son of John)
Joseph Ensor
John Cotterill
John Hendrickson
William Baines
John Parks (son of John)
Edmond Parks, Sr.
Daniel Scott Watkins
Isaac Wright (son of Wm.)
Thomas Brownlee
John Frame
Benjamin Beavens
Samuel Stansbury, Jr.
John Stone Gorffiss
Greenbury Mildnes
Nathan Wright
Halden Waters
Richard Jones
Richard Croxall
John Cug
John Bevan

36

SIGNERS FOR THE REMOVAL OF THE COUNTY SEAT TO BALTIMORE TOWN (1768)

Patrick Lynch
Christian Davis
George Wales
Abraham Pines
Abraham Asher
Thomas Edwards
R. Campbell Thompson
William Monty. Biggs
John Rutledge
William Williams
Charles Babington
Joseph Crook
Edmund Parks, Jr.
John Jarman
John Denton
John Waller
Thomas Sligh
Samuel Dorsey, Jr.
Joseph Beaun
John Parks, Sr.
Aquila Parks
Elisha Parks
James Nicholson
Moses Galloway
William Wright
Benjamin Mead
Laban Parks
Ojiles Stevens
William Stevens
Robert Jarman
William Quine, Jr.
Isaac Green
John Jones, Jr.
Mose Greer
Joshua Barton
Weyemouth Shaw
Hugh Deen
James Tudder
Edward Willson
William Paslett
Joshua Tuder
James Robinson
Thomas Fitch
William Miser
Edward Preston
Jonas League
Thomas Baulght
(Petition endorsed by
   Moses Galloway)

Thomas Howel
David James
James Finley
G. Robinson
Gideon Cleave

James Hope
John Hope
William Beatty
Constantine O'Donnal
Mordecai Amos
Daniel McComas
Samuel Ashmead (Deer
   Creek)
John Davis
John Parsons
Barnabas McNamee
Joshua Amos
John Lang (Long)
James Perine
John Morgan
Evan Evans
Isaac Parsons
Hugh Ortton
Thomas Cunningham
(Petition endorsed by
   Samuel Ashmead)

Isaac Walters
Thomas Sotherland
John James
Thomas James
William James, Sr.
(Petition not endorsed)

Richard Chenoweth
Richard Chenoweth, Jr.
William Parrish
Edward Parrish
Vincent Bosley
(Petition endorsed by
   Samuel Price)

Solomon Hillen
Richard Parrish
John Lewis (son of
   Henry)
John Ocakon
Francis Lockard
John Brown (son of
   Abell)
Robart English
Gilbert Israel
Edward Parrish
Robert Chapman
Andrew Ebard
Robert Weer
Hugh Keen
J. Rowles
Joshua Owings, Jr.
Joseph Davison

David Bradford
(Petition not endorsed)

R. Richards
Joseph Cole
Richard Cross
John Wheeler
George Wheeler
William Keith
William Boreing
John Cumings
George Groomrine
John Hall (son of Joshua)
Joseph Scott
Thomas Quarterman
Christopher Vaughan
John Shrimplins
John Ozbin
James Murray
Henry Peregoy
Christian Shilling
Frederick Decker
Henry Wade
Richrd Bond
William Murray
James Boreing
Reubin Boring
Francis Dawes
John Myers
Daniel Long
James Hendriks
Samuel Tanner
Thomas Allison
John Meharge
John Turner
Richard Graham
James Graham
James Kelley
Thomas Story
John Scales
John Cox
Absalom Barney
William Morrow
George Everhart
John Murray
John Plowman
George Merryman
John Brown
(Petition endorsed by
   Capt. Richard Richards)

John Conaway
Charles Conaway
(Petition endorsed by
   William Lux)

Henry Dorsey, Jr.
(Mutilated petition; at
least five names torn
away)
Jacob Ybach (Jacob
Ebaugh?)
Isaac Meyer
Johannes Gittinger
Dietrich Reinharth
Hannes Mehl
Christian Daker
Andres Welti
William Schrotter
Peder Faubel (Peter
Fowble?)
Johannes Rodenberger
Johannes Weber
John Dilley, Jr.
Phillip Bohm
Stoffel Ge---ier(?)
Heinrich zur Buchen
Henry Crottingar
Christoffel Sch---(?)
Philip Lorentz Franck
Johan Hass
Jacob Stein
Georg Philipp Manchen
John Minkey
Friederich Schneider
Hannes Dilli
Conrath Dorrmbach
Jacob Fowble
Martin Schneider
Jakon Rind (or Kind)
Carle Schind (Schmid?)
Wendel C---(?)
Joseph Mathias
Johannes Kirbel
Fillipp Lautenschleger
Heinrich Feder
Hanss Adam Munsch
Johan Hennen Mull
Michell Hany
Johanes Horch
John Gill, Jr.
William Cole, Sr.
Stephen Gill (son of
John)
Nicolaus Franckfurter
Adam Mieller
Peder Francks (Peter
Frank?)
Henrich Heyt(?)
George Meyers
Jacob Cotner

Jacob Draisch
John Henrix
Michel Fischer
Johannes Schauer
Jacob Zabf
Willm. Ma--t(?)
Philip Diehl
Henrich Utz
George Fisher
Ludwig Ritt---(?)
Frantz Schuster
Conrad ---(?)
George Walter
Henry Minkey
Frantz Gross
John Burns
Michael Born
Anthon Noll
Stoffel Gru
George Wollery
Stoffel Mohr
John Hawn
Ludwick Shuster
Gorg Koberstein
Frantz Adelsperger
Christian Adrion
Peter Stump
Friedrich ---(?)
Michael Rub
Balser Hardman
Thomas Littell
Jacob Rul
Michael Smith
Jacob Rub
Christian Schaffer
Jacob Schaffer
Miechel Dietz
Heinrich Wihrheim
(Petition endorsed by
George Myers)

William Blizard
William Scarfe
William Brown
Robert Dinsmoor
Henry Naff
John Sellman
Benjamin Maddock
Robert Walker
Philip Walker
Joseph Walker
Morrice Gosnell
Thomas Schales
John Hiser
Christopher Roads

William Logsdon
John Fowler
Jos. Arnold
Benjamin Arnold
Frederick Goble, Sr.
Frederick Goble, Jr.
Keney Loweall
John Hayden
Arthur Betty
Samuel Alexander
Nathan West
James Dilling
Luther Loveall
Labun Welek
Samuel Lane
Dutton Lane
William King
Abraham Stevens
(Petition endorsed by
William Winchester)

John Stoler
Conrad Schmidt
Jacob Ruhbortz
Jorg ---ible(?)
Johannes Lantz
James Kidlay
Samuel Messersmith
Friedrich ---(?)
Carlsen Meyer
Friedrich ------(?)
Morice Wersler
Martin Tschudy
Johannes Breitenbach
Philip Littig
John Hawn
Andres Steiger
Johannes Bader
Migel Born
Lorentz Keller
Mich Eltrorbach
John Ross
John Martin Unger
Johan Philliph Birkefer
------ Blei-Schmidt(?)
Joseph Muller
Thomas Lowe
Elias Bayer
Johann Conrad Small
Peter Striehbeck
George Strobake
William -------(?)
Gisper Kiel
Charles Hissey
William Blohman
Mattheis Zimmerman
Friedrich Meyer der Junge

SIGNERS FOR THE REMOVAL OF THE COUNTY SEAT TO BALTIMORE TOWN (1768)

Ferig ---(?)
Martin Segeter
Christof Reiss
Hugh Watts
Phillip Chraise
Charl Henrch Muller
Tobias Renner
Georg Jaisser
Johannes Barrall
Georg Schack
John Brown
Charles Babington
Nichlais Muller
John Lane
Constantine Bull
William Hunt
Joshua Sharpless
Robert Wade
Milers Love
Gabriel Holland
Peter Litzinger
John Rouse
Rudolf Hug
Martin Stoller
David Parks
John Sank
Daniel Spengel
Thomas Askren
James Elkinson
John Stoler
Joseph Hug
Petter Kiener
Johannes Schranck
Henrich Bluherodt
Weinbert Tschudi
Lancelot Bennett
John Crosbye
William Burg Faw
(Petition endorsed by
  John Stoler)

Richard Davis
Joseph McDonell
Seth Hyatt
William ---(?)
John Logsdon, Jr.
William Logsdon
Jakob Cole
Sa. Chenoweth
Henry Griffith Dorsey,
  Sr.
Jon Chenoweth, Sr.
Jochim Jahn (Yochim Yahn)
William Parrish
Daniel Asban

Richard Richard
John Pasmin (Pasmire?)
Nathaniel Brothers
William Hutson
William Gill
Stephen Gill
Sebastian Frosch
Richard Joens (Jones?)
Richard Hooker
Thomas Bone (Bond?)
Danniel Lain
Edward Stocksdale
Thomas Hutson
Joh. Georg Herman
Andreas Herman
John Clark
John Nicholas
  Wuillanie, Jr.
Peder Uchlir
Hannes Werbel
Fridrick Chrissman
Leakin Dorsey
Michael Huff
Jere. Johnson
Henrich Hennistoffel
Lotowick Weaver
Jonathan West
Robert Cross
John Cross
William Cross
John Haile
Charles Gosnell
Arthur Faris
Carl Schibirtt
Joh. Caspar Kirchner,
  VDM
Henry Cotterill
Arthur Dunn
William Gosnell
M. Hammond
Nicklass Fleuer
Jonathan Griffith
James Chapman
Philip Ulrick
John Israel
Gorg Weber
Thomas Gist
John Helms
Willim Pasmire
Willim Pasmire, Jr.
Thomas Pasmire
Adam Starr
---(?) Smith
Jakob Gis (Git?)
Peder Noss

Jacob Allgeir
Petter Krammer
Joseph Schall
Dunking Ogg
Peter Snap
George Tanner
Johan Belzer, Jr.
Jacob Shrader
Philip Shrader
Peder Schl(?), Jr.
Adam Gantz
Daniel Zapff
Anthony Naryes
Nicol Grunn
Johannes Rester
Fillib Rester
Ja. John Rester
Edward Parrish
Johannes Summer
Henry Worril
Micahel Arnol
Jacob Dean
John Carten
Ludewig Ban
Thomas Tucker
Richard Clark
Adam Shippley
Jas. White
J. G. Willamer
Rudolf Braun
(Petition endorsed by
  John Riston)

Richard McCallister
Philip Coale
James Calhoun
Fridrich Eichelberger
Charles Wildbonn
Robert Irwin
Frantz Noll
Michael Danner
Johannes Spittler
Georg Petter Baum
Johann Georg Gelwicks
Lewis Adam Antony
Philip Franer
Jacob Miller
William Hendrix
Hinman Woften
Caspar Krapf
John Lodgson
George Ruhl
Simon Swaub
Georg Winebrenner
Christian Kraf (Graf?)

SIGNERS FOR THE REMOVAL OF THE COUNTY SEAT TO BALTIMORE TOWN (1768)

Hannes Seri(?)
Johannes ---Schatz(?)
Samuel Haller
Carl Gelwicks
Jacob Reisser
Frantz Heim
Christian Hoover
Abraham Holl
Henrych Beyer
Christian Mehlheim
Johannes Heuster
Jacob Bary
Philip Mayer
Jacob Moaler
Marks Imlar
Edward Digges
John Jotter
Henry Bowman
Georg Weiss
Henry Sturgeon
Jacob Belss
Nickles Kleh
Nicholas Fisher
Georg Koch
Adam Forny
Friederich Sauer
Christoffel Stiehl
(Petition endorsed by
  Richard McCallister)

Benedict Swope
Daniel Bower (Bowers)
Samuel Owings
Herman Fischer
Joseph Harney
Diter Berger
Carret Wilson (Pilson)
Jeremiah Morris
Adam Reicther
Jannir Hass
Jacob Jentes
Adam Beyer
John Wells
John Botts
Georg Beber
Christofel Grammer
Thomas Watson
Robert Davis
Dungen Ogg
William Hobkings
Ettwert Stockstell, Sr.
  (Edward Stocksdale?)
James Irwin
Nathan Chopman (Chapman)
Paul Gorner (Garner)

John Doyl
Philip Salter
William Tio
Phillip Borter
Charles Clark
John McCinsey
Henry Worrel, Jr.
Philip Weber
Phillip McCole
Froutz Frish
Samuel Mackey
Benjamin Dunkan
Michel Gor
Matthias Rhode
Philip Hall
Isaac Hammond
William Bentley
Benjamin Bond
John Lamars
John Bentley
William Winchester
Nathaniel Davis
Samuel Mannon
John Durbin
John Chenoweth
Joseph White
Charles Howard
(Petition endorsed by
  Daniel Bowers)

Joseph Sutton
Josias Grover
Luke Wylie, Jr.
(Endorsement illegible)
George Risteau
Thomas Owings
Robert Thrap
Henry Garken
Loveless Gorsuch
(Petition endorsed by
  George Risteau and
  Benjamin Rogers)

Benjamin Ogg
Henry Butler
Samson Tuchstone
David Forsey
William Naygers
Wilhelm Hoban
Samuel Barker
Johannes Grothaus
Thomas Redbon
John Greathous
Thomas Buckingham
Richard Cruchly

James Stevens
George Dorsey
Adam Shipley
Richard Barnes
Charles Welsh
John Arnal
Benjamin Clay
Leven Porter
John Holbrock
John Shevers
Thomas Shevers
Francis Davis, Sr.
Phillip Porter
Joseph Linthicum
Neall Clark
Thomas Clark
Robert Bly
Jacob Fradrick (wagonner)
Nathan Todd
William Ginkings
Benjamin Knight
William Wilson (of
  Burnthouse Woods)
James Morray (Murray) (of
  Burnthouse Woods)
John Cooper
William Benett
Edward Hewitt
Benedick Lucas
Thomas Sellman
Daniel Carr
Henry Slack
William Graves
John Hood, Jr.
Samuel Shipley, Jr.
John Hood
George Shipley
Andro-- ---ichens(?)
Jorg Ganss
Michal Ganss
Jacob Ganss
Benjamin Barley
William Hartlegane
Gilbert Younger
Joseph Gosnell
Edward Leatherwood
Ezekiel Evans
Henry Young
Samuel Leatherwood
Thomas Franklin
Philemon Branes
Indemion Baker, Jr.
John Wildman
John Nelson
Ezekiel Beavin

SIGNERS FOR THE REMOVAL OF THE COUNTY SEAT TO BALTIMORE TOWN (1768)

Mical Huff
John Welker
John Scholes, Jr.
Robart Jarden
Lodowick Weaver
Lenard Hobs
Adam Faeruber
(Name of endorser not
  given)

James Calder
Paul Adams
A. Eaglestone
John Randle
James Ogleby
Jonathan Hanson, Jr.
Joseph Bosley, Jr.
Walter Ogle
William Wyle
Thomas J---(?)

Joshua ---(?)
(Not endorsed)
Michel Knight
George Knight
David Knight
William Mahann
James Anderson
Nathan Johns
Skipwith Coale
John Manhaum
William Parriss
William Peton
John Jones
Joseph Hop---(?)
Will Co---(?)
Henry Purssey
Zachariah Allen
Thomas Goodin
James Boodin
Robert West

Stephen Fisher
William Cowen
Samuel McWilliams
(Petition endorsed by
  Samuel Harris)

Samuel Miller
Charles Bailey
Charles Worthington, Sr.
Jono. Adam Messel
Alexander Martin
George Gooden
Philip Coale
Will Clarke
Hugh Reed
Benjamin Deavers
Torrance Oboil
John Wilson
(Petition endorsed by
  Jeremiah Sheridine)

SIGNERS AGAINST THE REMOVAL OF THE COUNTY SEAT TO BALTIMORE TOWN (1768)

Greenbury Dorsey, Jr.
John Brickerton
John Garrettson
John Beedle Hall
George Copeland
William Bradford, Jr.
George Patterson
Richard Dallam
Thomas White
Levin Mathews
John Day (son of Edward)
William Arnold
John Hall of Cranberry
Isaac Webster
Edward Hall
John Paca
James Moore
William Hill
Samuel Budd
Richard Willmott
Benjamin Wheeler
Hugh Deans
James Webster
John Patterson
John Love
Daniel Preston
William Bradford
Garrett Garrettson
Micajah Greenfield
Henry Garland

Francis Garland
Alexr. McComas (son
  John)
Alexander McComas, Jr.
Aquila Nelson
Gilbert Crockett
John McComas (son
  William)
Gabril Swan
Jacob Horwood (Harwood)
Henry Robinson
William Gallion
Moses Loney
Thomas Hampson
Thomas Magee
David McCracken
James Hullet
Nathan Gallion
Asbery Cord
Thomas Brown
John Bott
James Stewart
Jacob Gallion
William Anderson
William McIlhaney
Kent Mitchell, Jr.
Richard Garrettson
Aquila Hall
Daniel Ruff
Moses Ruth

John Blackburn
Mordecai Durham
Phil. Henderson
John Jackman
Joseph Johnson
Aquila Hall, Jr.
Andrew Lendrum
Charles Vashon
Thomas Everitt
John Mitchell
James Wetherall
Thomas Mitchell
Joseph Barns
Samuel Thompson
John Wilkerson
Francis Leeshody
Henry Slight
John Wood
Walter Tolley
Jos. Carvil Hall
Aaron McComas
Bartas Piners
William Andick
Robert Saunders
John Ogden
Charles Menagh
Reubin Skinner
Richard Peery
John Toomy
Cornelius Skinner

John Skinner
John Ouin
(Petition not endorsed)

James Phillips
James Lenegin (Senegin)
James Osborn
James Osborn, Jr.
Cyrus Osborn
William Osborn
Henry Rhodes
John Lee
George Holandsworth
Joseph Prearecatt
James McCracken
John Durham (plasterer)
Francis Billingsley
Alexander Smith
John Michell (Michael)
Mathew Creswell
Thomas Bryerly
Joseph Smith (blacksmith)
Daniel Scott, son of
 James
James Smith, Jr.
William Jones (carpenter)
Richard Robartson, Sr.
James Wetherall
Edward Jackman
Theophilus Baker
Barsill Billingsley
David Clark
Joshua Dourham (Durham)
Daniel Duskin
Willia Murffy (Murphy)
John Murrfy (Murphy)
Jacob Bond, Jr.
George Little
Isaac Whitaker
John Chauncey
James Chauncey
William Hollis, Jr.
John Herbert
Anthony Drew
Michael Kinnard
Caleb Beck
Thomas Bleany (Blaney)
Ozwin Sutton
Nicholas Baker
John Hanna
William Harrison
William Willson
William Hanna
Philip Quinlan
George Wright
Henry Green

Leonard Green
Henry Cooper
John Shinton
Richard Worrell
Barnet Johnson
Robert Johnson
William Johnson
William Ramsay
Robert Clark
Lewis Putee (Puttee)
Archibald ---(?)
John Mitchell
Henry Jarman
John Swinerd
William Manley
George Chansey
Gilbert Vansicklen
Richard Vansicklen
Hollis Hanson
Thomas Price
John Hanson
John Donavin
John Fokner
John Hanson, Jr.
Nathan Horner
Morriss Dickson
James Norriss
John Mitchell, Sr.
William Smith
Hugh Bay
John Elis (Ellis)
James Faris
James Holmes
James Sincler
John Callender
Robert Callender
Charles Taylor
John Lynch
George Lange
William Grafton
John Michael, Sr.
George Carothers
William Keen
John Rhoads, Jr.
Timothy Neve
James Wilgus
Robert Dobens
William Kelley
William Johnson
James Little
James Little
Abram Norriss
Charles Ward
David Maskembel
James Watson

Hugh Hawkins
William Deall
John Hays
William Welsh
Isaac Trotter
Alexander Ewing
James Smith
William Moore
James Muller
Thomas Hanna
John Hill
Robert Robarts
Walter Billingslea
George Pusey
James ---(?)
James Jones
Job Barns
Thomas Jones (mason)
Ezekil Jones
Amos Jones
Robert Hawkins, Sr.
Richard Hawkins
William Campbell
Andrew Haslet
(Petition not endorsed)

Henry Dougherty
William Sims
James McNabb
William Wells
Moses Lockerd
Paul Wantz, Sr.
Christoff Benz, Sr.
John Renshaw
Thomas Ruth
William Ellets
Richard Wells, Sr.
Thomas Jones (mason)
Richard James
Ezekiel Jones
Amos Jones
Alexander Murey
John Draper
William Barnhill
John McCollough, Sr.
John McCollough, Jr.
Samuel McChesney
Michael Archdeakin
Mr. John West
Mr. Robert Cooke
Nathaniel Sims
James Thompson
Andrew Wolcot
Joseph Joans (Jones?)
Alexeander Murrey

Joseph Hansen
Nathan Laughlin
John Muller
Thomas Willson
Thomas Foster
William Porter
John Lynch
Nathan Litton
Richard Ross
Zachariah Allen
James Jones
John Wilson
William Carroll
Thomas Hawkins
James Maxwell
John McDaid
Danuel McDaid
James Black
William Coale, Jr.
John Beaver
William Hopkins
Joseph Wilson, Sr.
Daniel McDade
John McDade
Thomas Bishop
Thomas Johnson
James Hutcheson
Manasseh Finney
James Gordon
John McBride
John Finney
Ralph Sims
William Wilkinson
John Wineman
Andrew Kinnar
Daniel Campbell
Thomas McCallak
James Stephan
William Wray
Eduard Stepleton
George Guyn
Thomas Sims
Walter Robison
Daniel Campbell
Felixe Cosgrif
Samuel Campbell
James Fisher
Stephen Fisher
Garret Croeson
Thomas Maxwell
David Maxwell
Joseph Renshaw
James Parks
John Montgomery
William Montgomery

John McCall
Benjamin Jones
Robert Lyons
William Hopkins, Jr.
(Petition not endorsed)

Benedict Wheeler
Dixson Stansbury, Jr.
James Barton
Enoch James
Thomas Wheeler
William Armstrong
Thomas Bleakleay
Philip Calvin
Richard Robinson, Jr.
Edward Norris
Thomas Welsh
Shepard Armstrong
William Bay
Joseph Thomas
William Bay, Jr.
Abraham Whitaker
Jacob Bond
James Hodgkins
Thomas Simmons
James Ewing
Robert Camble
  (Campbell)
Mebrel Ellott (Elliott)
Eduard Riley
James Elliott
Thomas Miles, Jr.
Thomas Miles (son of
  Peter)
Peter Carlisle
William Robinson, Jr.
Robert Clarke
Daniel Thompson
John Dale
Thomas Street
Thomas Bussey
Samuel Standeford, Jr.
William Dammit, Jr.
John Standeford (son of
  Sam)
Joseph Norris (son of
  Edward)
Richard Hope, Jr.
William Nelson
James Hope, Sr.
James Amos
Alexander McMaster
Thomas McMaster
John Stro
William Stro

William Williams
Thomas Hutchins
Thomas Franklin
Daniel Shaw
Bennett Bussey
Thonas Miles
John Smith
Thomas Elliott
John Craft
John Gray
James Maddin
Jonathon Lyon
Aquila Clark
William Norris
Asel Hitchcock
Alexander Thompson
James Wilson
Jno. Chocke
Joshua Chocke
William Everett
Samuel Hannah
John Hannah
Richard Everett
Samuel Everitt
Walter Rice
Robert Amoss
Thomas Amos
William Ady
John Giles
George Clarke
William James
Aquila MacComas
Peter Perine
Charles Robinson
John Demoss
Daniel Tredway
John Bryarly
(Petition not endorsed)

Edward Garrettson
Benjamin Hanson
John Henry
Sam Kimble
Richard Monk
Belser Michel (Balsher
  Michael)
Edward Vann
James Barnes
John Kirkpatrick
John Creighton
Dan Hair
William Loney
Gregory Barns
Abraham Cord
George Budd

43

Patrick Smith
George Reed
Peter Sullivane
Robart Darbe (Darby?)
James Hill (son of
  William)
John Hill
John Ford
Pearey Fouller
Abraham Banks
Danell Jud
Elihu Hall Bay or Elihu
  Hall (Bay)
Thomas Gash
Moes Colems (Moses
  Collins?)
Morres Collens (Morris
  Collins)
Samuel Webster, Sr.
William Robinson Presbury
John Deaver (joiner)
William Presbury (mason)
William Ralph
Thomas Presbury
Thomas McBride
William Augustus Smith
Richard Bennett
Richard Hill
James Thrift
Francis Deacon
Edward Mitchell
Francis Riley
James Taylor
Alexander Downey
William Downey
Thomas Wilson
Richard Webster
Joseph Puntenney
John Watkins
Edward Evans
Thomas Jones
John Armstrong
John Money
John Loney
John Hall Hughs
James Armstrong
Joseph Rabes
Joab Barns
Samuel Webster
Archibald Beaty
Samuel Cartey
William Parry
Kent Mitchell
Thomas Tredway
Mathew McClentok

Amos Hollis
George Chancey, Jr.
Daniel Donohue
William Magill
Thomas Rodgers
Isaac Wood, Jr.
William Mitchell
Thomas Miller
James Seale
Richard Thrift
William Thomas
Thomas Mills
Nicholas Scaff
William Jameson
William Jennings
William Smith
William Dortridge
George Presbury
(Petition not endorsed)

James Richard
William Horton
Billingsely Roberts
William Amoss (son
  James)
Jno. Watters
Abraham Andrew
John Hughston
John Lusby
William Kitely
Walter James
Samuel Ricketts
John Reohds (Rhodes?)
Henry Mahorney
Francis Green Gilpin
Jonathan Kely (Kelly)
Luke Bond
Andrew Hall
Andrew Hall, Jr.
William Keley (Kelly)
Martin Preston
Barnard Clement Preston
Walter Marton (Martin)
James Marton (Martin)
John Barnhows
John Beale Howard
William Debrular
Stephen Pribble
J. Norris (son of
  Benj.)
Alexander Cowan
Clement Lewis
John Green
John Norris (son
  Edward)

William Amoss
James Norris
Robert Amoss
William Gillmore
Simon Reine (Perine?)
Peter Reine (Perine?)
John Norris
Benjamin Norris (son of
  John)
William Norris (son of
  John)
Thomas Norris (son of
  Benj.)
Abraham Norris (son of
  Benj.)
William Jones
Francis Billingsley
Walter Billingsley
Jacob Bull
Edmund Bull
James Munday
James Lytle
George Lytle
Thomas Hutchins (son
  Nickles)
Josa. Bond
James Amoss, Jr.
Benjamin Amos (son of
  James)
William Bull
Buckler Bond
Edward Cripple
John Norris (son of John)
Daniel Treadway (Tredway)
Thos. Tredway (son of
  Daniel)
John Hillary
Patrick McCardel
John Ellis
Hugh Kernachum
Daniel Fralia
Colmer Canlee
James Monahan
Patrick Flanagan
John Garson
Robert Whiteford
Morris Baker
Morris Baker, Jr.
William Baker, Jr.
Charles Baker (son of
  Morris)
Daniel Thomas
John Howard
James Amos
John Kidd

Thomas Johnson
Robert Bishop
Barnet Johnson
William Buntinge
John Dale
Walter Tolley, Jr.
Spence Legoe
James Sanders
John Twedel
Edward Norris
William Downs
Jno. Tutton
Benjamin Howard
Lemuel Howard
Samuel Durham
Samuel Durham, Jr.
James Durham
Mordecai Durham
Joshua Durham
John Durham
David Durham
Aquila Durham
Benjamin Norris
John Green
Dan Norris
John Taylor
James Whitaker
Isaac Whitaker
Robert Travis
Edward Robinson
Nathaniel Yarly
Thomas Saunders
Edward Saunders
Joseph Saunders
Joshua Saunders
Thomas James
Vinson Richardson
Samuel Richardson
Benjamin Richardson
Daniel Preston
Benjamin Amoss
Thomas Richardson
Thos. Richardson Jr.
Asel Hitchcock
James Carroll
James Carroll, Jr.
Peter Carroll
William Deale
Daniel Duskins
Godfrey Watters
Henry Watters
Nicholas Watters
Stephen Watters
Thomas Bay
Thomas Bay, Jr.

Lewis Dunham
Andrew Taas
Johns Montgomery
John McKnight
The next five names had
  lines drawn throuh
  them:
Mordecai Amoss
John Amoss
Wm. Mccomas (son of
  John)
Wm. McComas (son of
  Dan.)
Daniel McComas
Abram Hughes
Esram Hughes
Isaac Garrett
John Garrett
Thomas Rowntree
William S. Cator
William Linday
John Bay
(Petition not endorsed)

Daniel Kenly
John Lathim
Thomas Boyle
Reinerd Potts
Michael Gilbert
Parker Gilbert
Charles Gilbert
Jeremiah Cook
John Hall (Swan Town)
Abraham Guyton
Thomas Kennedy
Abraham Robinson
James Fitzsimmons
Robert Cunningham
George Steuart
Thomas Harris, Jr.
Mathew McClentok
William Semple
Benjamin Culver
Robert Culver
Edward Ramsey
William Horton
Henry Knight
Robert Megay (McGay),
  Jr.
Isaac Umbel
John Umbel
John Megay (McGay)
James Horner
William Mekem (McKim)
Enuck (Enoch) West

James Pritchard
David Sweeney, Jr.
Rawland Sheneer
John Litton
Samuel Smith
Elijah Beck
Charles Beck
John McComas (son of
  Daniel)
Daniel Pritchard
James Pritchard

George Botts
Samuel Swaurt
Richard Spencer
James Sparold
Jno. Gallion
William Brickell
P. Gaddis
John Henry
William Beton
Matthew Sweeny
Abraham Robinson
John Robinson
Isaac Robinson
John Rodgers
Jacob Giles
Gilbert Donahue
Amos Cord
John Hall
Jno. Mathews
John Lee Webster
James Mather
Joseph Gibbons
William Ford
Andrew Tate
Benjamin Scott
John Twadel
Robert Scott
Robert Scott, jr.
Thomas Mills
Thomas Strong
Thomas Downs
Thomas Durbin
Samuel Griffith
Alexander McComas
Solomon McComas
Thomas Durben
(Petition not endorsed)

William Wilson, Jr.
  (sadler)
Jno. Browne
Aquila Duley
William Boardsman

45

Josias William Dallam
John Gardner
John McGay
Samuel Gallion
Clothworthy Cunningham
Joseph Stiles
James Mathews
Thomas Smithson
Edward Ward, Jr.
James Kennedy
Jno. McLane
Thomas Wilson
James Gallion, Sr.
Alexander Hanna
John Cretin
Samalt(?) Welborn
David Durham
Henry Ruff
John Bennet
Peter Bennet
Joseph Buley
Daniel Carlin
John Lusby
Benjamin Green
William Hollis
Grafton Preston
Thomas Bond
Aquila Paca
Gerard Hopkins
William Johnson
William Webb
David Davis
John Willmott
Francis Holland
James Quinlin
Dines (Dennis) Cain
James McCermak
Thomas Ross
Charles Vashon
James Dickson
Benedict Legoe
William Scott
Nathaniel Smith
Francis Leeshody
Thomas Hill
Henry McBride
Archibald Johnson
John Johnson
Ralph Smith
James Yoe
Robert Stephenson
Samuel Smith
Jonathan Starkey
William Bond
George Knotts

Ephraim Knotts
Solomon Brown
Ralph Smith, Jr.
Henry Smith
John Moore
(Endorsed by the Upper
    House of Assembly 6
    June 1768. Signed by
    U. Scott, Clerk)

James Simms
John Jolley
Thomas West
William Morgan
Samuel Jinkins
   (Jenkins)
Francis Jinkins
   (Jenkins)
James Fisher
Edward Reily
Josiah Lee
James Rigbie
Joseph Brawnly
   (Brownly)
James Hinds
Robert Dunn
Alexander Clay
Robert Bryarly
Edmund Bull
William McClure
Samuel Webb, Jr.
James Major
Charles Sims
Jonathan Jones Smith,
   or Jonathan Jones
   (smith)
William Fisher
Thomas Wheeler
Ignatius Wheeler
William Husband
John Bull
Samuel Lee
Alexander Rigdon
Thomas Baker Rigdon
John Worthington
Joseph Waters
Samuel Litten
N. Rigbie
Joseph Wilson, Jr.
James Wilson
Robert Tarbert
Henry Croft
John McFadin
Josias Scott
James McCandlee

William Clake (Clarke?)
Richard Kroesen
James Walker
John Smith
John Hast
David Bartley
Isaack Umbul
James Litten
John Umbel
Robart Bradin
John Harris
Robart Mils
Thomas Harris
Samuel Shaw
Simon Dennie
James Death, Sr.
Edward Death
Ephraim Gover
William Richardson (son
   of Thos.)
James Hicks
David Berry
John Morgan
Patrick Quigley
John Glan (Glen?)
John Jones
Samuel Wilson
William Bennington
Robert Elder
Thomas Jones
William Fisher, Jr.
Joseph Hopkins, Sr.
Joseph Hopkins, Jr.
Samuel Hopkins
Phelix Donnoly (Felix
   Donnelly)
Francis Donnelly
James Cain
Benjamin Wheeler
Josias Wheeler
Edward Prigg
Jesse Foster
James Billingsley
Samuel Forwood
Joseph Forwood
Thomas Archer
James Death
John McCulloch
John Forwood
William Forwood
Edward Morgan
Robert Crawford
Richard Lyon
Samuel Webb
Zacarias Spencer

SIGNERS AGAINST THE REMOVAL OF THE COUNTY SEAT TO BALTIMORE TOWN (1768)

John O'Neil
Patrick Fowler
James Martin
Abraham Johnson
Francis Neill
John Scarrel
Matthew McClure
John Wilson
Barnard Preston
Gershin Silver

William Wilson
Samuel Wilson
William Wilson, Jr.
Joseph Jonston
Robert Jeffery
Henry Dunkin
Henry Bath
John Kroesen
Nicholas Kroesen
Buchanan Smith

Jno. Reddick
Samuel Jeffery
Valliant Nettenfield
Jno. Nelson
William Smithson
Samuel Bayles
Benjamin Bayles
Samuel Bayles, Jr.
(Petition not endorsed)

PETITION FOR PUBLIC ROAD FROM ROCK RUN, 1771

A petition of sundry inhabitants of Baltimore and York Counties was read before the General Assembly of Maryland on October 18, 1771, praying for a road to be laid out from Rock Run on the Susquehannah River to Foy's Landing. The following persons were summoned to testify in this matter. (Archives of Maryland, Vol. 63, pp. 12, 13, 14, 20, 173)

William Cox
James Webster
Jeremiah Sheredine
Daniel Preston, Sr.
Andrew Lendrum
Richard Seward
William Husbands
William Welch
David Clarke
Philip Coale (Cecil Co.)

Isaac Webster
Thomas Smith
Nathan Rigbie
John Wilson
John Tolley
Oliver White
James Fisher
Samuel Hopkins
Thomas Taylor
Nathaniel Giles

A LIST OF LETTERS LEFT IN BALTIMORE IN 1773

In the very first issue of the Maryland Journal and Baltimore Advertiser on August 20, 1773 we find a notice of Baltimore's first post office. At the time, the town did not have a regular mail service, so William Adams volunteered to receive, and hold until called for, letters for Baltimore and vicinity. The following is a list of letters left at William Adams' in Baltimore, by the Frederick-Town Post, as published in George McCreary's The Ancient and Honorable Mechanical Company of Baltimore, (1901), pp. 16-17.

William Andrews, Back River Neck, Baltimore County.
John Barrow, near Upper Cross Roads, Baltimore County.
George Bramwell, Patapsco.
Benjamin Bale, Baltimore.
Charles Collins, Baltimore.
Lawrence Carroll, hatter, Baltimore.
Captain James Colden, near Baltimore.

James Carroll, in Strabane Twp., York County, Penn.
Mrs. Esther Dennis, at Col. Dennis' in St. Martin's, Somerset County, Maryland.
Barney Doherty, Baltimore.
John Finn, Baltimore.
John Fitzsimmons, Baltimore.
James Flemming, Baltimore.

A LIST OF LETTERS LEFT IN BALTIMORE IN 1773

James Geehin, in Baltimore.
George Hail, Baltimore.
John Jones, Baltimore.
Henry Johns, Baltimore.
William Langrall, in Dorchester
County.
Thomas Montgomery, Baltimore.
Frank Manning, Baltimore.
Thomas M'Culeth, near Rock Run.

William Ray, near the Ball Fryer Ferry
in Baltimore County.
(Note: This is the Bald Friar
Ferry, now in Harford Co.)
Michael Reily, Baltimore.
Daniel Robertson, Baltimore.
John Grant Rencher, Baltimore.
James Smith, Baltimore.
Thomas Ward, at Rogers' Mills,
Gunpowder Falls.
Sarah Woodfield, Baltimore County.

RECORD BOOK OF BALTIMORE LODGE OF MASONS NO. 16 IN 1773

The membership record book of the Baltimore Lodge of Masons No. 16
(1773-1780) is in the Manuscript Division of the Maryland Historical Society
Library in Baltimore (MS.107). It contains lists of members and their dates
of entrances, degrees received, resignations and deaths from 1773 to 1780.
The following were members in 1773.

Robert Moore.
Alexander Stenhouse.
Charles F. Wiesenthal.
John Boyd - declined being a member by
his own request on September 12,
1780.
James Somervell.
Alexander McMechan - died in Baltimore
on January 19, 1776.
Ivie Hair - entered May 17, 1773; past
as a fellow craft on June 21, 1773;
raised to degree of master mason on
September 28, 1773; died in the West
Indies (uncertain when died).
Alexander Cowan - entered May 10,
1774; past as a fellow craft on July
4, 1774; raised to degree of master
mason on October 5, 1774.
Ebenezer Mackie.

Samuel Hay - entered December 30,
1774; past as a fellow craft on
January 10, 1775; raised to degree
of master mason on January 23, 1775.
Jonathan Plowman - entered being
before a modern apprentice, 1775;
past as a fellow craft on April 9,
1776; died on May 22, 1776.
Thomas Brareton (Brereton) - admitted
a member being a regular ancient
master mason, December 27, 1774;
declined being a member by his own
request, September 8, 1778.
Thomas Ewing - admitted a member being
a regular ancient master mason, his
first time appearing March 14, 1775,
a subscriber for the warrant; died -
lost on his passage to France in
1777.

These petitions of the court were abstracted from Baltimore County Court Proceedings as published in the Calendar of Maryland State Papers--The Black Books for the years 1773-1774. For the court cases they listed Justices and Jurors for the cases cited.

Proprietary vs. Negro Charles and Negro Ben who were charged and found guilty of assaulting their master James Calder, on February 22, 1773. Both were sentenced to be hanged.

JUSTICES	SHERRIFF	JURORS
Thomas Franklin	John Robert Holliday	Thomas Owings
William Young		Abraham Whitaker (of Abraham)
Benjamin Rogers	PROSECUTOR	Simon Vashon
William Otley	Thomas Jenings	Daniel Hughes
Jonathan Plowman		James Moore, Jr.
John Moale	JURORS	Hercules Courtney
Andrew Buchanan	William Worthington	Absolom Price
William Goodwin	Henry Weatherell	Joseph Miller
	William Demmitt	John Merryman, Jr.

Proprietary vs. Negro Hercules, property of James Russell and Company, charged and found guilty of stealing a horse belonging to Corbin Lee, on October 8, 1773. He was sentenced to be hanged.

JUSTICES	SHERIFF	JURORS
Benjamin Rogers	John Robert Holliday	Buckler Bond
Andrew Buchanan		Mordecai Amos
Jonathan Plowman	PROSECUTOR	James Greenfield
Thomas Sollers	Thomas Jenings	William Hunter
John Moale		Samuel Litten
William Buchanan	JURORS	Maybury Helms
Isaac Van Bibber	Jeremiah Johnson	John Spicer
	Thomas Chinowith	Benjamin Bowen
	Thomas Rutter	William Amos

Proprietary vs. Enoch McDonald and Rebecca, his wife, who were charged with having beaten to death Charity Stoble on October 7, 1774. They were found guilty and sentenced to be hanged, but a subsequent plea for pardon "since they never intended the death of the child" was granted because "they were recommended as fit objects of mercy by the justices and foreman of the jury."

JUSTICES	SHERIFF	JURORS
John Moale	Robert Christie, Jr.	William Weare
Isaac Van Bibber		John Walsh
James Calhoun	ATTORNEY-GENERAL	Valerius Dukehart
Hercules Courtney	Thomas Jenings	Thomas Hutchings
John Craddock		Thomas Constable
Thomas Sollers		Daniel Hughes
Andrew Buchanan		James Frankin
Jonathan Plowman		Thomas Hutchings
William Spear	JURORS	William Lux
William Buchanan	Charles Young (foreman)	
John Smith	John Gray	
William Russell	Beal Randall	CLERK
George G. Presbury	William Demmitt	A. Lawson

OFFICERS OF THE COURT AND JURIES

Proprietary vs. Negro Dick, slave of William Russell, who assaulted Mary Godson and found guilty of stealing money and various articles from her on October 8, 1774; to be hanged.

JUSTICES
John Moale
Isaac Van Bibber
James Calhoun
Hercules Courtney
John Craddock
Thomas Sollers
Andrew Buchanan
Jonathan Plowman
William Spear
William Buchanan
John Smith
William Russell

SHERIFFS
John Christie, Jr.
John Robert Holliday

JURORS
Charles Young
John Gray
Beal Randall
William Demmitt
William Weare
Jacob Walsh
Valerius Dukehart
Thomas Hutchings
Joshua Bond
Nathan Griffith
John Read
John Bond

CLERK
A. Lawson

ATTORNEY-GENERAL
Thomas Jenings

A LIST OF TAXABLES IN BACK RIVER UPPER HUNDRED IN 1773
TAKEN BY WILLIAM HUTSON

Armstrong, William
Anthony, John
Armstrong, David; Robert Danch; Negro
  Hager
Aston, Peter Sr.; Peter Aston, Jr.
Aston, Joseph; Edward Dinsarn
  (Finsarn)
Aburd, William
Ashman, George Jr.; William Cutam;
  Anthony Burten; Nathaniel Coub;
  Negro Hercules
Ansil, Henry; Foblue Leadluce
Bagford, William; Richard Hisor;
  Negroes: Harry, Hannah
Burnem, John
Bosley, Walter; Negroes: Cate(1),
  Parraway, Ruth, Cate (2)
Bowen, Mary (widow); Nathan Bowen;
  Negroes: Baddoah, George
Brown, William
Burgess, Joseph
Beasy, John
Bowen, Benjamin; Josias Bowen; Samuel
  Manum; Thomas Walcraft; Negroes:
  Simon, David, Chloe, Simeon

Bowen, Solomon; John Bowen; Solomon
  Bowen; Negroes: Simon, Luce
Black, Samuel
Bond, Nicodemus
Bell, William
Bilson, John
Brady, James
Britain (Boitan?) , Nicholas; Negroes
  Cock, Sall
Burgess, Thomas; William Finley;
  Daniel Browen
Bond, Benjamin; Negro Bugy
Bond, John Jr.; John Bond; Negroes:
  Hannah, Luce
Bond, Josnue; William Crock
Bond, Thomas (Qtr.); John Baxter; John
  Pinder; Negro London
Barham, Joseph
Bosley, Joseph; Joshua Bosley; William
  Bosley; Stephen Barrott; Negroes:
  Page, Nan, Meriah, Tom, Priss, Dinah
Boring, James
Bond, Edward
Belt, Richard; William Hill; Wm.
  Montgomery; Francis Smith (Hmith?)

Buchanan, Andrew at his quarters;
Joshua Jones; Jasper Smith; Negroes:
Dick(1), Cate, Ralph, Dick(2), Moll

Britain, Nathaniel (Boitain?); Samuel
Smith; Negroes: George, Peter,
Hannera

Buchanan, Archibald at his quarter;
Nicholas Hale, son of George;
William; James; Henry; Negroes:
Lander, Prince, Joney, Saxney,
Sanah, Moll

Colegate, Richard; Negroes: Seserona,
Jem, Sal, Sue, Sale

Condon, William (Britain Ridge);
Negroes Hercules, Hannah

Cole, Samuel (Britain Ridge); Phillip
Cole; Negro Harry

Chinworth, Richard Jr.; Arthur
Chinworth; William Chinworth; Thomas
Chinworth

Coles, Slathan; Richard Wheeler;
Negroes: Boson, Lydia

Cole, Rachel (widow of Denis); William
Cooper; William Hill

Cole, Mary (widow); Ninirant Cole;
Negro Cone

Chambers, James

Cockey, John; Thomas Webster; Thomas
Hersy; Thomas Draper; Edward Night;
William Collins; Negro Nan

Carrier, Thomas; Peter Aston, security

Cockey, William; Edward Flannagan;
Rowland Bates; Negroes: Jack, Sam,
Ja, Bett

Cloon (?), Thomas

Cole, Thomas Jr., Levy free(?) –
William Richardson; William Russell

Cromwell, Elizabeth (widow); John
Pindell, Jr.; Negroes: Cack, Nathan,
Tom, Charles

Cradock, John; Darby Jenner; John
Seaboy; Richard Morgan; John Quin;
Richard Piddle; Negro Boatswain

Cromwell, Joseph; Phillip Cromwell;
Richard Cromwell; Negroes: Hardy,
Crehal

Cockey, Edward, Joshua Cockey;
Negroes: Easter, Juday

Carroll, Charles Esq. at his quarter –
Coles Caves; Andrew Scandal; Joe
Clark; Samuel Miller; Negroes:
Sandigo, Willigre, Nedilent,
(unclear), Deb, Easter, Sue, Nell,
Subinah, Tody, Brister, Natt, Isaac,

Moll(1), Moll(2), Peg, Cote, Dinah,
(torn)

Cockey, Thomas Sr.; Thomas Cockey;
James Space; Negroes: Jonathan,
Boson, Burnam, (unclear), Haly(?),
Cook, Jack

Colegate, John Sr., John Colegate; 5
Negroes

Chillem, William

Cannida (Cannilla?), Thomas

Cromwell, Stephen; Jeremiah Tomson;
Hercules Stone; Negroes: Will,
Barrett

Carnan, Charles; Richard (torn);
Thomas Jonas (Jones?); John Gorden;
Anthony Ryan; Negroes: Nero,
Berkshire, Daniel, Kitt, (unclear),
Rachel, Hannah

Daughaday, Richard; Negroes York,
Dinah

Daughaday, John; Patrick Maxarin; Four
negroes

Deye, Penelope; Negroes: Sam, Peter,
Jack, Rachel, Leah, Mariah, Sarah

Deye, Thomas Cockey; Negroes: Jack,
Austin, Amber, Caesar(1), George,
Taffy, Sue, Kisey, Sarah, Sall, Dan,
Ester, Caesar(2), Charles, Champion,
Jacob, Ben, Hannah, Bett, Levy, Nan

Ethatan, Joshua

Edmiston, Wm. (The Rev.); Negroes Ned,
Margret

Fancut, William

Fort, Richard; Henry Leve (Love?)

Fort, Samuel

Ford, Thomas Sr.
Thomas Ford
(?)-----popa
Negro Sarah

Ford, Stephen
Joseph Ford

Fishpaugh, John; Negro Dick

---(?), Benjamin

Flatt, Thomas

Ford, John Sr.; John Ford; Joshua
Ford; Negroes: Jack, Comfort

Gorden, John

George, Still

Gorsuch, Charles; Norman Gorsuch

Gorsuch, Loveles(?); Thomas Gorsuch;
Negro Dinah

Green, George Jr.; Negroes: Toby,
Cates Gott, Richard

Gist, Thomas Jr.; Timothy Shahanthe;
Abraham Buchly; Edward; Negro Baum

Gillard, George

Galhamton, Thomas

Galloway, Fiaca (widow); Negro Alice

Griffith, Nathan (at his qtr.); James Trapnel; John; Daniel; Pary; Negro Nan(1); Negro Nan(2)

Gill, Stephen (of John); Thomas Stacy; William; Negro Luce Stepney

Gill, Stephen Sr.; Edward Gill; Jonathan Easton

Gilmore, Thomas

Gott, Samuel; Richard Gott; Negroes: York, Cock, James, Dinah

Gott, Anthony; Negro Hager

Griffith, George

Gorsuch, John

Gorsuch, William; Charles Gorsuch

Govane, James; John Deaver; 10 negroes

Gill, John Jr.; Joseph Clark; Thomas Thorp; Negroes Bombro, Dye, Rachel

Gill, William

Gill, John Jr.; John Garby; Negroes: Tom, Will, London, Bob

Hisor, Samuel

Hale, George Sr.; Henry Hale; Joseph Hale; Shadroth Hale; Morris Pope

Hale, George Jr.; William O Harry; Negro Jane

Hale, Nicholas

Hearoy, William; John Smith; James Leary

Hammond, George; William Howard

Hall, Phillip; Joseph Hoskins; William Cullins; Negro Florah

Hunt, Samuel; Phineas Hunt; Timothy Whiger; Negroes: Jack, Tom, Sue

Hopkins, John; Thomas House; Negroes: Charge, Potchane

Hopkins, Richard; Nicholas Hopkins; 9 negroes

Haines, James

Heart, Joseph; John Acton

Hunt, Job; William McKoy; Negroes: Ned, Tamer, Rachel

Hutson, William; Thomas Hutson; Charles Lockart

Hubbert, John; Samuel Owings; Jr., Security

Hopkins, Sarah; Negroes: Hostin, Charles, Caesar, Norce, Moll, Grace

Holliday, John Robt.; William Welch; William Allen;

William Rack, David Tool, Wm. Springate, Richard

Wheeler; Negroes: Toby, Tom, Jem, Caltimore, Dinah, Flora

Hale, Ned; Shadrach Hale; Negro Luke

Jent, Thomas; John Bricken; William Tomless

Jones, William

Jones, Joshua

Johnson, George (on Britain Ridge)

King, William; Joseph Hammond

Kemp, John; Samuel Bowen

Kelley, James; Roger Parritt

Kitten, Thomas; John Phunfy; Isaac Wheeler; Timothy

Lee, William

Ledger, John

Lewis, Dunham

Lux, Darby; James Easam; Hopkin Hopkins; Negroes: Roger, Phillis, Beck, Hagar

More, William

Males, John

Mathews, Oliver; William Mathews; Thomas Middleton; Francis Scantree; Daniel Swift

Morford, Thomas; Stephen Morford

Moale, John (Gunpowder Qtr.); Negroes: Hercules, Godfrey, Minervy

Morris, Jeremiah; James Fir; Nathan Weber

Motherby, Charles; Levy Free; Negroes: Jaminer, Tom

Neatherclift, Wm.; Thomas Farmer

Norris, Joseph; John Rud; Negro Mary

Nicholson, Benjamin at Newfoundland Quarter; Edmond George; Wm. Scolecraft; Negro Anthony

Owings, Richard (of Stephen); Negro Jim

Oran, Henry Wright

Odle, William

Owan, John; John Jones

Owings, Caleb (of Stephen)

Owings, Samuel Sr.; 7 negroes

Owings, Bale; John Seapler, Negroes: Wilks, Rachel

Owings, John Cockey; Richard Atkins; John Taylor; Paul Bess; Negroes: Jack, Jenny

Pindell, John Sr.; Negroes: Moll, Nan

Pierce, Philip Grofford

Price, Stephen; Negroes: Juda, Como

Price, Mordecai (of John); John Turringly; John Rolph; Richard Goodman; Robert Ley; Negroes: Loff, Edward

Philpot, John (at Adbuts Quarter);
John Bond, Jr.; Clift Aserbant;
Negroes: Henry; Mark, Rickey,
William, Sam, Moll
Parkes, David
Pindell, Phillip
Pierce, William
Perrigo, James; Robert Read
Price, William; Negroes: Bramo, Farmer
Price, John Sr.; Benjamin Price;
Negroes: York, Tony, Coray, Hannah,
Fanch
Pitts, John; Henry Bond; Negroes:
Jack, Nan, Hannah
Patton, Abrahaml Nicholas McKoy
Powel, Benjamin; John Drualte; William
Hedges; John Seaden; Charles Dayly
Raven, Sarah (widow of Abraham); 6
negroes
Ragon, Timothey
Risteau, George (at Gunpowder Qtr.);
Negroes: Caesar, Sam, Jude
Roach, Samuel
Roberts, Thomas
Randall, William; John Hiser; George
Carr; Negroes: Baltimore, Dick;
Jacob; Cann; Bep
Ridgley, Charles; William Cloman; John
Corns; Negroes: Captain, Frank,
Dick, Harry, Hester, Paterson,
James, Cate(1), Phillis, Cate(2),
Tony
Ridgley, Charles, Captain at
Northamton Qtr.; Samuel Merry; John
the Wagoner; George Goodwin; Edward
Welch; Duch Henry; Shepard;; Samuel;
Dile; John Bowest; Denis; Jack Gum;
Coleman; Michael; Slight; Negroes:
Bob, Marane, Casly
Ridgley, Charles, Captain, and Company
at the Northamton Fce.; Henry
Howard; Benjamin Deaver; Caleb
Warfield; John Vaughn; B. Legget;
Daniel Barker; Philip Beal; Richard
Gough; Johnus White; John McCown;
Joseph Allen; William Onion ;
Charles Doud; Joseph Harvey; Michael
Martain; Timothy Murphy; Samuel
Coil; John Dehoddy; Edw. Corckland;
James Roany; Barney Quin; William
Stevens; Thos. Ellishear; Samuel
Fisher; Edmond Gunshaw; John Puit;
Thos. (?)nahory; Martin Poltis;
Henry Riddon; Dennis White; Wm.
McConnel; Joseph Wood; Daniel Boot;

Thomas Davy; Wm. Connelly; William
Roe; John Fonhue; Negroes: Toby,
Helton, Joe, Lyn, Tom, Jupiter,
Teaner, Hannah, Jonathan, Dan
Sparks, William Sr.; William Sparks,
Jr.; William Heling
Stephenson, Joshua; John Loyed
Stephenson, Henry; Nicholas
Stephenson; Jeremiah Sweny; Negro
Hannah
Stansbury, Thomas (son of John, could
by Thos.); Edward Loyd; Negro Domer
Stansbury, Thomas Sr.; Benjamin
Stansbury; John Stansbury; Negro
Golar; Nick, Sam, Jude, Pegg
Sankes, John
Sigaper, John
Slater, James
Steal, John
Stephenson, Henry (son of Edward);
William; Negro Sarah
Sollars, John
Sollars, Benjamin
Sater, Henry; William Hollis; Negroes:
Hester, Hannah
Sater, John
Simpson, John
Shaw, Joseph; John Shaw
Tipton, Jonathan
Tipton, Aquila
Tipton, William; Joshua Tipton;
Nicholas Tipton
Thomson, Cuthbert
Talbott, Edward; John Talbott;
Benjamin Talbott; John Whethers; 4
negroes
Tobin, James
Trapnell, Vincent; Henry Cloman;
William Chapman
Tipton, John; Tobias Tipton
Taylor, Henry
Tipton, Thomas
Tilley, Edward; William Druett;
Negroes: Joe, Harry, Daniel, Florah,
Fanny, Bett
Wells, Ann (widow); John Thomas
Walker, Thomas; Negro Hannah
West, Jonathan
Worthington, Wm. (Qtr.); Edward
Mansfield; Negro Joe; Hannah
Willmott, Robert; John Willmott;
Negroes: Jim, Jack, Easter, Fanny,
Passure

A LIST OF TAXABLES IN BACK RIVER UPPER HUNDRED IN 1773

Willmott, John Sr.; Aquila Willmott;
 Negroes: George, Pompy, Hannah,
 Comfort, Lucy
Willmott, John Jr.; Richard Nesbit
Wheeler, Ruth (widow); Negro Alice
Walker, Charles (Qtrs.); John
 Wilshire; James Murphy; William
 Island; Negro Nan
Worthington, Samuel; Thomas Groves;
 John Price; George Miller; Roger
 Bulmore; Negroes: Lewis, Tolly, Tom,
 (torn), Robert, Brown, Sall, Poll,
 Bett, old cook
Wintinger, Bowner; Timothy Sha
Wilson, Jacob; Thomas Canada
Wood, James; Samuel Hale
Wheeler, William Sr.
Wheeler, Solomon; Joseph Wheeler;
 Negro Jenny
Wheeler, William; Whacan Wheeler
Williams, Edward; George Hammond,
 Security
Whiten, William
Woolf, Michael
Yon, John; John Taylor
Yawn, Yocum
Younce, Phelter

Cromwell, Nathan; Negroes: Oliver,
 Tom, Sam, Piping, Arch, Press
Chapman, William; Jonathan West,
 Security
Darling, Thomas; John Pindle, Sr. (or
 Pindell)
Murphey, Dennis; William Hutson,
 Security
Evins, Joseph
Marse, Harcalas; Charles Carnan,
 Security
Bond, Shadrach
Clarke, Arthur; Henry Sater, Security
Macarthas, Callagan; Henry Sater,
 Security

On the back of one of the above lists
 is the following note:
BACK RIVER UPPER: Taxes and Additional
 List = 840. Examined by And.
 Buchanan and Jas. Gittings. Examined
 and 19 Taxables added twice.

A LIST OF TAXABLES IN BACK RIVER LOWER HUNDRED 1773 TAKEN BY DOMINICK B. PARTRIDGE, CONSTABLE, JULY, 1773

All, Benjamin
Annice, Joshua
Boson, James
Biddison, Jarvis; Daniel Biddison;
 Negroes: Febe, Rachel, Abey
Biddison, Thomas; Thomas Biddison;
 Negro Luce
Burgain, Thomas; Emanuel Abbs
Brown, Dixon; Dixon Brown; James
 Isaacs; Negroes: Vulcan, Dick, Doll,
 Leah
Bush, Benjamin; Negroes: Dublin, Beck
Boren, James
Clark, Samuel; Negroes: Reding, Venut,
 Biner
Carback, Valentine
Carter, Richard; Negroes: Hannah, Nan
Carter, Joseph
Coe, William; John Thompson
Duke, Charles; Thomas Mcionaly(?)
Duke, Christopher; Negroes: Caleb,
 Page
Dicker, Henry

Davis, Robert; Negroes: Dinah, Sam
Davis, Thomas
Daughaday, Joseph
Eagleston, Thomas; Negro Moses
Fitch, William; Henry Whys
Fitch, Robert
Fitch, William
Fuit, Thomas
Floid, Thomas
Frinsham, Henry (or Funsham)
Fowler, William; Negro Easter
Fuce, William
Fowler, Richard
German, Benjamin
Groves, William
Growy(?), Thomas (Graves? Groves?)
Graves/Groves?, John
Gash, Conduice; Philip Gash; Nicholas
 Gash; Wm. McGlauhlin
Gregory, John
Gregory, James
Glendenning, (Clendenning?) William
Grimbs, Nicholas

A LIST OF TAXABLES IN BACK RIVER LOWER HUNDRED 1773

Hill, Joseph
Hardester, Lemuel
Harryman, George; William Clarke;
  Negroes: Toby, Caesar, Jeffry,
  Easter,Hagar
Harryman, Thomas
Harvey, Robert
Hatton, Acquilla
Hillen, Sollomon; Thomas Mathews;
  William Merison; Negroes: Jamet (1),
  Jamet (2), Doll, Grace
Harryman, John; Negro Cazer
Holland, Gabriel
Howlet, John; Joseph Langdon; Negro
  Sam
Hottman (Holtman?), Jacob
Harryman, Charles; Josias Harryman;
  Negro Hagar
Ireland, Richard Jr.
Johnson, Ephraim
Johnson, Joseph
Johnson, John
Johnson, William
Kingsbury Furnace; George Matthews;
  James Smith; James Robinson, Sr.;
  James Robinson, Jr.; Richard
  Chinworth; Caleb Harryman; Negroes:
  Bob, Ralph, Scipio, Gold, Chintz,
  Cyrus, Daniel, Frederick, Story,
  Ceazer (1); Beazy, William, Thom
  (1), Cleanis, Jame, Thom (2), Sambo,
  Prince, Bristol, Dick (1), Mark,
  Duncan, Peter, Will, Ceazer (2),
  Joe, Dick (2), Coffee, Zua, Kate,
  Ruth, Bett, Jenny, Phillis (and 5
  more unnamed)
Lancashire Furnace - Edmond Warriener;
  Richard Gibbins; William Rock;
  Thomas Carbach; Charles Maxfield;
  William Berry; Henry Young; John
  Murray; Robert Sims; Henry Jackson;
  Negroes: Kate, Hannible, Brook,
  Peter (1), Frank, Peter (2), Chuff,
  Phillip, Gay, Sam, Guy, Hazard,
  Prince, Chester, Wallace, Dick,
  Lancashir, Ceazer, Scipio, Emanuel,
  James, Sampson, Mingo, George, Ben,
  Prima, Hannah, Esther, Phillis,
  Marsa, Priss, Lette (and 10 more not
  named)
Mattox, John; William Mattox
Murray, John
Martin, Nathaniel; Negroes: Trace,
  James, Will, Nan, Sall, Daphna,
  Beck, Dinah

McAnnikin, John; John Long; Negroes:
  Seal, Sall
Mumer, David; Michael Casener
McCluer, John; Thomas McCluer
Marcer, John; Negroes: Tom, Ben, Dick,
  James, William, Phill, Hannible,
  Liddy, Kate
McNutt, William
Miles, Peter; Thomas Miles
Oram, Henry
Parlett, William; William Parlett
Pattyson, John; William Pattyson
Parlett, Charles
Partridge, M. Dobery; Negro London
Right, William
Rush, William
Randall, George; Wm. Chaplain; Sam
  Welshire
Sanden, Benjamin
Stansbury, Charles; Thomas Quitt;
  Negro Fann
Shields, Phillip
Stansbury, Richardson; Negro Luce
Sims, Thomas
Sindall, Samuel; William Sindall
Stansbury, John; Joseph Stansbury;
  John Ivery; Negroes Phill, Sue, Doll
Short, Jacob
Sandom, William
Story, Joseph
Sedwick, Benjamin
Stansbury, Edmund; John Jeffner; John
  Bush; Negroes: Will, Jude
Taylor, James; Negro Choice
Turner, Francis; Mathew Turner
Turner, Joseph
Turner, William
Taylor, Richard; William Leet
Taylor, Joseph; Negroes: Peter, Night,
  Clate, Hannah, Nann, Jack, London,
  Flora (and 7 more not named)
Taylor, Samuel
Wigley, Edward; Edward Wigley; Isaac
  Wigley
White, Luke; Negro Clear
Warrington, Henry
Welch, Phillip

Note on the reverse side:
  Back River Lower: 294 and 7
  additional.301. Examined by William
  Buchanan and Isaac Van Bibber.

A LIST OF TAXABLES IN BALTIMORE TOWN WEST HUNDRED, 1773
TAKEN BY JOHN STOLER, CONSTABLE

(The number after each name indicates the number of taxables in each house. Only the name of the family head is given.)

Armstrong, James 1
Adam, William 3
Ash, Lawrence 1
Armstrong, John 1
Ashburner & Place 1
Ackerman, George 2
Appleman, Conrod 1
Apple, Christian 2
Allen, Robert 1
Allen, Edward 3

Brown, Jacob 2
Brown, Michael 1
Boyd, James 1
Brand, Adam 2
Braithenback, John 1
Brunner, John 1
Barcy, Lewis 1
Blaishiraid, Henry 1
Bower, Edward 3
Barnyby, Elias 2
Bayly, James 1
Bowen, John, Barber 1
Burgess, Joseph 3
Bayly, Thomas 1
Brown, John 1
Boyd, John, Doctor 1
Baint, Frederick 1
Burk, John, Barber 1
Brierton, Captain 1
Barney, William 2
Buchanan, William 5
Black, Hugh 1
Belt, Charles,
Cabinetmaker 1

Craig, John 4
Clows, William 1
Cannon, John 2
Cos, James 8
Calhoun, James 1
Culthan 3
Clarke, James 2
Cranath, Lemuel 1
Chase, Jeremiah 1
Cos, Thos. Arrison 1
Carmickael 1
Christie, Robt.Jr. 5
Chambers, James 2
Christie, James Jr. 6
Clements, John 5
Carson, James 2
Carson, Samuel 1

Douglas, Sewall Geo. 4
Douglas, William 1
Duhart, Valesius 2
Dailley, Dinus 1
Dickens, William 2
Dugan, Cumberland 1
Duke, Thomas Patt 1

Edwards, James 4
Eickelberger, Jacob 1
Eickelberger, Barnt 1
Elgenson, James 1
Egan, Nicholas 1
Ebrell, Samuel

Frowell, John 1
Frelch, Christian 1
File, John 2

Garts, Charles 1
Graybill, Philip 2
Gaston, James 2
Garritson, Cornelius 1
Gordon, John, Sadler 3
Galdwell, John 1
Growen, Rudolph 2
Gorsuch, Robert 1
Gartner, George 1
Goddard, William 4
Garthson, George 1

Harrison, Thomas 9
Hutchings, William 1
Hopkins, Philip 1
Heagen, Erder 1
Hart, Jacob 2
Hart, John 7
Howard, William 1
Hoffman, Andrew 1
Hughs, Daniel 3
Hownd, William 2
Holliday, James,
  Shoemaker 4
Harris, David 1
Heatherington and
  Weatherburer 2
Hopkins, Gerrard 5
Hall, Walt 2
Hughes, Christopher 3
Horsselbach, Catharine
  2
Haithshoe, Catharine 1

Jones, Thomas 4
Juday, Nicholas 1
Juday, Winbart 1
Johnston, Christopher 2
Jones, Nicholas 1
Jones, Thomas (dupl.) 4

Keener, Peter 1
Keepet, Jacob 4
Kraither, Jacob 2
Kiser, Mark 1
Kennedy, James, Dr. 3

Larsh, Valentine 1
Lewin, Gabriel 1
Lowry, Henry 3
Laindecker, Simon 1
Long, Robert 1
Lindenbeck, George 2
Labatt, Ignatius 2
Low, Thomas 1
Leavely, William 3
Little, John 2
Leman, Richard 4
Langston, James 1

McCabe, John 1
Marshall, Thomas 5
Mathison, Evan 4
Mogenhemer, Gilbert 3
Miller, Philip 1
McMacken, Alex. 1
Massersmith, Samuel 4
Main, Alexander 1
Mayjer, Frederic 1
Marshall, William 3
McClure, David 2
Mops, Frederic 2
McKim, John 2
Markley, Conrod 1
McClure, John 1
Marmer, Francis 1
Massy, William 2
Morrison, Joseph 1
Mordecai, Mordeca 1
McLevn, Alexander 1
Meyer, Frederic 5
Moale, Richard 12
Moore, Wm. Jr. 10
Moore, Wm. Sr. 2
McClannel 2
Moor, Robert 2
Moor, Martin 2

Neese, Christopher 1
Neall, Capt. 1

O'Neal, Felix 1
Owings, Samuel 1
O'Neal, William 3

Purviance, Samuel   3
Purviance, Robert   3
Preistman, George   3
Patton, Mathew   4

Richardson, William   6
Richardson, Aubery   3
Rick, John   2
Rusk, William   3
Rusk, David   4
Rogers, Philip   5
Rogers, Joseph
  Brass Foundry   1
Russell, Henry Jr.   1
Russell, William   3
Redy, Samuel   1
Richinson, Benjamin   2
Ram, Jacob   2
Ross, John, Captain   1
Ross, George, Capt.   1
Ridges, William   1

Shrine, John   2
Skull, William   2
Sanderson, Francis   5
Smith, James   1
Somergell, James   2

Sley, John   2
Shlaymaker2
Starrup, Jacob   2
Shields, Caleb   3
Sheuth, William   1
Saegeser, Martin   1
Stribeck, Peter   1
Strutt, John   2
Sterratt, James   3
Smith, Thomas   1
Steiger, Andrew   5
Shragly,   2
Scath, John   1
Sheaff & Phile   1
Spencer, William   1
Sinkelair, William   1
Smith, Francis   5
Smith, Nathaniel   3
Smith, John   3
Shields, David   3
Spear, William   6

Towson, John   2
Thomas, Philip
Trygell, George   1
Triplett, Md (?)   3
Terbeck, Michael 1
Tewett, Thomas 2
Thompson, Henry 4
Taffleby, George 1

Usher, Thomas 4

Vashon, Simon 2

Winshler, Marites 1
Wiesenthall, Chas. 2
Walsh, Jacob 5
Walker, Robert 1
Walker, James 1
Worthington, Thos. 2
Walsh, John 2
Wolfe, Michael 1
Wender, Christopher 2
Wigeldorf, Henry 2
Westby, Hugh 1
Woolsey, George 1
Westby, William 4

Young, Charles 2
Yonigling, Abraham 1

Additional List: (?)
  hile, John 1
Allen, Solomon 1
Chamier, Daniel, and a
  serving man, and negro
  woman
Good, William 1
May, Anthoney
Moal, Richard; Negro
  Liberty 1

Signed by John Stoler.
  Baltimore Town West ..
  481. Examined by John
  Moale and Andrew
  Buchanan.

LIST OF TAXABLES IN DELAWARE HUNDRED, BALTIMORE COUNTY, 1773

Arnold, Joseph
Arnold, Benjamin
Arnold, William
Andison, William

Buckingham, Francis Sr.; Bisalam
  Buckingham
Brothers, Francis
Buckingham, John Jr.
Bardel, John
Bardeley, James
Bardeley, John
Brothers, Thomas
Buckingham, William
Baley, William
Basman, Joseph; Jack Hannah
Basman, Thomas

Buckingham, Benjamin; George
  Buckingham
Buckingham, Benj. Jr.; Zeb.
  Buckingham; Benjamin Buckingham,
  Securites
Barnes, James; Caley Barnes; Samuel
  David
Barnes, Richard; Aquila Barns
Barnes, Philiman
Brown, Abell Jr.; William Purer; James
  Oitter
Brown, John; Patrick May; Tom
Brown, James; John Charter
Brown, Samuel; John Home; Charles
  Knight
Brown, David; John Hammersbale; James
  Grant; John Roule; Fib---(torn)
Barnes, Lego; Nicholas Selby, Security
Brown, Alex. Sr.; John Bates: Tom,
  Tobey, Roger, Peter, Pompey, Ginney

Borning, William; Demon
Bennit, Thomas; Mark Smith
Bennit, Mary; Benjamin Bennit; Gruney
-----(?)
Bennit, William; William Ellace
Bennit, Samuel; John Jay; Cornealus
Bend
Barns, Adam
Binout, Joshua; William Heal
Bayan, Thomas

Cook, John, of Thos.
Collins, Patrick; Wm. Hardegile
Cole, William (Qtr.); Francis Harris;
William Masey; Harry Easta
Cook, Wm., of Thos.; John Cook, Jr.
Christman, John; John Day
Conaway, Charles; John Cebs
Chapman, Rigen
Chapman, Robert
Chapman, John
Cooper, John Sr.
Chapman, Luke; Charles Chapman
Crows, John
Clarey, Benjamin; Benjamin Clarey;
Morrice Inglish
Clark, Wm., of John
Cook, John Sr.; John Cook
Cinled, John

Deaver, Philip; Abigil; Grace
Davise, John
Dorsey, Jonsey; Thomas Mauway; Sam;
Bin; Rachel
Dorsey, Edward; Edward Dorsey; John
Goodlan; Wm. Shavens; William
Price; Joseph Holdin; Comfort
Dorsey, Basel (Qtr.); Thomas Gilbert;
Henry Gilbert
Dillin, James
Dewell, John
Dorsey, Caly
Debeny, John
Davison, Joseph
Davis, Walter; Charles Row
Daniel, Michal
Dorsey, Nicholas; Abrim, Soloman
Dorsey, Charles (of Nich.); Joseph
Chapman; John Carter; John Langley;
George Miller; Absilam Frisel
Dorsey, Nicholas Jr.; William Aston;
John Martin; Thomas Miller
Dorsey, John (Qtr.); Ka(?)es Conener;
Edward Gattle; Thomas Giffiry; John

Poe; John Mikes; John Cocks; Richard
Williams; Harry Cater Cub
Dorsey, Ely (Qtr.); John Randle; Will;
Joe
Dorsey, Ely

Eavins, John
Eavins, Tobe
Edwards, John
Eavins, Thomas
Ellis, Obidiar
Elder, John; Leonard; Willis; Robert;
Sook; Sue
Elder, Owen; Isack; Luce

Frisel, John; Edward Scarf
Fisher, Peter
Foster, Thomas
Fips, James
Foular, John
Franklin, Charles
Frisel, Abrim
Franklin, Thomas

Gilbert, Jacob
Gasaway, Thomas (Qt); William Moore;
Francis Cunner
Glover, John; John Nats; John Power
Gersiler, Wernel; Daniel Davise
Grimis, Richard; Henry Lark
George, Peter
Goff, Henry (Qtr.); Boston Frog; Wm.
Richison; Patrick Welsh; Charles
Fortin; Jiry Pegg
Gersiler, John
Gorsuch, Nathan; Harry; Jack
Gladman, John; Mic(?) Gladman
Gilliss, John (Qtr); William Gilpin;
Daniel Kiley; Joseph Neal; Peter
Milibet; Daniel Harvey; Peter; Tom
Grimis, James; James Rorson
Grate, Houk Armon
Green, John
(?)---, Richard

Hawkins, Rigin
Hawkins, William
Hains, Jacob
Hains, Antoney
Hardigle, William
Hutson, Robert (Qtr.); Samuel Brown
Hawkins, John; William Marks, Security
Hamburton, James
Hickman, Nicholas
Hook, Jacob Sr.; Jacob Hook, Jr.

Hadin, William

Hammon, Isock; Patrick Burns; Thomas
  Standley

Hooker, Richard Sr.; Aquila Hooker;
  Richard Hooker

Hooker, Barney

Hoobs, John

Howard, Joseph (Qtr.); Richard Welch;
  Matthew Green; Glascow Fillice

Hill, Thomas

Hammond, Regin; John Booth; Toney;
  London; Jack; Robert; Sidey; Luce

Hust, Edward

Jones, Richard

Jurden, Robert; William Jurden;
  Thomas Jurden

Jacobs, Richard (Qt); Nace; Ned; Bess

Jagriff, William

Jacobs, John

Jeinkins, Thomas

Jacks, Thomas

Kelley, Charles; Moses Kelley

Kinston, George; Thomas Foster,
  Security

Knight, John

Longworth, Solomon

Linsey, John; John Davise

Linsey, Anthoney; Samuel Lambert

Letherwood, Samuel

Logston, Lawrence

Logue, James

Logston, Lego

Lucus, Benjamin

Lucus, Thomas

Lucus, Thomas

Lawrence, Benjamin; Thomas Glyn; John
  Staford; Jack; Hager

Matocks, Benjamin

Martin, Charles

Marks, William

Moore, John

McDaniel, Joseph

McColarster, Robert

McColans, James; Robert McColarster,
  Security

Melton, William

Mattocks, William

Mattocks, Mual

Miriman (Merryman); Samuel Jr. (Qtr);
  Mortiene Miriman; Jack

Mirssir (Mercer), Luke; Willdim
  Mirssir; Andrew Mirssir; Richard
  Mirssir; John Steward; Richard;
  France

Missir, Francis Jr.; Evin Smith

Miller, George

Miller, Daniel

Mash, John

Michlifish, David

Mirshual, Robert

Neff, Henry; John Neff

Nash, John

Nicom, Henry

Ogg, William

Ogg, Dunkin

Ogg, Clin (Elin?); Hictor; Abegel; Nan

Owings, Christian; Hugh Armstrong;
  Tom; Jery; Cate; Sambo

Owings, Richard (son of Samuel); James
  Riley; John Highnmarsh; Timothy
  Philips

Oldwer, Samuel

Pirantont, William

Parish, William

Piut, Charles; Ned Bird

Poor, Peter; William Lay; John Rom

Poole, Richard

Pidicourt, Nicholas

Poole, Joseph

Philips, Thomas; Robert Cly; Thomas
  Redman

Porter, Nathan; Jack (torn)

Richison, John; Wm. Hardigiler,
  Security

Rooker, John; John Nash (Secty)

Stevenson, Henry (Qtr); Robert Shote;
  Charles Hood

Slidockyou (?)

Silmon, John; John Silmon; Philis

Shipley, Richard; John Hegothay;
  Umphisy Smith; Con; John Huney;
  Samuel Pirsefull; James Bachild;
  Mirimian Duningham; Hager

Shildin, James

Steavns(Stearns?), Thomas

Steavns(Stearns?), Julius

Strickler, Thomas

Swope, Jacob; Joe Rose

Stevenson, John (at Qtr); Joseph
  Chiswald; Miles Coner; Patrick
  Toules; John Ragin; Dinis Howley;
  Minto; Nirou

Stoxtol, Solomon; Jacob; Jack; Sal
Shipley, Eziacal
Scolis, John
Spirrer, Grinsbery; James Blare
Sadler, William
Suby, Nicholas
Shipley, George (Qtr); Joshua Porter;
  Thomas Rice; Thomas Conoway;
  Martain McDaniel
Shipley, Samuel Jr.; John Samson
Shipley, Samuel Sr.; Samuel Shipley;
  William Thomas
Shipley, Greenberry
Slack, Henry
Silman, Thomas; William Silman; Harry
Shipley, Aman
Shipley, Adam
Shipley, Apsulum
Snoden, John Babtis; Thomas Cattle,
  Charles; Harry

Todd, Nathan; Joseph Banks
Todd, John; John Taler
Talbert, Richard; John Dok
Twice (Twise, Tevis?); Robert Twise;
  Benjamin Twice; John Pans; Henry
  Smith
Tivis (Tevis), Peter; Joseph Peacock;
  Robet Riden
Twise (Tevis?) Nathan; John Lockard
Towson, John; Jack

Wirps, John
Ware, John
Wheleman, John
Wilson, Greenbery
Walker, Joseph; John Edwards, Security
Walker, Robert; John Walker
Wagin, William
Wartin, Robert
Wilmoth, John (Qtr); Jiry; Bess; Dinis
  Downey
Wheller, Edward
Warril, William
Wilson, William Sr.
Wilson, William Jr.; David Stiles
Wilkir, John
Word, Francis; William Se(?) us
Welsh, John; Some of the names were
  torn in half: Henry ---ker; Ambr-
  Gorgown; John ---caden; John
  ---gace; John ---rase; James Smith;
  James Ordan; Thos. Magtrhlin; Peter
  Perrin; Joseph Drakens; Hav...(torn)
  George; Mas(?)ry; Obed; Betty; Nancy

On Reverse side: Delaware Hundred
Taxes 462 examined by JSH. The Hole
Amount of Taxes is 501: Richard
Owings, son of Sam.

LIST OF TAXABLES IN DEPTFORD HUNDRED (BALTIMORE TOWN) BY GEORGE (NAME TORN) M, CONSTABLE, 1773

Anderson, James
Arinils, Skinner; Negro woman

Brown, Benjamin
Beech, George
Bride, Henry
Beamont, Elizabeth; Servant man
Belsoror, John
Bourton, Richard; John Kalahor; 3
  servants
Burtice, Samuel
Browning, Thomas; Sidney, George

Cowin, Alexander
Courtney, Harkelus
Coward, Dugan; Negro Will
Cattle, John; Man Davy
Chester, Joseph; James Stoaks; Andam
  Cornop
Coulsch, John
Craford, Patrick
Clark, Richard

Davy, Alexander
Dickeson, Britingham; Negroes: Will,
  George; John Benstine; William
  Scott; John Owings; R. Hingston;
  William Salmon; William Hamonon; 5
  whites
Dunn, Charles
Dungan, Daniel
Dunn, John
Davison, John
Davis, William; son John; 3 servants

Elliot, Thomas, 4 negroes
Forgison, Hugh
Fuller, William
Forgison, Cumberland
Fisher, James

Grist, Isaac

Hoak, Anthony; George Adams; Philip
  Sitsley; John Lemon; Rudolf Ealing;
  Christan Sbygle

Harris, Edward
Harrison, John
Hollinsworth, Jessee; 2 servants; 1
  negro
Houlton, William; son John
Hays, William; 5 servants
Helm, George; John Young; Jos.
  Fletchers

Inlows, Abraham; boy Stephen; Thomas
  Morris

Johns, Acquila; 1 negro
Johnston, Charles
Johnston, Barney
Judy, Martin; 1 servant man
James, Micajaw
Jacobs, William

Kelly, Dinis
Kearers, John; Man Pitt
Kirk, Samson

Leeth, Alexander; Negro woman
Lookis, Bateel
Lovett, Charles
Luorn, Francis
Louderman, George
Leavlin, Henry
Laurence, Henry
Lydwich, Phillip
Long, Robert
Long, Thomas

Morgin, James; William Wood; John
  Ervin (Erwin); Abssoman McCoy;
  Negroes: Matt, Dick; George
  Laurance; Negro Charles; Daniel
  Minor; Negro Jim
McKinley, Anthony
Martin, Christifer
McIlroy, Fergison
Maunk, Henry
Moartion, Robert
McQuillin, Redin(?)
McCoy, Francis

Nouland, Alexander
Nelson, Benjamin; Joseph Cromwell;
  William Camble; Peter Hoaks; John
  Sims; John Sollers; William
  McGrall; Livin Willson; James Sharp

Orrick, Widow; 2 negroes

Patton, George; 1 servant man

Rylee, Henry
Russie, James
Reardon, Michel

Spencer, Benjamin
Shake(Spake?), George, Blacksmith
Stahr, George, laborer
Simmons, John
Smith, John; son George; Negro woman
Simerman, Matthias
Scaff, William

Tull, Handy
Toole, James
Trimble, William

Van Bibber, Abraham; Negroes: Dick,
  Poll, Luke
Van Bibber, Isaac; Negroes: Pompy,
  Reason, Tom, Dick
Vandeford, John; 1 servant man; 1
  apprentice

Welsley, Christian
Wells, George; servant James; James
  Gray; John Chester

Wells, Henry; Negro woman
Willson, Jesse
Wale, John
Ware, Samuel

Additional List:
Craford, Patrick
Taylor, Alexander
McQuilin, Relin for Mikell McLure
Morgin, Wm. security for Wm. McCray

Burtice, Samuel, security for man
  Gahagam
Craford, Patrick (looks like a
  duplication of the above named Pat.
  Craford)

On the reverse side: Deptford
  Hundred: 184, Add'l 3 = 187.
examined by William Buchanan (Other
  examiner's name unclear)

LIST OF TAXABLES IN GUNPOWDER UPPER HUNDRED, BALTIMORE COUNTY, TAKEN BY
SUTTON GUDGEON, 1773

Allbird, Thomas
Agent, James; James Leeson
Albright, Joseph
Allinder, Joshua
Allin, William; Thomas Hooking

Bean, John
Barton, Asahel; Negro Jenny
Bashet, Richard; Alexander Language;
  Richard Bashet; Mathew Culbert;
  John Buffet
Burton, William
Bonida, James
Burton, Joseph
Baxter, Samuel
Bausley, James; Joseph Hone; William
  Standy
Butler, Thomas, Security for Hugh
  McKernon
Baker, Samuel; John Baker
Bausly, James (of Chas.); Joseph
  Moore; Negroes: Ben, John
Boyce, Rebecca (widow); Ben Boyce;
  Negroes: Frank, Tom, Andrew, Harry,
  Abraham, John, Charles, Nan (1),
  Cave, Nan (2), Lucy; Sarah
  Solesbury
Brown, George
Bussey, Edward Sr.; Negroes: Dick,
  Mezingo, Dol, Hannah
Bussey, Jesse; Negroes: Tom, Charles,
  Hannah
Baker, Charles Jr.; William Down;
  Negro Pot
Baker, Charles Sr.; Negroes: Sezar,
  Philis, George, Hager, Roger, Sye
Barrow, John (Security); John Barrow,
  Jr.; Negroes Pol (could be Thomas
  Pol); William Sparrow; Hopkins
Bradley, Thomas; John Butler;
  Benjamin Mathers

Baker, Charles (of Fidly); Negro Moll
Boyce, Thomas
Baker, James; John Dungan; John
  Dennis; Edward Humpreys; Negroes:
  Pompey, Cate
B--?--shaw, Jacob
Brown, Henry

Combs, Coleman
Counselman, George
Counsins, George
Crudgton, George; Negro Frank
Cooper, Joseph
Corbley, Nicholas
Corbin, Abraham; Wm. Latchfoot;
  Timothy Derford
Coal, William
Corbin, Nathan
Cromwell, William; Negroes: Harry,
  John, William, Nan, Diana
Clay, Abraham; Henry Clay; William
  Griffin
Cullom, William
Carnowl, William
Chamberlain, Thomas
Cammell, Charles
Coal, George
Chance, Jeremiah
Coskery, Arthur; Francis Coskery;
  Thomas Butress; Negroes: Adam, Rose
Chamberlain, John; Philip Chamberlain;
  James Chamberlain; Henry Brown;
  Negroes: Dimbo, Cato, Dick, Sampson,
  Will, Lucia, Maria
Chamberlain, Samuel; Mark Warrel; John
  Bartlam
Chamberlain, Abraham; John Mubui(?)

Dowty, Thomas

Dulaney, Walter, at Qtr., and Peter Squire, Overseer; Negroes: Cooper, Charles, Pompey, Frank, Ben, Harry, Bet (Bes?), Cate, Racher, Nell, Sarah
Dulany, Walter, at Qtr. and Charles Wells, Overseer; Samuel Chuen; Joseph West; Peter Hickby; Negroes: Simon, Punch, Cesar, Joe, Will, John, Jack, Phil, Dol, Rachel, Bec, Hegar, Sal
Deason, Enoch
Donnelly, John (Sec); John McCann; James Smith
Dimmitt, James; Richard McKenly; Robert Smith
Darnell, Henry Bennet; Negroes: Peter, George, John, Tom, Ben, Sue (1), Peg, Sue (2), Sall, Grace, Sue (3), James, Peter
Dean, Emanuel
Dorsey, Jno. Hammond; Negroes: Sam, James, Isaac,Jack, Glasgow, Natt, Nan, Hannah, Heger, Grace, Salle; Richard Mell's
Dean, Hugh Rev'd.; Charles Manners; Negroes: Nads, Tom, Ned, George, Jem, Rachel, Jean, Flora, Sue
Ede, William; Daniel Newman; Richard Bartley
Edwards, John
Ensor, Wm.(Security); Wm. Ensor, Jr.; Charles Deason
Elliott, James Sr.; William Elliott
Elliott, James Jr.
Elliott, John; James Magragh
Enlows, William
Enlows, John

Flukes, William
Franklin, James; Samuel Crook; Jno. Ward; James Laurence; Patrick McCloon; Daniel Gill; Negro Tom Troausberry
Farrell, James
Franklin, Thomas, Major; Thomas Franklin, Jr.; Negroes: Tony, Sam, Harry, Simon, Luke, Dick, Joseph, Hannah, Bet, Bine, Esther, Lucy, Little, Lucy; Jenny Dedford
Flanagan, Patrick; Patrick Flanagan
Ford, Joseph

Gad, William
Green, Abel
Gittings, James, Esq.; James Dewhurst; Joseph Kimbo; Joseph

Clayton; John Blacksmith; John Draper; John Strong; Michael Maningo; Timothy Mahony; Negroes: James, Ben, Arch, Cato, Joshua, Ralph, Jack, Sam, Major, Esther, Hannah, Judy, Cate, Flora; Laurance
Craft, overseer; Negroes: Tom, Cesar, Jack, Sal, Diana
Guiton, Henry; John McMonce; Negro Diana
Green, Clement; Negro Pug
Golway (Galway), Aquila; William Waddard; Negro Harry; 6 for Zebulon Hicks
Gutridge, Edward; John Gutridge
Grover, William; John Hash
Green, Thomas; William Ryan
Guiton, Benjamin Jr.
Guiton, Benjamin Sr.; Negro John Opel; Norwich
Green, George
Golding, Jno.; Charles Manners; Negroes: Nads, Tom, Ned, George, Jem, Rachel, Jean, Flora, Sue
Gittings, Asahel

Hendon, Henry, Secy. for Jno. Clark
Hunter, George Sr.; George Hunter, Jr.; James Hunter; Samuel Hunter; Benjamin Turner; Thomas Holt; Thomas Ask
Hunter, Jonathan; Philip Griffith; Edward Ryan; Michael Hart; Frank Wilkins
Householder, Henry Sr., Secy. for Peter Quigley
Householder, Henry Jr., Secy. for Patrick Danly
Holland, Jno. Sr.
Holland, Jno. Jr.
Harwood, Richard Sr.; Jno. Harwood
Howard, J. Beale Jr.; James Lathrum; Negroes: Frilas, Gaying, Burrow, Jobel, Hannah
Howard, John, Capt.; Negroes: James, Harry, Cate, Rachel
Hunter, Peter (Secy); Luke Jennings; William Blake; George Scarf; Phil Ward; Jno. Presbury
Howard, Thomas; Gassaway, and Jno. Taylor, overseer; Negroes: Harry, Keener, Phillis
Hilton, Joseph; Benjamin Adair
Hunt, Simon
Howard, Robert

Hall, William
Helfry, John
Hendon, Richard
Hooper, Jno.
Hopkins, Ezekiel; Negroes: Lucy,
   Hannah
Holland, Thomas
Herrinton, William; George Randal;
   John Saunders
Herrinton, Zebulon
Hilton, John Sr.; John Hilton Jr;
   James Hilton; William Lawson; Henry
   Condron

Johnston, Robert; James Watkins
Jones, Rachel; John Jones; Negroes:
   Frank, Hannah, Hegar
Jenkins, Michael; Negroes: Mark, Sam,
   Paul, Sal, (torn)
Jenkins, Jonathis; James Flaherty;
   James Fitzgerald; Negroes: Bob, Tom
James, Jno. Smith; Gregory White;
   Negro Jack

Kelly, Fred
Kemp, Hercules; William Kemp

Linton, Aron
Lynch, Brady
Lucas, Thomas; Negroes: Will, Sambo
Legit, Sutton
Legit, James
Legit, Joshua; Negro Tom
Lynch, William, Security for Henry
   Jacobs; Negro Tom

Mathers, Jno.
Mallet, William; Jno. Carson; Peter
   Stafford; Arthur Carter
Mash, Thomas; John Mash; Edward Tyler
McCaslin, Henry; Jacob McCaslin;
   Elisha McCaslin; Thomas Whitly
McClung, John; William Bonsil
Miller, Theophilus; James Miller
Magnus, John
Milliman, Charles; Joseph Barton
Mullin, James
Moore, James

Page, Jno.
Palmer, Samuel
Perdue, Walter; John Loon; Negroes:
   James, Hager; Thomas Agent
Picket, William
Philip, Isaac

Preston, Thomas

Omitted from the first:
Gittings, Thomas; James Gittings;
   Negroes: Jack, Primus, Moll, Jenny,
   Silas
Gordon, Charles; William Gordon; John
   Gordon; James Gordon
Greenfield, James; Mickiah Greenfield
Goodin, William; Abraham Lynch; John
   Whitton; James Cocker; Nicholas
   Shier; Negroes: Sam, Jude
Gushard, Sarah (widow); Negroes:
   Charles, Jem

Reeves, Thomas
Richards, Isaac; Thomas Rutter; John
   Richards
Rogers, Benjamin, Mill; William Riley;
   Phil Hodge; Richard Tate; Wm.
   Stackpole; Negro Abraham
Rucko---(?) (torn)
Ryland, Nicholas
Richards, William
Roberts, Leven; Negro Hanna
Rogers, Thomas
Ridgly, Charles (Qt); Robert Shaw;
   William Taylor; Timothy Wren; George
   Ogle; William Gilburn; Richard
   Harvey; Negroes: Ben, London, Cesar,
   Farar
Rutledge, Ephraim; Dick Jaisham
Riley, John; William Riley
Rollins, Abraham

Nichols, Thomas Sr.; John Craig
Nichols, Thomas Jr.

Sanks, Zecherie; Edward Gibins
Standiford, William; James Standiford;
   Negroes: Peter, Mingo, Pug, Edward,
   Abbington
Samson, Emanuel
Shanly, John
Standiford, Jno.; William Rose; James
   Cook; Edward Hunt
Standiford, Aquila; Negroes: Rose,
   Abigail
Sturk, John
Standiford, Abraham; Thomas Woodin
Serjeant, William, Security for Strapt
   Fosil
Smith, Joshua; Henry Smith; Negro
   Celia; James Barry
Starky, Jonathan; Negro Harry

LIST OF TAXABLES IN GUNPOWDER UPPER HUNDRED, 1773

White, John; Security for John
Stutter; Jacob Householder
Wilson, John Sr.; John Wilson;
Gittings Wilson; Negroes: Mack,
Davy, Naas, Plato, Lisha, Jenny,
Sal
Wilson, Benhid; Negroes: Adam, Ben,
Solomon, Die, Cassasty, Dina, Nell
Wright, Abraham; Solomon Wright;
Thomas Kenny; Negro Celia
Wright, Jno.
Watson, Thomas
Wright, Sarah, widow; Abraham Wright
Watkins, Samuel; Negroes: Captain,
Phillis
Walton, John
Ward, John (unclear)

Young, Clary (widow), Security for
James Watkins; William Godgrace;
Negroes: Dan, James, Harry, Sue,
Moll, Bec, Nan, Poll, Diana

Yoe, James; Negroes: Joe, Pug
Young, Robert

Young, Samuel; Dirum Pleaqasque,
Overseer; Thomas Parpeld; Frank
Gunnell; Negroes: Harry, Samson,
Moll, Sal (1), James, Sal (2), Bet,
Lucy, Dick

Names omitted before:
Tolly, Walter Jr., Security for
William Nixon and Thos. Maroon; John
Simmons; William Curdle; Negroes:
Peter, Tony, Jenny
Tolly, Walter Sr.; Wm. Everitt,
overseer; Negroes: Peter, Harry,
Judy, Venus
Threadaway, Thomas (or Treadaway,
Thomas); Negroes: Old Fillis, Young
Fillis, Cesar, Stephney, Jessy

On reverse side: amount of taxables
is 610 plus 4 additional for a total
of 614. However, it further shows
that Gunpowder Upper taxables
numbered 613 when examined by B.
Rogers, James Gittings, and "R.C."

LIST OF TAXES IN MIDDLE RIVER LOWER HUNDRED, TAKEN BY WALTER JAMES, CONSTABLE, FOR THE YEAR 1773

Andrews, William; Negroes: Grace,
Isaac, Longo, Toby, Martin,
Malborough, Robin, Will, Sil, Luce,
Judey, Phillis; Charles Hill; John
Bolton; Negroes: Pompey, Fanny,
Cook, Sue, Tom, Celar
Ayers, Thomas
Arnold, James
Asher, Abraham; Negro Choice
Anders, Abraham
Allender, William; Negroes: Primas,
Ceasar, Clove

Brittain, Abraham; William Brittain;
Negroes: Simon, Benn, Isaac, Hannah
Bevan, William
Bevan, Benjamin
Bevan, John; John Bevan, Jr.
Betson, Thomas
Brannen, Thomas; Christopher Dives,
Secy.
Bevan, Joseph
Brannan, James
Bunting, William
Brown, William; James Hill

Bevans, Jesher
Bond, Elizabeth; James Bond; Negroes:
Harry, Cate, Feby, Nell
Bayley, Thomas; Negroes: Simon, Ned,
Bet
Barton, Aquila
Barton, Selah
Barton, Joshua
Brittain, Nicholas (Qt); William
Cirbe; Charles Powell; John Murry
Bond, Thomas; John Coke
Bond, William
Buck, John; Joshua Buck; Negroes:
Cook, Coffee, Step, Luca, Hannah

Crook, Joseph; John Quay; Negro Jim
Colvin, Phillip
Chine, Roderick; Negroes: Joe, Poll
Christopher, John; John Cua (Qua?)
Cromwell, Richard; John Asher
Cockey, John
Cross, John
Carter, William
Cartwright, Abraham
Clark, Benjamin
Chapman, Thomas

65

Day, Edward; Negroes: Ben, Peter, Joe, Jack, Sambo, Dick, Flora; Joseph Jennings; Richard Dixon
Dives, Christopher
Dorney, James
Denton, John
Dairs, Thomas
Denton, William

Edwards, Edward

Fowler, Richard
Flowerty, John
Frederick, John
Foster, William

Grover, George
Grecor(?), John
Griffis, Edward; Hugh Kinsey; John
Grimes, Reson
Galloway, Moses; John Galloway; James Galloway; Caleb, Bob, Murrea, Bell
Galloway, William
Griffin, John

Holmes, Thomas; Geo. Gouldsmith Presbury, secy.
Hendrixson, John; Negro Jerry
Hendrixson, Garret
Hendrixson, Matthis; Negro Dina
Hughs, Solomon
Hatton, Unity; Benjamin W--(?); Negro Peter
Hatton, Cheney
Horton, Elizabeth; Daniel Hach
Harryman, Robert
Holebrooks, Jacob
Hughs (nothing else)

Jarman, William
Jarman, Abraham
James, Walter; 1 Negro servant
Jarman, John; Negroes: Harry, Clove
Jones, John; Negro Sharlott

Killman, Thomas

League, Luke; John Jones
League, James; Negro Nan
League, Nathan
League, Josias
League, Moses; John Hatton; Samuel Stone; Negro Will

McCoben, John
Mildews, Aquila; Berry Mildews
Mack, James
Medes, Benjamin; Negroes: Jeffery, Jongo, Luce

Nicholson, Nathan; George Bowles; John Mully; John Turner; Negroes: Able, Jude, Harry

Perkins,, William
Presbury, Geo. Gould.; William Hunt; Negroes: Jupiter, Nan, Rachel, June
Procter, Giles; Joseph Procter
Parks, John (son of Edmund)
Parks, Edward Jr.
Parker, Thomas
Peterson, Jarret; Adam Peterson
Pennington, John
Parks, John; Aquila Parks; John Parks; James Allchurch; John Parks, security
Peckard, William; John Griffin, security

Rumage, Adam; William Savory
Rame, John
Rutledge, Elizabeth; John Rutledge; James Fuld
Ra, Tobias (unclear)
Roberts, Benjamin
Raven, William; Negro Peg
Raven, Luke; Negroes: Dina, Pompy
Raven, Luke security for John Cotreel
Reese, Adam; Negroes: Daniel, Peter, Grace, Rachel, Luce, Simon, Kiss, Jack

Summers, Jabob James Standford
Shawan, Daniel
Swilivan, William
Sudden, John; John Bellamy
Sudden, James; John Raile
Saunders, John; Jacob Holebrooks, security
Sinclair, Moses; Negroes: Priss, Moses
Sout, Joseph
Summers, John; John Summers,Jr.; Negro Toby

Taylor, James
Thompson, John
Tolley, Walter; James Adams; Negroes: Morah, Sande, Daniel, Frank, Morah, Harry, Peter, Cupit, Batria, Venus, Judah, Hannah
Todd, William

Waller, John
Worthington, Vachel; Elisha Parks;
  Negroes: Uington, Adam, Jerry,
  Murrea, Alce, Tamor
Wilson, John; Negro Fye
Wilson, Garrett
Whaland, Patrick; James Whaland;
  Negro Dick
West, Benjamin
Waters, William
Wise, Edward
Watkins, Daniel; Negro Mingo
Wright, William
Wright, Joseph
Wright, Abraham

Living at Linghams Neck, Corbin Lee,
  Security: William Wood; John Clay;
  George Sank; Charles Franklin;
  James Woolfe; James Huron; John
  Woller; Thomas Elliott; Robert
  Cantling; Nicholas Allender; John
  Buckley; John Trumain (Truman);
  John Rock; Fidal Rock; Frederick
  Rock

An Account of Taxables at Nottingham
  Forges: James Skinner; Francis
  Downing; Robert Stewart; Hugh
  Stewart; John Collins (hammer);
  John Collins (refiner); Daniel
  Dulany; Samuel Moor; Thomas
  McLachlane; John Hurtze

An Account of Negroes at Nottingham
  Forges: Moses, Roger, George,
  Harry, Mount, Old Paul, Vulcan,
  Allick, London, Paris, Sam, Arrow,
  Paul, Pompy, Stafford, Hector,
  Will, Ewer, Jacob, Old Hercules,
  Hercules, Joe, Toney, Andrew,
  Buchanan, Jerry, Russell, Sam, Tom,
  Mintoe, Michael, Mingo, Boatswain,
  Jacob, Chester, Litchfield, Peter,
  Charles, Quibus,

Nedd, Tom, Downing, Bob, Ditts,
  Hagar, Jenny, Cash, Lydia, Phebe,
  Pamela

An Account of Taxables Belonging To
  Corbin Lee: Sangoe, Sam, Dick,
  Moses, Cobber, Roger, Coffee,
  Bencrue, George, Will, Bob, Basil,
  Sarah, Nann, Sophia, Bell, Sue,
  Dinah

An Account of Tasables At Nottingham
  Furnace: John Owings; Henry Hay;
  John Hughes; Richard Jones; Jonas
  Jones; Richard Willis; George
  Townsend; Amos Holebrook; William
  Miser; Charles Hughes; George Spier;
  Benjamin Powell; Thomas Wells; John
  Woodthey; Thomas Aram; Edward Hart;
  John Hencasil

An Account of Negroes at Nottingham
  Furnace: Dick, Will, York, Sango,
  Jack, Jack Boy, Pompy, Toney,
  Paddell; "Amount Brought Up":
  Charles (Owings); Jack (Owings); Sam
  (Bond); Tom; Cankie; Hannah; Sarah;
  Emy; Phillis; Grace; Hamie (Hughes);
  Kitt; Peter; Dick (Crola); Jack
  (Law--n)

The following names were added at the
  end of the list (apparently out of
  order):
Abercrombie, Robert
Andrew, William Jr.
Diven, Mary; Negro Hannah
French, Otho
Jones, Thomas

On Reverse side: "Middle River Lower
  Taxes 419. Exd JBH & TF."

Benson, Benjamin
Bosley, Caleb; Negro Packhp(?)
Bosley, Elizabeth; Zedbedey Bosley;
  Thomas Bandele; Negroes: Benjamin,
  Robert, Hannah
Brooks, Charles; Servant Moses
Brooks, Samuel
Bosley, William; Moses Boon; Negro
  James
Bosley, John; Gyles Baker; James
  Brooks; Negroes: Singolow, Petter,
  Harry
Benixt, Barney; Thomas Colwell
Bosley, Walter
Bosley, Elizabeth (widow of Charles
  Bosley); Negroes: Peter, Jack
Bosley, Joseph; Green Bosley; James
  Domene; Negroes: Dick, Ben, Hagar
Birum, John
Ball, Joseph

Corbin, Benjamin; Ezekiel Corbin
Cyous(Cyrus?), Benj.
Chennaweth, John; James Morgin
Corbin, Edward; Richard Baskett;
  Abraham Green
Corbin, Vinson
Commins, Robert; Larrance McNeal
Cole, Thomas; Mordeyca Cole; Negroes:
  Paco, James, Ammy, Peter, Ceedy,
  Sarah, Candis, Mando
Culisson, William; Joshua Culisson;
  John Brooks
Clossey, John
Cole, Abraham; Negro Sarah

Dilling, Moses

Elender, Frederick; Servant Brion
Ensor, Elizabeth; Darby Ensor; Joseph
  Winks; Negro Cate
Ensor, George; John Maloney; Negro
  (no name)
Ensor, Abraham; Richard Wood; Wm.
  Goodfellow; William Orched; Thomas
  Hewes; John Goodman; David Longley;
  John Stiles; Negro Toney
Edwards, Benjamin

Foster, John; John Haywood; Negroes:
  Coyle, Ruth, Lucy

Green, Isaac; John Stevens; Negro
  Tamer

Gorsuch, Thomas Jr.; Niclass Otway
Gorsuch, Thomas; John Homes; James
  Ireland; Negroes: Harry, Kate
Green, John
Greenbury Green;l Lemuell Green
Gorsuch, John, Censor (probably is
  "Senior"); Steven Gorsuch; Negroes:
  John, Sinkler, Dick, Sambeau, Beka,
  Matter
Gorsuch, Charles; Charles Gorsuch;
  Servant Joseph; Negroes: Jack, Moses
Gorsuch, Charles, son of John Gorsuch;
  Thomas Crocker; W. Frisbe
Gorsuch, John "the smithe"
Griffith, Abraham; James Bowlle; James
  Towers; Isaac Griffith
Gorsuch, John, son of Thomas Gorsuch,
  his Quarter.; William Howard;
  William Wareley; Negroes: Charles,
  George, Poll, Simon, Hannah, (torn)

Hooker, Benjamin; Negroes: Budge,
  Abraham
Hunter, William; John Burtles
Hix, Jacob; Mathew Etharley
Hale, Thomas
Hicks, Labon; Henry Hicks
Herrenon, Nicklass; John Hipwell;
  Negro Congo
Harryman, George; Benjamin Hipwell;
  Negroes: Jace, Hagar
Herrenton, Temperance; Abell
  Herrenton; John Wilson; Negro Fan
Hall, Joshua; Joshua Hall; Thomas
  Hall; Thomas Aleem; Samuel Burkit;
  Negroes: Rosey, Eve, Rachell, Fan,
  Etter, Beck
Hix, Nemiah
Hix, Abraham; Servant Thomas

James, Walter; Servant William
Joy, Peter

Linch, James; Richard Anderson
Lemmon, Alexous; Joseph Allen
Lemmon, John; Negro Beck

Merryman, Chage (?); Walter Herclies;
  Michell Nisid; Isaac Morrow; Edward
  David
Mellecain, William
Moor, John
Meloney, William

Merryman, Nicklass; Thomas Johnston;
John Waller; John Hood; Negroes:
Charles, Ned, Tom, Kate, Sarah
Merryman, John Jr.; John Price; James
Collings; Frances Johnson; Negroes:
Rachel, Dinere
Merryman, John Sr.; James Coffey;
Negroes: Dick, Coffey, Jacob, Kate,
Hager
May, John
Merryman, Benjamin; James Wood;
Joseph Marmun; Negroes: Harry,
Cloes
Merryman, Elijah; Moses Hobins; Negro
Sandey
Mathews, Thomas; Mordaca Mathews;
Samuel Hill; Richard Woolley

Norton, Isaac; John Nox

Obrion, William
Orrick, Nicklass; Patrick Burk; John
Coulion
Ogleby, James

Perrygoy, Joseph; Wm. Perrygoy; Wm.
Wheeler; Negroes: Tumer, Vade
Price, Benjamin; Thomas Price;
Negroes: Jacob, Semer, Jude
Price, Mordecai; Henry Wilmot; John
Clark; Negroes: Deman, Fanny
Price, Samuel; Negroes: Coxey, Jack,
Sammey, Tom, Hannah
Rodgers, Benjamin, his quarter;
Joseph Fox; Frances Dille; James
Rion; Richard James; William
Megurk; Thomas Turmtory; Wm.
Chandler; Luke Stansbury; Negroes:
Cate, Dan, Betty, Cleare, Cato,
Dice, William, George
Reves, Rodger
Rees, Daniel; Robert Squires; Geo.
Parington
Roades, Richard; William Barber;
Servant Mathew
Rouland, Thomas; Samuel Rouland

Stansbury, Samuel; Robert Williams;
Edward Williams

Stansbury, Samuel Jr.; Negro Sceasor
Stansbury, Kale; William Stansbury;
Jeremiah Neagor (Negro Jeremiah?)
Sanos, Ellexander
Samuel, Miles (?)
Stevens, Edward
Savage, Hill
Stansbury, Joseph; Negro Presto
Scote, Abraham; William Haley
Stiner, Jacob
Smith, Andrew; Servant Peter
Smith, Daniel; Daniel Smith

Trapling, William; William Trapling;
Mark Farling; William Goodman;
William Mooney
Tarbott, Vincent; Negro Cato
Tipton, Samuel; Samuel Tipton;
Negroes: Cato, Simon, Bloner, Fanne
Trasey, Benjamin
Thomas, John; John Thomas; Daniel
Thomas

Varham, Guss; Edward Parrish; Negroes:
Die, Bet

Wheeler, Benjamin; William Wheeler
(torn) McCload; Negroes: (unclear),
Semer, John, Bec, Ruth
Welch, Joshua
Wheeler, Nathan; Samuel Nappit;
Negroes: George, Abigail
Wantland, Thomas; Abraham Wantland;
Thomas Foster
Walker, Joseph; George Walker; Daniel
Walker
Wantland, James

ADDITIONAL NAMES:
Groombridge, James
Green, Thomas
Trasey, Edward
Wetherenton, William; Charles Prosser;
Negroes: George, Peter, Hannah

Note: Middle River Upper Hundred
Amount of Taxables: 344. Examined by
Isaac Van Bibber.

Armstrong, Michiel
Adams, Paul
Aldon, Charles
Alter, Christian

Barnet, Andrew
Butler, William
Brook, Humphrey
Barrick, John; Stosel Nice, Secy.
Bell, William; Michiel Murrer
Bell, Richard; John Bell, Secy.
Barney, Benjamin
Boone, Thomas; John Boone; William
  Boone; Negroes: Jacob, Leedy,
  Rachell, Hagar
Barger, Tector; Isaac Due
Brown, Isaac
Beach, Thomas
Butler, Mary; Negroes: Jacob, Beck
Barnet, Baker
Buchanan, Elenor; Indian Harry;
  Negroes: Harry, Phil, Nat, Ruby,
  Philis, Kath

Cambell, Alex; Robert McKim, Secy.
Calwell, James
Cromwell, Richard; Negroes: Charles,
  Ben, Manor, Ruth

Due, Robert; William Caffray; William
  Joyce; Tom Kelley; Timothy Cowen;
  James Murphey
Downs, William; Michael Gardner,
  Secy.
Dunn, Arthur; Henry Rutter, Secy.
Dunn, Henry; Michael Grainor, Secy.
Dimmit, John
Dunahour, George; Jacob Miers, Secy.
Drake, Francis

Enders, Jacob

Flour, John
Fright, Robert; Andrew Moore
Flarring, William

Gardner, Michiel
Grimes, John
Grainer, Michiel; John Brown; John
  Glove
Gering, Andrew
Green, Thomas
Gardner, John; Isaac Wheeler; John
  Rauls

How, Edward; Sam How, Sr.; Sam How,
  Jr.
Hewet, Jacob; James Ares; Tom Arton;
  Negro Nan
Hisor, Gasper
Hook, Rodall; Tom Caster; Francis
  Spade; George Pasley; Tom Blakely
Hisor, Samuel; William Butler,
  Security
Hook, Jacob Jr.; William May
Hale, Stephen
Hoppum, William; Negro Manor
Helms, Lenard
Helms, Mabery Sr.; Negroes: Peter,
  Charles, Jinny, Tamer, Hager
Helms, Mabery Jr.; Negro Hager
Hooper, John
Hanson, Edward; James Johil; Daniel
  Wilsh; Mark Jackson; John St. John;
  Negro Rachiel

Jeffrees, Richard
Johnson, Thomas; Alexd. Wilson;
  Negroes: Dick, Caleb, Simon, Hagar,
  Morear
Jackson, Marshall; William Butler,
  Security

Kenaday, Thomas

Longley, Benjamin
Leaf, Jacob
Lary, Jerimiah
Louden, George; John Gardner
Lance, Martin; Jacob Miers, Secy.
Lowery, Edward
Lawson, Alexandria; Negroes: Will,
  Sam, Anthony, Hannah, Firdah, Mary

McKim, Robert
McGrew, Robert
Miller, William
Murphy, John
McColister, Joseph
Mabery, Alexander; John Grimes, Secy.
McKnight, William; William Pipe; Negro
  Hannah
Meals, John
Miers, Jacob; Negroes: Jacob, Michiel,
  Tolley
Moakel, James
Mournan, Samuel; Mich'l Horn; Negro
  Jacob

Nichols, John
Nice, Stoffell

Oursler, Elic

Procter, Jonathan
Price, Abraham; Isaih Price; John
  Farconer; James Sanders; Negro Moll
Price, Amon
Parker, George; Frederick Theames,
  Security
Pluck, John
Polen, William
Patterson, Thomas
Pinny, Henry
Pimtany (Puntany), Edward

Read, John; Negro Jones
Rutter, Henry
Ritter, Anthony; John Ritter; Tom
  Ritter
Rutter, Thomas; Negroes: Pool, Joe,
  Jeane
Rutter, Mary; Negroes: Essex, Hagar
Rodwell, Godfrey
Right, Thomas
Ridgely's Quarter; Roger and Edif

Smith, Nicholas
Smith, John
Sumore, John
Stoler, Martin
Stergin, Robert; William Rutter,
  Security
Spring, James; Samuel Welsh, Security
Stocker, Joseph
Spicer, John; Valentine Spicer; Negro
  Sam

Taylor, John
Towson, Esekial; John Murphey
Theames, Fredrick
Trumbal, John

Welsh, James; Negroes: Dick, Tillis
Ware, Edward
Wooding, Solomon
Wooley, Joseph; Robert Fright,
  Security

Wooding, John; John Wooding, Jr.;
  Negroes: Ben, Rachel
Wooding, Stephen
Ward, Thomas

Yaram, Thomas
Young, Jacob Jr.
Young, Jacob, Sr.; Negroes: Toby,
  Tuce, Tanny
Young, Edward; Jacob Young, Security
Young, John

List of Taxes in Middlesex Taken by
  John Gardner at Mr. Carroll's at
  Mount Clare, 1773: Tery Malone;
  Thomas Huggins; Negroes: Abram,
  Dick, David, Charles, Nick, Guy,
  Timbols, Jingo, Harry, James,
  Christmas, Ned, Will, George,
  Charles, Pugg, Lucy, Tom

Additional List:
Smith, Joseph; Nich'l Smith, Security
Warren, Jacob
Davis, Richard; John Gardner, Security
Bryan, Charles
Burk, John; Michiel Gardner, Security
Bell, Edward; John Gardner, Security
Kerns, James *
Barker, Job *
(* to Wm. Flurron)
Parrish, Robert; Lenard Helms,
  Security
Goodwin, Pleasant; Negroes: Paul, Nan
Goodwin, William; Negro Peg

Taxes at M. R. Forge: Franklin James;
  Sam Leach; Thomas Rogers; Thomas
  Renolls; John Brown; James Mays;
  Negroes: Mingo, Jim (1), Ben, Jacob,
  Jack (1), Jack (2), Will (1), Will
  (2), Shadwell, Tony, Andrew, Jim(2),
  Abraham, Joel, Moses, Jack (3), Joe,
  Mark, George, Charles, Massy, Ben,
  Jov, Michiel, Patt, Hister, Kate,
  Henry

On reverse side: Middlesex: 246 + 29.
  Total 275. Examined by B. Rogers,
  William Buchanan

Anderson, William; Servants: William, Peter
Anderson, Abraham
Anderson, Benjamin; William Anderson; Joshua Anderson; Slave Hammer
Allison, Alexander
Allender, William; Slave Cato
Armstrong, Solomon
Armstrong, George
Armstrong, Nehemiah
Airs, John
Airs, Jeremiah Sr.
Airs, Jeremiah Jr.
Almoney, John; Servant Jacob
Anderson, Thomas; Richard; Joseph; Phillis
Andrew, Dillion (Dillon?); Thomas Evison, Secy.

Beard, John Adams
Burns, John
Bossley, Elizabeth, widow of James; James Bossley; Slaves: Beck, Booze, Sam
Bull, Isaac; Jacob Bull
Bossley, Vinston; Slave Peg
Bacon, John; Servants: Samuel, John
Bell, John
Boyd, Robert
Bosley, Elijah; John; Jack; Barrick; Cong; Hagar
Baxter, William
Bossley, James; Bob; Sarah; Gray; Jack; Durner; Bet; Moll; Tom
Bossley, Elizabeth
Bossley, Ezekiel; Servants: John, Will, Doll
Bossley, Elizabeth, widow of Charles; Seasar; Robin; Tom; Hannah
Bossmun, Edward; James; John; William; Slave Cate
Burck, Uleck; Servant Joe
Black, William

Carland, James
Cook, John
Cross, John
Crosslan, Thomas
Collet, Moses
Commins, Anthony; George; Phillis
Christison, John; Wm. Christison; Servant John
Currier, William

Daley, Jacob
Dimmit, John; Servant John
Dixon, John; Thomas Dixon; Servants: John 1, John 2
Dicken, John; Slaves: Harry, Ceebee

Ellet, George
Ellet, James; James Ellet
Edwards, William Sr.
Edwards, William Jr.
Evison, Thomas

Forster, Benedick
Fleehart, Joshua
Fugate, Edward; Servant Tom
Flin, Nicholus
Franklin, Joseph
Fuller, Nichol(torn)
Fortine, Bridg--hard

Gutterage, James
Grice, Jacob
Grover, Josiahs
Gibs, Aaron
Galloway, Thomas; Thomas Galloway; Servants: Andrew, Tom
Gullivur, Thomas
Griggory, William
Grice, William
Goodwin, Rachel, widow of Job; August
Gothart, William
Goins, James; Richard Deaver; Slaves: Dames, Ben, Jean
Green, William Sr.
Gossage, Benjamin; Servant George
Gulliver, Thomas Jr.
Green, Isaac
Goodman, William; Walter Odel

Hughes, John Sr.; Slave Phillis
Hughes, Thomas
Hughes, John Jr.
Hughes, James
Hughes, Elijah
Haze, James
Haze, Abraham
Hunt, Thomas
Hill, John
Hansin, Benjamin
Hutchans, Richard
Hutchans, Nicholas Sr.
Hutchans, John
Hutchans, Nicholas Jr.; Slave Mun
Hutchans, Thomas; Servant Mark
Hoddy, Richard

Hicks, Isaac; Thomas Hicks; Isaac
  Hicks; Slaves: Tuleb, Grace

John, Kelley; John Kelley(?); John
  the Dutchman; Slaves: Jean, Thebes
Johnson, Aaron, Servant, Henry
Jones, Richard, son of Richard;
  Joseph Jones; Derry; Seasar; Moll;
  Mina
Johnson, David; Servant Lucas
Johnson, William; James Johnson; John
  Johnson; Servants George
Johnson, Luke; Servant John
Johnson, Jacob
Johnson, David Weaver; Servants:
  James, Alexander
Jones, Richard, son of Arter Slave
  Jack
Johnson, Nathan; William Johnson
Johnson, Phillip

Kane, John; Davison McGaw; James
  McGaw
Kelley, Thomas
Kelsey, William; Servant John

Lytle, George; Thomas Lytle; Servant
  William
Lytle, James (1)
Lytle, James (2)
Lawson, John; Slave Seasar
Leesh, Benjamin
Love, Robert; Servant Watkins

Mitchel, Robert
Morris, John
Mainer, Richard
McDannale, Chornalius; John
  McDannale; Servant John
McBoyce, James
McClung, Adam; Servant John
McClung, Robert; Servants: John,
  Richard
Marshall, Thomas; Slaves: Berry,
  Sause, Moll
Marshall, Isaac
Marshall, John
Moore, James, Doctor
Myers, George
Meridath, Samuel; Servants: John,
  George; Samuel Meridath
McGaw, Adam; Slaves: James, Tom
Mutchner, Christopher

Norris, Joseph; Slaves: Tom, Sam, Nat
Norris, James; Servant William
Norris, Ann (widow); Servant John
  Frank
Nelson, William; Servant John
Nowlin, James
Norris, John; Servants: Jack, John

Palmore, George
Patterson, William
Pickard, Joseph
Patric, John; Servant Patric
Purdue, Laban; Servant John
Price, Nesus; Slave Tonee
Pocock, James; Larres; Hester
Pitchto, Philip Love
Pocock, Daniel; Servants: Robert, John
Pocock, John; Servant Murfie
Pierce, Thomas
Pierce, William
Parrish, Joseph
Parrish, Edward
Parrish, William; Nicholas Parrish;
  Slave Dick
Price, Thomas; Servant Godfrie
Price, Samuel; Servants: George (1),
  George (2)

Riston, Benjamin; Slave Hagar
Riston, Abraham
Richardson, Zaceheriah
Ryce, James
Reed, Joseph
Richardson, James
Richardson, John
Rhubee, Thomas Jr.
Rutledge, Michel
Rutledge, John
Rutledge, Abraham; Slaves: Peter, Sam,
  Doll, Pheebee
Richardson, William
Richardson, John
Reed, High (Hugh?)
Ritchardson, Roberts; Wm. Ritchardson;
  Roberts
Riston, Thomas; Slaves: Squash, Sue,
  Bess
Randel, Thomas; Charles Randel; John
Rite, Bloss; James; Mize; Phillip
Rhodgers, Thomas
Rhodgers, William

Shaw, Daniel; Slaves: James, Tim,
  Dinah, Grace
Stewart, John; Charles; John; Dinay

Smith, Robert
Sutten, Samuel
Standiford, Jacob
Standiford, John (son of John);
  Servant John
Standiford, Vinston
Standiford, Israel
Shields, John; Slaves: Messer,
  Dublin, Will
Standiford, Shelton
Stansbury, Dixson Sr.; Valintine;
  Hagur; Harry
Stansbury, Dixson Jr.; Servant
  Richard
Sampson, Richard
Slade, William Jr.; Servant John
Shipley, Benjaman; Benjaman Shipley;
  Eli Shipley
Slade, Josiahs; Nicholus Slade;
  Servants: John, William
Slade, William Jr.; Slaves: Pollipus,
  Murreeur
Slade, William Sr.; Servant George
Sinckler, William Jr.; Slaves:
  George, Tim, Peg
Shepherd, John; Slaves: Harry, Beck,
  Junur, Hanner
Stansbury, Edward
Stephens, Ephraim

Tarmun, William
Tarmun, Benjaman
Trace, Tage
Tate, John
Talbot, Bellenda, widow; Edward
  Caleham; Slaves: George, Sam, Jack,
  Beck, Murreeur
Talbot, Sulphia; John Talbot; Johnson
  Airs; Jean; Cate

Touzer, Ritchard

Voshel, Augusteen

Wile, Abel
Wile, Vinston; Slave Vembar
Wile, Joshua
Wile, William; Benjamin Wile; Servant
  Hugh
Wilie, Benjamin Jr.
Wilie, Benjamin Sr.
Wilie, Aquila; Josiahs Sparks
Williams, Thomas
Wodley, Samuel
Woldley, John
Wodley, Francis
Wood, William
Woods, Henery
West, David
Winks, Joseph
Wilson, John
Wilson, James
Wodsworth (Sic)
Ward, John
Watson, William; John Watson; Servant
  John
Watson, William Jr.
Wilee, Casandrew; Luke Wilee;
  Greenbury Wilee; Seasar; Jack;
  Hazard
Wilee, Walter; Servant Robert

On reverse side: Mine Run, Examined
  by Thos. Sellers: 415; John Weeks 1;
  Richard Forlenbred 1; Daniel Curtus
  4 – 424
Examined by John Moale: 424.Error in
  this list, 3 taxes too much.R C
  examined.

Addilspader, Francis; Thomas
  Adilspader
Armeguish, Christopher
Armagush, Stophel

Boreing, Joshua; John More; Negro
  Savy
Boreing, Absalam
Boreing, Elizabeth; Thomas Boreing
Bever, John
Boreing, James; James Boreing
Boreing, Thomas
Buzzard, Jacob
Bull, William
Bull, John
Baugham, Simon
Boblets, Charles
Bossum, Charles; Joseph, white hand
Bond, Benjamin; Negro Rachel;
  Jonathan, worker
Bond, Thomas
Bosley, Thomas; Negroes: Bob; Hagar;
  Jack Conner
Barker, John
Burns, John
Ball, Peter; Thomas Ball
Busby, John; John Busby; Abraham
Buns (Burs?), Adam
Barny, Absalam; Absalam Barny; Negro
  Sary
Burnes, John; Thomas Dowel
Burnes, James
Baley, Adam
Brown, John
Butler, Edward
Bosley, Gedden; William Mason

Coltritor, John; Barnit Houke
Crew, William
Cox, Jacob
Cox, Zebediah
Copperstone, George; John Word
Catyear, Stophel
Crottinger, Henry
Crepaugham, Cunerd
Chilcoat, John Jr.; Dennis Mallence;
  Thomas Caver; John white hand
Chilcoat, Joshua
Chilcoat, John Sr.; Silvana Sonecroft
Cole, Henry
Curby, Antony
Cables, Robert; Samuel Cables;
  Benjamin Cables; Abraham Thomas;
  Stephen Lsawed(?)

Cole, Mordecai; Absalam Boreing; John
  Cannady; Negro Linen
Cole, Christopher; Christopher Cole;
  Negroes: Harry, Nell
Cole, Ezekiel; Thomsa Dieson
Cole, Charles
Curtingner, Jacob
Crohan, Mathew
Cummings, Robert
Cullins, Thomas
Culleson, Jos.
Clater, Edward
Carr, Juller; Negro Sam
Carr, Joshua
Crop, Sollemon; Benjamin Crop; Erzeril
Cuper, James
Cross, Benjamin
Collet, Daniel; Moses Collet
Colder, James; Negro Dick
Couch, Michel
Coss, Henry; Edward Jonson; John
  Proddon

Dowel, Jonathan
Deed, Michel
Dilley, John
Day, Thomas
Doter (Doton?), Edw.
Dawes, Francis; John Miller; Thomas
  Caper; Thomas Scot; Samuel Scot
Dawnny, Thomas; Nolter Dawnny; Michel
  Horn
Dausey, Elisha; James and Mack, white
  hands; Negroes: Seazer, Ruth
Daniels, Jonathan
Davis, John; John Davis; William Davis
David, Price (David Price?)

Eatheryourn, Christopher; J.
  Eatheryourn
Edwards, John
Ensor, John; John Morgin; Negro Dove

Frasher, John
Fowble, Jacob; Henry Moback
Fowble, Peter; Michel Fowble; Melken
  Fowble
France, John
France, Henry
Feather, Henry; Philip Feather; Adam
  Feather
Ford, Mordecai; Negroes: Jason, Jeff,
  Diner
Fite, Henry; Peter Fite; Andrew Fite
F(torn)te, Wolly

F(torn)ord, William

Gittinger, John; Henry Gittinger
Garlots, Henry
Gill, Stephen
Gill, Edward; George Fullfort; Negro
  Matiller
Grofrap, Richard
Greedree, William
Grimes, James; William Wood; Thomas
  Vane
Gadd, Absalam
Gapot, Martin
Groxson, John
Green, Joshua
Gibbens, Thomas

Hardin, William
Hare, Stopel; Philip
Hartson, David
Hale, Tilley
Hale, Thomas
Hale, Charles; Nicholas Hale
Hale, Henry
Hanns, Michel
Hawkins, Thomas
Howmiller, George
Hose, John; John Pacler; Philip
  Grosus
Hale, Mathew
Hill, John
Hall, John of Joshua; James Arviss;
  Thomas Chapman; Negro Beck
Hudlestone, Robert
Husk, Bennit
Hardister, Henry
Hoopman, Babury; John Hoopman
Hartman, Francis; (name of white
hand unclear)
Hicks, John
Highet, Christopher
Hare, John

Johnson, Jeremiah; John Willmouth;
  Charles Darrick; William Lolle;
  William Brucks; William Prese;
  Negro Rachel
Jones, William

Lutes, John
Lubdon, Thomas
Loughslagle, Henry
Lowler, James
Long, Henry
Lemhood, Henry

Lemmon, Alexis; Negro Florence

Murray, Wheeler
More, Stophel
Maryman, William
Maryman, George
Minkey, Philip
Mehand, John; Lewick Wampler
Melone, Michel
Mecomsque, Daniel; James Addes
Mecomsque, John; (name torn off)
Mathew, Thomas
Malled, John
Mallonnee, John
Madlecort, John
Mathew, Richard
Marchel, Thomas
Markey, John; John Markey
Morgin, James
Miller, Elizabeth; John Miller
Martin, Charles
Myers, Lorrance
Mallan, Thomas

Nace, Peter
Nideven, Mordecai
Nole, Anthony

Peddicoart, John
Prince, Henry
Powman, Daniel
Parish, John; Mordecai Parish
Price, John Jr.; Jones; Smith
Petts, Lues; George Bace
Parish, John
Peneton, Daniel; John Allen; Patrick,
  a white hand
Purkepile, Andrew; Chris. Purkepile
Purce, John
Purkepile, William

Rollins, Richard; Negro Jack
Richard, Richard
Rogers, Benjamin Esq, Quarter at the
  Great Meadows; Negroes: Phil, Phan
Riseton, John; Thomas Riseton
Rinehart, Avarone
Rogers, Benjamin Esq; Christ. Singary;
  Negroes: Jacob, Limus, Charles, Als;
  David Fahan

Shilling, Christopher; William
  Shilling
Shaver, Jacob
Siddin, John

Scoffield, John; William Scoffield
Sap, Peter
Scott, Joseph
Shall, Joseph
Stansbruary, Thomas; Thomas Dring
Stillis, Philip
Scipper, James
Smith, Charles
Singary, Christopher; Negro
  (unclear); Robert Fisher
Spindle, Jacob
Stansbruary, William; Negro Thom
Stansbruary, Joseph; Negro Briston
Spindle, Jacob

Tipton, Jonathan
Tipton, Briant
Tracey, Bassil
Teffenner, Cateven; Michel Teffenner
Tipton, Mordecai; Quillar Tipton;
  Jacob Abrerum
Tanner, George
Tipton, Samuel; Richard Bare
Tipton, Thomas
Tracey, John
Tracey, Wornil

Vaughan, Christopher; Richard Vaughan;
  Negro Pri (Pru)
Vaughan, Suredine (Sheredine?)

Woodcock, Robert
Whareham, Henry
Wisnal, Mathias; Ales Ashwith; Hewonan
  Melon
Weaver, John
Wolfort, Frederick
Wolfe, Jacob
Wotlen, Thomas; James Smith
W (torn) tlee, William

Names Out of Order:
Cullison, Jos.
Reeth, William
Reeth, John
Reed, John

On the reverse side: North Hundred —
  Taxes: 336, Exam. by William B.

LIST OF TAXES TAKEN IN BY NATHAN PERRIGO, CONSTABLE OF
PATAPSCO LOWER HUNDRED FOR THE YEAR OF OUR LORD GOD 1773

Arrowsmith, Samuel
Arnall, Joshua
Arnall, Peter
Ammick, Nicholas

Bowen, Edward; Negroes: Ceasor, Pegg
Bowen, Absalam
Battee, Ferdenanda; Negroes: Jack,
  Genny
Blansford, John
Bowen, Josias; Negroes: Davey, Joe,
  Ben, Will, Lucey
Baxter, Edmond
Briant, James; Negroes: Ceasor, Jude
Beckney, John
Beddy, Petter
Bowen, Samuel

Colegate, Thomas; Richard Aylward;
  John Butterworth; Mullatto Genney
Colegate, Thomas, Secty.
Coppersmith, Peter
Cochran, William
Collins, John; John Lindsey, secty.
Cloey, John
Clark, John

Colespell, Thomas
Cunningham, James
Caplinger, John; Nicholas Ammick,
  Security

Davis, Daniel
Davis, Anne; Negro Sam
Dillan, Patrick; Moses Machubin, scty.
Davis, Christian; Negro Seasor
Dicks, Richard

Eglestone, Abraham; Negroes: Nell,
  Phillice, Tobe
Ensor, Abraham; John Aldredge; William
  Bushop; Negroes: Sam, Waco, Harry,
  Pegg
Eglestone, Benjamin; Anthony Bolling
Evans, Job
Evans, Daniel; Tom
Egletson, Jonathan
Eddards, Williams
Eddards, Thomas; William Eddards,
  scty.

Fulter, Michel
Ford, Loyd; (torn)i Ford
Ford, Loyd Jr.; Loyd Ford, Sr.,
  Security

Green, Robert
Green, Solomon
Green, Moses
Green, Abraham
Green, Many (Mary?); Negro Robert
Green, Josias; Mary Green, Security
Gray, Lynch; Edward Watts, Security
Gray, Ephraim
Gray, Zachariah
Green, Venson
Gatch, Thomas; Negroes: Petter,
  Phillis, Hagar
Goshage, Charles Qtr; Negroes: Jack,
  Fanny
Goshage, David; Isaac Turner, Darby
  Lowrey, John McKnight, Joseph
  Streetor, Petter Vininger; Negroes:
  Simon, Vinder
Goshage, John; Negro Hazard
Grits, Lewis
George, John
Garman, John
Gardner, Nicholas
Garretson, Job; Negro Ben
Grimes, James; John Grimes
Goswick, Aquilla

Hicumbottom, Joel; John Hicumbottom
Hisca, Felty
Homes, William
Hail, John   ·
Hanson, Jonathan Sr.; Simon Hanson;
  John Loom; William Gillin; Negroes:
  Jack, Ceasor, Priss
Hanson, Jonathan Jr.; Thomas Riley
Hail, William; Charles Rogers,
  Security

Joyce, William

Keias, Joseph
Kindley, M James or James McKinley

Loves, Miles; Robert Fenton; Negro
  Diner
Leech, John
Lawson, Alexander, Qtr.; Thos. Comly,
  overseer; James Maguire; Negroes:
  Will, Soll, Abraham, Jem, Lucy,
  Jenny
Lynch, William; Dennis McCarty;
  Negroes: Will, Ned, Jack, Sam,
  Catto, Bold

Lynax, Nathan
Linnox, Richardson

Lynch, Robuck; Patrick Lynch; William
  Lynch; Negroes: Tob, Jack, Harry,
  Hagor, Nann, Judey, Ruth
Lynch, Isaac; Patrick Lynch, scty.
Lindsy, John
Lux, Darby; Richard Holden, slave;
  Negro Anthoney
Limes, Christopher at his Mill;
  William Trwith; John White; John
  Liver; Edward McLaughlin; James
  Briant; John Bowing
Leakin, James

Mason, Alexander; Thomas Todd,
  Security
Machubin, Moses; Negroes: Mingo,
  Thomas, Hector, Ceasor, Harry,
  James, Edenborah
Mock, Paston
Martin, Nathaniel; Negro Diner
Machubin, William; Negroes: Mingo,
  Charles, Samuel, Benjamin, Jean
Merryman, Aberilah, widow; Negroes:
  Ben, Toney, Flora, Lib, Hannar
Merryman, Joseph; Martin, his man
Madwell, James; Jeffry, his brother

Norwood, Nicholas; John Toombs; John
  Allcraft; Henry Middleton; Negro
  Jenny
Nail (Neil), Aurther
Neill, John

Oyston, Lawrence; Negroes: Coose,
  Hannar
Oyston, John
Oak, John
Orum, John
Oyston, Lawrence; Negroes: Goose,
  Hannar
Oyston, John
Oak, John
Orum, John

Perrigo, Nathan; Negro Ruth
Perrigo, John
Petty, Horrace; Tobias Stansbury,
  Security
Partridge, William; Negro Bristo
Partridge, Anne; John Partridge;
  Negroes Dick, Deb
Pingell, Andrew
Perrigo, Nathan; Negro Ruth
Perigo, John
Petty, Horrace; Tobias Stansbury,
  Security

78

Partridge, William; Negro Bristo
Partridge, Anne; John Partridge;
  Negroes: Dick, Deb
Pingell, Andrew

Ridgley, Charles; Negroes: Jack,
  Will, London, Dick, Sarah, Judia;
  White servants: Adam Bayles, James
  Bradley, Elias Button, Richard
  Hull, Tim Hurley, Samuel Bugh(?),
  Daniel Davis, Larry Garbin, Derby
  Kelly, Mathew Moade, Daniel
  Gallion, John McGinwish
Roles, Richard
Ryder, Andrew; William Wood; Owen
  Crow; Negroes: Toby, James, Cloe
Ruck, Thomas
Redacore, Jacob
Rogers, Charles; Negroes: Shopher,
  George, Cato, Nan, Cole

Smith, Charles
Sweeting, Edward; Negroes: Jacob,
  Jemima, Mathews
Stansbury, Daniel; Negroes: Pegg,
  Geen
Smith, Samuel; William Baley
Shaw, Thomas; Knightsmith
Shaw, Nathan
Shaw, Thomas; Negro Lucy
Sulewan, Darby; Thomas Shaw, Security
Spriggs, Richard; Ferdinand Battee,
  Overseer; Negroes: Will(1),
  Will(2), Will(3), Bob, Jacob,
  Dinah, Syke, Rachel, Sall
Slater, William
Stansbury, Richard
Spriggs, Samuel; Richard Stansbury,
  Security
Sollers, Joseph; Francis Gersh
Serjant, John
Sollers, Thomas; John Watley; Thomas
  Stevens; Negroes: Roger, Nall,
  Rosile, Dick, Pegg, Beck
Sollers, Labrith; George Barland;
  Negroes: Nick, George, Ned, Chance,
  Dick, Sarah, Beck, June, Jenny,
  Cloe
Stansbury, Tobias; James Maguire; Two
  Negroes
Stansbury, George; Negroes: Jack,
  Maria
Sollers, Heighe; Negroes: Samson,
  Deb, Ketch, Sarah
Sendall, Jacob; Jacob Sendall
Stokes, James

Smith, John Aderson; Meshach Hail;
  John Dareity; Rich. Atterdson;
  Negroes: Tom, Qular, Tab
Stevenson, Richard King; Negroes:
  Marget, Cato, Hager
Stevenson, Sater; John the Gardner;
  Negro Ester

Todd, Thomas; Thomas Hamner, Overseer;
  Martha Skiffington; Edward Maloon;
  Peter Skully; John Shill; Negroes:
  Sam, Toby, Able, Hannar, Hager,
  Dinah, Esther
Thackhan, William; Edward Sweeting,
  Security
Throton, Luke; William Tillburry;
  Negroes: Seasor, Pearo, Harry,
  Hanner, Jean, Geminar
Tolbert, Rebecca; Benjamin Tolbert
Todd, Lancelot
Todd, Thomas, Carpenter
Taylor, Charles; John Taylor; Negro
  Diner

Villin, John
Vensell, Charles; Margit Harner,
  Security

Woodard, John; Negroes: Jerry, Phillis
Wheatherton, Mary; Negroes: Tom, Pone,
  Dick, William, Tom, Comfort, Clow
Watts, Edward
Wilkinson, William; Daniel Bucklar;
  Negroes: Eady, Hannah, Luse,
  Barthene, Cuffy, Sam, Dick, Cane
Watts, John
With, William; Rebecca Talbot, secty.
Walker, David
Wheeler, John
Woohey, Petter; Philip Woohey
Walles, William Taxes in all: 391
Wise, Lue Signed: Nathan Perrigo

  An Additional List of Taxes Taken in
  Patapsco Lower Hundred
  By Nathan Perrigo, Constable

Armatage, John
Brock, Rachel, widow; Negro Jim
Bush, James; Thomas Gatch, scty.
Brian, James Jr.; David Walker, scty.
Carter, William; James Madwell, scty.
Fahey, Patrick
Fletcher, Robert
Gadcomb, John; Abraham Egleston,

LIST OF TAXABLES OF PATAPSCO LOWER HUNDRED, 1773

Mall, Thomas; Joel Hickenbottom,
  Security
Oyston, Gabriel; John Watts, Security
Roddy, John; Rachel Baxter, Security
Randall, George; Wm. McChubin,
  Security
Smith, John
Todd, Richard; David Walker, Security
Trotton, Luke; Negro Luke

Rogers, Benjamin Qtr; Negroes: Susar,
  Pegg

Taxes in All: 17

On Reverse side: Additional List 17
  + 391 = 408.
Examined by Thomas Sollers. Examined
  by B. Rogers.

A LIST OF TAXABLES FOR PATAPSCO UPPER HUNDRED, IN BALTIMORE COUNTY TAKEN BY ABRAHAM WALKER, CONSTABLE, 1773

A (torn) on, Richard
(probably Ashton?)

Banniker, Benjamin
Baker, Nicholas; Elam Baker
Barton, James Sr.; Benjamin Barton
Barton, James Jr.
Black, William
Brightley, Matthias
Brown, Luke; Negro Sarah
Bazil, Ezekiel; William Marr
Black, Joshua; Moses Black, Secty.
Bailey, John; John Nusom Bailey;
  George Bailey; Negroes: Arthur,
  Sharper, Hannah, Kate
Bailey, Sarah; Negro Bonn
Brooks, Clement; Thomas Lingham;
  Walter Parker; John Ghiselin;
  William Jessop; William Woston,
  Jr.; William Woston, Sr.; Nathaniel
  Woston; John Cook; Robert Joachim;
  Barnabas Loveman; Charles Brady;
  John Phinemore; Joseph Roberts;
  Thomas Hignot; Thomas Grant; Samuel
  Perry; Michael Drury; Thomas
  Sarles; John Daridge; Joseph
  Stevens; Thomas Bock; Philip
  Clarke; Samuel John Lurridge; Negro
  Jerry; Negro Jacob; William Pain;
  William Lucas; Patrick Corban; John
  Sylvester; Joseph Jenkins; John
  Lewis; William Turner; David Haile;
  Joseph Nicholas; William Matthews;
  David Morgan; John Lawlar; Negroes:
  Andrew, Adam, Benn, Cesar, Cato,
  Colonel, Crusole, Dennis, Grace,
  Hannah, Joseph, Juda(1), Jack,
  Juda(2), Jacob, Jeffery, Kate,
  Mary, Milla, Marshal, Nick, Nephew,
  Nanny, Poll(1), Pegg, Poll(2),

  Prince, Patrick, Rachael, Sam,
  Sarah, Sue, Sal, Tom(1), Tom(2),
  Tom(3), Will
Brooks, Clement; Negroes: Peter,
  George, Nero, James, Dide

Croxal, Charles; Negroes: Charles,
  Will, Esther, Bridget, Tom, Benn,
  Kate, Aminta, Bett
Calvert, John; 14 Negroes (no names
  given)
Creswell, William
Connaway, John; John Connaway
Cornelius, John; Wm. Cornelius; John
  Cornelius
Cromwell, Oliver; James Cromwell;
  James Browning; John Cromwell

Dorsey's Forge: Elam Bailey; James
  Crow; Ezekiel Wilson; Philip Neau;
  Thomas Wood; Robert Buckel; William
  Nailer; John Jenkins; Era Evans;
  James Atwood; John Goodard; William
  Nailer; Eoelin Smith, Thomas Ellis,
  and 9 negroes.
Dilworth, William; Joseph Dunbar
Dawn, Thomas
Dulaney, Daniel Esq.; Thos. Wm.
  Perber, and 5 Negroes

Ellicott, John; Samuel Godfrey;
  Jonathan Ellicott; Michael Monks
English, Robert; Patrick Noel

Flood, William

Grondia, John; Richard Williams;
  Thomas Spicer; Peter Matthews;
  William Hancock
Griffin, Thomas; Negro Chloe
Gardener, John
Greah, Jacob; Jacob Greah

Hessey, Henry
Hessey, Charles
Hussh, Valentine; Peter Hussh; John
  Hussh
Hood, James
Hippenhammer, Andrew; Andrew
  Hippenhammer
Henry, Isaac
Heath, William; Joseph Bailey, and 5
  Negroes

Jarvis, William

Lewis, Charles; Thomas Smith
Lewis, John
Lott, Samuel
Lewing, James
Limbrey, Andrew; Andrew Limbrey
Lewis, Edward
Lloyd, Thomas; John Mahony; Hugh
  McMullen; Negroes: Harry, Beck,
  Toney
Lewis, Henry
Lighthisor, George; Michael Richards,
  Security

Mackubin, Zachariah; 9 Negroes (no
  names given)
Moale, John Qtr.; James Stewart;
  Thomas Hiscock; 5 Negroes listed
McKinley, Daniel for Taylor, Thornton
  and Calvert; 8 Negroes listed
Miller, Johanna; William Miller; John
  Miller
Miller, Joseph
Miller, Godlip
Morris, Edward
McKeil, Patrick; George Teale,
  Security
Matthews, William
Morelon, Samuel; Greenberry Morelon

Norwood, Mary; James Wardon; Negroes:
  Pompey, Low
Norwood, Samuel, son of Edward;
  George Hall; Thomas Jones; James
  Bunion; 4 Negroes

Owens, John
Owens, Lancelot; Thomas Baldwin
Owens, Ellen; 3 Negroes

Peak, George
Penn, John Sr.; John Penn
Pierpoint, Charles Jr.; John Pierpoint
Partridge, Joseph
Penn, Reason; James Thompson; Thomas
  Hand; Negro Jenny
Patterson, Joseph
Pierpoint, Charles Sr.; Negroes: Sam,
  Boatswain

Ridgeley, Charles, son of William,
  exer. to Samuel Norwood, decd.;
  Richard Wilmott; John Braddon; 10
  Negroes
Ryan, John; Thomas Robinson
Reed, John; George Reed; John Reed
Reed, John Jr.
Richard, Michael
Robinson, Joseph
Read (Reed), Jacob; Charles Pierpoint,
  Security
Strackell, John; Frank Stanley; 3
  Negroes
Stinchcomb, John Sr.; Maclane
  Stinchcomb; 4 Negroes
Stimper, Charles
Smith, Adam; John Reed, Security

Teale, Emmanuel; Lloyd Teale
Teale, Edward; William Edge; Negro
  Jane
Teale, George; William Ferrol;
  Negroes: James, Amber

Williams, William; Negroes: James,
  Margaret
White, Elisha; Otho White; John White
Walker, Alexander
Wells, Benjamin; Negro Alexander
Wilderman, Jacob; Jacob Wilderman
Walker, Abraham; John Daniel; Joseph
  Barns

Zimmerman, George; John Stempel;
  Thomas Stone
(End of List: No Tally Given)

A LIST OF TAXABLES BELONGING TO PIPE CREEK HUNDRED

BY WILLIAM KELLEY, JR., 1773

Algier, Jacob
Alinck, William
Ambrous, William Jr.
Ambrous, William; William Mash
Algier, John

Berky, Christian
Blizard, William
Blizard, John
Baker, Isaus
Baker, Morris; Meshak Baker
Belt, John; Nathan Belt; Joseph Belt
Brown, John Jr.
Brothers, Tobias
Brown, Rudolph
Boy (Bay), Jeremiah
Baker, Henry
Bagster, Greenbury
Belt, Leonard; William Biset
Biddle, John
Bartly, Archibald
Bords, Philip
Bidler, John
Burns, John; John Turner; Antony (no last name)
Burns, Michael
Butler, Henry; Peter Makincim
Brown, John; Henry Brown
Brown, William
Baumgardiner, John
Black, John

Corbin, William; Negro Roger
Corbin, John
Chapman, William
Commel, Martin
Cramer, Peter
Cuper, Finechance; Valentine Cuper

Durbin, Christopher
Del, Michael
Densmore, Robert
Day, Mark
Day (?), Richard
Day, Matthew
Deal, William
David, Henry; James Estub
Deker, Frederick; John Read
Deker, Rudolph

Epercu (Upperco?), Jacob
Everhart, George
Epaugh, Jacob; Negro Harry

Elms, John; Michael (no last name)
Ekler, Jacob
Ekler, Ulrick; Daniel (no last name)

Fisher, Michael; Paul Hern
Frasher, John; William Russell
Frank, Peter; Phillip Frank; Daniel Peck
Felty, Felix
Fisher, George; David Fisher; George Fisher
Fisher, John

Gill, Thomas; Negroes: Hannah, Nan
Grace, Francis; John Grace
Graham, Richard; Thomas Moore; John Ward

Hooker, Richard
Homes, James
Hase, Joseph
Hicks, Steven
Hostleter, Corstenau
Hooker, Thomas
Hudgel, Joseph
Henestophel, Henry; John Henestophel; Wm. Henestophel
Higings, John
Hooke (Houck) Barnet
Horn, Michael
Hemp Christopher

James, Thomas

Kelley, William; Daniel Pavy
Kelley, Joshua
Kifer, Finsance

Loveall, Zebulon
Loveall, Ethan; Richard Gilcote
Loveall, Luthan
Loveall, Henry
Loveall, William
Lane, Samuel
Lane, Samuel Jr.
Lane, Abraham
Louderslaer, Philip; Geo. Louderslaer
Lipe, Conrad
Lane, Dutton; 6 Negroes

Morrow, William
Murry, Ruth; 5 Negroes
Murry, James; William Adkison
Murry, Christopher; Philip Maisin; Elam Cruther; Negro Ledy

82

A LIST OF TAXABLES BELONGING TO PIPE CREEK HUNDRED

Miller, Adam
Murry, John; James Flemmen; Gobin
  Sullivan; Samuel Manton; John
  Phillips; 3 Negroes
Murry, Shadrack
Myers, Isaac
Myers, George; Henry Fuller; William
  Price
Murry, John

Ozband, Joseph
Ozband, John; Edward Pope
Ozband, Daniel; Walter Hill
Oats, Henry; Coate Lip (?)
Oats, Jacob
Oats, Peter

Plowman, Jonathan
Plowman, James; Henry Green
Pussy, George; William Driver
Pirely, Ludwich
Pirely, Conrad
Parrish, Joseph; William Jenkins
Plowman, John
Pechy, Peter; Peter Pechy
Pixler, Jacob

Rutter, Ludwich; Michael Rutter
Richard (Richart), John
Rinehart, Teltrich
Rupe, Jacob
Richards, Richard; Nicholas Richards;
  James Story
Sturns, Abraham
Sap, George
Stones, Thomas
Slanis, George
Slider, Christopher
Snap, Peter; Peter Snap
Starner, John
Shaver, Jacob; John Shaver

Snider, Frederick; Michael Snider
Snider, Martin
Switeser, Ludwich
Scales, John
Story, Thomas
Sap, Daniel; Frederick Sap
Sap, John
Sap, Jacob
Sap, Daniel Jr.
Sence, Christian
Steclor, Simon
Swank, Conrad
Slagle, Peter
Srier, Andrew
Srote, Stoppel
Srier, Loudwich
Swots (Swarts), John
Spours, (no first name)

Tomer, Christian; John Tomer
Trash, Jacob
Turner, John
Tousan, Thomas Sr.; Joshua Tousan
Tousan, Thomas Jr.

West, Thomas
Wade, Henry
Williams, John
Ward, Richard
Wittman, Peter
West, Thomas
Welch, Laban
Welty, Margret; Nicholas Kiser
Wineman, Barnet
Wever, Philip; Stophel (unclear)
Wells, John
Wooding, Steven; John Harves

On the reverse side: Pipe Creek
    Taxes......236.....Examined J B N

A LIST OF TAXABLES TAKEN IN WESTMINSTER HUNDRED IN 1773
BY HENRY MINSPAKER, CONSTABLE

Ashburner & Place; Thomas Langton;
  John German; John Evans; Edward
  Edwards
Anderson, Daniel
Alldrige, John
Armstrong, James
Antony, John
Alexander, Mark; George Welsh

Alexander, Robert; Negroes: Gabriel,
  Binah, Lucy, Nan
Allen, William
Allen, Owen; William Gibson; John
  Gibson
Allen, William

Buchanan, Andrew; Negroes: Belle,
  Rachel, Ameliah, Jack

83

Buchanan, Archibald; Abraham Rister; 3 Negroes
Barrier, Antony
Bolser, Casper
Burlington, Casper
Burlington, Curtis
Barnet, Daniel; Patrick Shean; Charles Shiel; Samuel Thompson; Negro Cloe
Bowly, Daniel; Nicholas Ruxton Moore
Brown, Henry
Brown, John
Busrow, Joseph
Babine, John
Buchanan, Loyd; Extr. for Negro Sarah
Bissho, Paul
Bryan, Thomas
Brawney, Thomas

Caldwell, James
Curtis, John
Carroll, Daniel; Boy Hugh; Negro Dinah
Chase, Rev. Thomas; Negroes: Peg, Rachel, Jacob
Cullin, Daniel
Citseselman, Andrew; Bolser Warner
Chalmers, George; Thomas Alnut
Clement, John for James Brown
Cheston, James; Daniel Cheston; Abaniah Cannada; Thomas Wilkinson
Cox, Merryman
Cromwell, Richard
Carson, Samuel; Henry Champion; Negroes: Bet, Judah
Constable, Thomas; William Miller; Joist Lidwick; Thomas Roach; John Ryer; John Noys; Alexander McKurdy; James Kennedy
Collins, William; Servant man John
Colbert, William

Deshail, Luis
Drumbrow, Adam
Davis, Richard Capt.; Negroes: Gress, Prissilla
Dagen, George; Negro Fanny
Derumple, John; James Williams; John Sanders; Negroes: Tom, Flora
Depea, John
Durant, John
Deliar, Peter
Davis, Robert
Donnellen, Thomas
Dick, William

Duglass, William

Eaton, William
Easton, Edward
Ewall, John; Negro Sarah
Ennace, Jonathan; Joshua Ennace; James Ennace
Erbeck, Leonard; Fredk. Rockhart

Fonarden, Adam; Apprentice boy Jacob
Frymiller, Joseph
Frazer, James
Flanagan, John; James Berry
Fisher, Michael
Farfet, Thomas
Farley, Thomas

Gervis, Benjamin
Grant, Daniel; Jacob Miller; Mathew Warberton; Phillip Donnly; George Eharse; Let Ragon
Gray, James
Graves, George
Gibney, Hugh
Gough, Harry Dorsey; Thomas Rossiter; Negroes: Dick, Will, Hagar, Beck, Lucke
Gaye, John
Greene, Job
Gutrow, John
Gutrow, Joseph
Gutche, John
German, John
Grangeir, Joseph
Gray, John; John Cockran
Galbreath, Mrs. for Negro Dinah
Goodwin, William; Roderick McKezzie; Negro Phebe

Hook, Andrew; John Stewart; Thomas Holton
Hofman, Abakkuk
Howard, Cornelius; Negro Jason
Hostater, Francis
Hollingsworth, John
Herman, John
Holliday, John
Hiner, Nicholas
Higgins, Patrick
Hill, Richard
Hartvey, Viddie
Harris, William; Conrad Hush; Jessy Sharpless
Hammond, William

Jones, Benjamin
J---(torn), George; Andrew Gribbell
Joyce, Joseph
Jacoby, John Leonard; Henry Augustine
Jennings, Jonathan
James, Isaac

King, Benjamin
Keap, Daniel
Kefer, John; Michael Peck
Keener, Melker; Christian Keener; Man
  Benjamin
Kennaday, Murdock; William King

Limes, Christopher; John Roil; John
  Smith; David Creater; James Keaf;
  David Coleman; Jeremiah Swain; John
  Strawback; Man Thomas
Lara, Cornelius
Lawson & Hudson for Nat Bond
Lownes, James
Lawson, James; Boy Joe; Negro Poll
Lockerman, John
Laboon, John Joseph
Lashaway, John
Long, Robert for Thomas Cole
Lenton, Thomas; Joseph Ellebaki(?);
  Isaac Taylor
Logan, Thomas
Lock, William
Lux, William; George Lux; Rawley
  Spinks; James Hagarthy; Roger
  Connelly; Jonathan Pilling; Darby
  Speeby (Speely); James Murrey;
  Negroes: Nan, Jenny(1), Cumbo,
  Silvia, Jenny(2), Peter, Tom,
  Mamell, Charles, Ben, Perry, Jack,

Munrow, Alexander
Main, Alexander
Mosman, Archibald
McGachen, William; Eve Hare
Murphey, Dennis
Miller, Garret
Minspaker, Henry
Maxfield, James
McClellan, John; Michael Connel; John
  Swindell; Negro Eshmael
Murphey, Joseph
Mockerboy, James; Negro Easter
McCannon, John
Myers, John Jeremiah; Negroes: Comb,
  Maria
Merryman, John; Gerrard Hopkins;
  Negro June

Maloy, John
Moale, John; Negroes: Jack, Lidia,
  Frank
Miller, Paul
Monsey, Samuel
Moltimore, Thomas
Morris, William

Nickelson, Benjamin; William
  Scrawfield; Negro Mary
Nice, David; John Talbort
Nott, Thomas

Oram, Henry

Pewter, Anthony
Pearson, John
Polamus, Joseph
Plum, Peter
Purre, Peter
Parot, Peter
Payne, William; Man Kit
Phipher, William
Procter, John; John Whitehead; William
  Morrish

Rabe, Adam; Benjamin Prump; Peter
  Prumner
Richards, Ammon
Rogers, Benjamin; Negroes: Rose, Nell,
  Ceaser, Peg; Jonas Jones
Ridgely, Charles, son of John; Willim
  Day; Robert Johnson; Negroes: Jack,
  Nero, Jacob, Sall, Cait, Jack
Reed, Edward
Rogers, Joseph
Riddle, James; Thomas Farrel; Patrick
  Magray
Riddle, John; Robert McConnel
Ross, John; Mulatto Bob
Rice, Lawrence; Benjamin Hunt
Rutter, Moses
R---(torn), Mary; Negro Boddy
Richards, Rhema (?)
Renalds, William

Smith, John Addison; Negro Peg
Stenhouse, Alexander (3 more unnamed)
Swarts, Charles
Smith, Conrad; Adam Smith; Thomas
  Packet; Frederick Keas; Negro Venice
Smith, David
Stevenson, John; Aaron Buth; John
  Ellis; Negro Jack

Stewart, David; John Plunket; Negro
  Rachel
Shaney, Daniel
Stover, John; Peter Wilmoth; Jacob
  Craver
Smith, Roland Sr.
Smith, Roland Jr.
Shemay, Sixton
Smith, William; James Smith
Stinson, William

Taylor, Jacob
Thew, David
Taylor, Robert
Trout, Martin
Tobin, Thomas
Tinker, William

Unger, Martin

Viley, James

Williams, Garret
Watts, Hugh
Williams, John; William Lawrence;
  Edmund Welsh; Martin Condon; George
  Cooper; Boy John
Wells, John; Negroes: Cato, Peter,
  Jacob
Winchester, John
White, Oliver
Woods, Robert
Welsh, Robert
Wedge, Simon
White, Simon
Whiney, Thomas
Wilson, William
Woodward, William

Young, Charles; Hans Creavey

Additional 1773 LIST:
Oliver Sold
Joseph White
Joseph White (of Oliver)
John Baptist Wolly
Joseph Babine (Babbine)
Matthew Miller
Peter Sollertine (unclear)
Francis Dashealy Dashiel
Andrew Harroon
Daniel Granger
Ruth Ennis (Jonathan's wife)
Thomas Dew, Wedstone Point; Negroes:
  Old Ben, Luck, James
Nathaniel Cromwell
Nicholas Moore - living with William
  Lux - before to Daniel Bowley
John Cunningham
Valentine Snider
John Arno
Samuel Munjoy
Joseph Wollis
John Asheare
Daniel Landrone
John Mathea
Paul Richards
John Grangers
Francis Luear
James Poulson
Lamapple Every
Richard Moale; William Hollet; Wm.
  Clatterbreck; David Jones; Man Tom
  and Dick
John Stableton
George Steel
Joseph Smith
Joseph Lemain
Robert Villis

Reverse side: Westminster 390 + 21
  Additional = 411. Examined by B.
  Rogers and Wm. B.

BALTIMORE INDEPENDENT CADETS, 1774

The following article is contained inside the cover of a book in the library of the Maryland Historical Society in Baltimore entitled <u>Baltimore Town and Baltimore County Committee of Observation Proceedings, 1774-1776</u>. It is an article about the formation of the "Baltimore Independent Cadets" in 1774 by some of the most spirited and respectable young men of the time, many of whom were transferred to the regular service during the Revolutionary War. It stated:

"We, the BALTIMORE INDEPENDENT CADETS, deeply impressed with a sense of the unhappy condition our suffering brethren of Boston---of the alarming conduct of General Gage--and the oppressive unconstitutional acts of Parliament to deprive us of liberty, and enforce slavery on his Majesty's loyal liege subjects of American in general; for the better security of our lives, liberties, and property, under such alarming circumstances, think it highly advisable and necessary that we form ourselves into a body or company, in order to learn military discipline, and to act in defence of our country, agreeable to the Resolves of the Continental Congress. And first, as dutiful subjects to King George the 3rd, our Royal Sovereign, we acknowledge all due allegiance, under whose banner we wish to support the dignity of his Crown, and the freedom and liberty of the Constitution. Secondly, we resolve after a company of sixty men shall have voluntarily subscribed their names to this paper, that public notice thereof shall be given, and a meeting called to elect the officers of said company, under whose command we desire to be led, and will strictly adhere to, under all the sacred ties of honour, and the love and justice due to ourselves and country; and in case of any emergency we will be ready to march to the assistance of our sister colonies, at the discretion and direction of our commanding officer so elected, and that in the space of forty-eight hours notice from said officer. Thirdly, we agree and firmly resolve to procure at our own expense, a uniform suit of clothes, (Reg'l.) Scarlet, turned up with buff, and trimmed with yellow metal, or gold buttons, white stockings, and black cloth half boots; likewise, a good gun with cartouch pouch, a pair of pistols, belt and cutlass, with four pounds of powder and sixteen pounds of lead, which shall be ready to equip ourselves with, on the shortest notice. And if default shall be found in either of us, contrary to the true intent and meaning of this engagement, we desire, and submit ourselves to a trial by court martial, whom we hereby fully authorise and empower to determine punishments, adequate to the crimes that may be committed, but not to extend to corporal punishment. Given under our hands, this third day of December, in the year of our Lord, one thousand seven hundred and seventy-four."

Mordecai Gist
A. McLure
James Clarke
Barnet Eichelberger
Richard Cary, Jr.
Christopher Hughes
William Beard
Henry Sheaf
Robert McKim
Alex. Donaldson
Walter Roe
William Sterett

Matthew Scott
John Spear
Philip Graybell
Thomas Russell
David Hopkins
John Lanavan
A. McKim
J. Riddle
Brian Philpot
Charles McConnell
Christopher Johnston
Thomas Ewing

BALTIMORE INDEPENDENT CADETS, 1774

John McLure
Samuel Smith
John Smith, Jr.
J. Kennedy
G. McCall
J. Hudson
Thomas Lansdale
J. Govane
William McCreary
Hugh Young
William Hammond
William Stone
Abraham Risteau
Moses Dailey
Robert Buchanan
George Lux
N. Ruxton Moore
David Plunket

Robert Patterson
Christopher Lion
Caleb Shields
David Evans
Simon Vashon
David McMechen
George Peter Keeport
John Weatherburn
Matthew Patton
Robert Long
Robert Brown
Hezekiah Waters
William Geaton
John Deitch
Thomas Jones
James Somervell
Joseph Magoffin
George Mathews

MEMBERS OF THE BALTIMORE COMMITTEE OF OBSERVATION, 1774

From the proceedings of this committee (a copy of which is in the Maryland Historical Society Library) the following inhabitants of Baltimore Town and Baltimore County were duly chosen to serve on the committee in accordance with the 11th Resolve of the Continental Congress, November 19, 1774:

Andrew Buchanan, Chairman, and Robert Alexander, Clerk.

BALTIMORE TOWN: Andrew Buchanan, Robert Alexander, William Lux, John Moale, John Merryman, Richard Moale, Jeremiah Townly Chase, Thomas Harrison, Archibald Buchanan, William Smith, James Calhoun, Benjamin Griffith, Gerrard Hopkins, William Spear, John Smith, Barnet Eichelberger, George Woolsey, Hercules Courtenay, Isaac Griest, Mark Alexander, Samuel Purviance, Jr., Francis Saunderson, Dr. John Boyd, George Lindenberger, Isaac Van Bibber, Philip Rogers, John Deaver, David McMechen, and Mordecai Gist.

PATAPSCO LOWER HUNDRED: Charles Ridgely and Thomas Sollers.

PATAPSCO UPPER HUNDRED: Zachariah McCubbin, Charles Ridgely (son of William), and Thomas Loyd.

BACK RIVER UPPER HUNDRED: Samuel Worthington, Benjamin Nicholson, T. C. Deye, John Cradock, Darby Lux, and William Randall.

BACK RIVER LOWER HUNDRED: John Mercer and Job Garretson.

MIDDLE RIVER UPPER HUNDRED: H.D. Gough and Walter Tolley Sr.

SOLDIERS DELIGHT HUNDRED: George Risteau, John Howard, Thomas Gist, Sr., Thomas Worthington, Nathan Cromwell and Nicholas Jones.

MIDDLESEX HUNDRED: Thomas Johnston and Mayberry Helm.

DELAWARE HUNDRED: John Welsh, Rezin Hammond and John Elder.

MEMBERS OF THE BALTIMORE COMMITTEE OF OBSERVATION, 1774

NORTH HUNDRED: Jeremiah Johnson and Elisha Dorsey.

PIPE CREEK HUNDRED: Richard Richards, Frederick Decker and Mordecai Hammond.

GUNPOWDER UPPER HUNDRED: Walter Tolley, Jr., James Gittings and Thomas Franklin.

MINE RUN HUNDRED: Dixon Stansbury, Jr. and Josias Slade.

"Resolved that the same or any seven of them have power to act in matters within the Town of Baltimore and that any five may act in matters without the said Town in the said County. Resolved that T. C. Deye, Capt. Charles Ridgely, Walter Tolley, Jr., Benjamin Nicholson, Samuel Worthington, John Moale, Doctor John Boyd, and William Buchanan, or any three of them, be a Committee to attend the General Meeting at Annapolis on Monday, the 24th of this month. Resolved that Robert Alexander, Samuel Purviance, Jr., Andrew Buchanan, Doctor John Boyd, John Moale, Jeremiah Townly Chase, William Buchanan and William Lux, be a Committee of Correspondence for Baltimore County and Baltimore Town, and that any four of them have power to act." November 21, 1774

TAXABLES IN ST. PAUL'S PARISH, BALTIMORE COUNTY, IN 1774

This list of taxables is recorded in Reverend Ethan Allen's book entitled Historical Sketches of St. Paul's Parish in Baltimore County, Maryland which he compiled in 1855. A copy is available in the Maryland Historical Society Library in Baltimore. Each person named therein is followed by a number which represents the number of taxables in his house. This list, in 1774, only gives the household head by name. The list also contains names of persons in Rev. Dr. West's list in the year 1786/7, and these names (marked with an * asterisk) appear to have been in St. Paul's in 1774 as well.

BALTIMORE WEST HUNDRED

John Armstrong, carpenter - 1, Capt. Solomon Allen - 1, Andrew Anderson - 1, Mary Arnson - 0, Rev. Patrick Allison - 1, Charles Armstrong - 1, John Atherton, carpenter - 2, John Adams - 1, William Adams - 3, Henry Augustine - 2, Conrod Appleman - 1, Michael Allen - 1, Edward Allen - 3, Christian Apple - 2. *James Alcock, *Christopher Adams, *George Ackinghead, *Mark Alexander, *David Armstrong.

John Badier, tanner - 1, Jacob Belmeyer - 1, Abraham Bathan - 1, John Boyd, Doctor - 2, Thomas Brereton - 2, John Bowen - 1, John Byrne, barber - 1, Henry Blychrod - 1, Levlin Barry - 1, Adam Brand - 1, Robert Buchanan of Wm.- 1, Samuel Butler, castmaker - 1, William & Andrew Barclay - 2, Michael Brown, butcher - 1, John Burk, barber - 3, Benjamin Buttersworth - 1, Michael Barry - 1, Nathaniel Bond - 1, Charles Babington - 1, William Boering - 1, Christiana Bransen - 0, John Burk, bricklayer - 1, Andrew Bonner, tanner - 2, Jacob Brown, baker - 3, Balser Bansell - 1, William Buchanan - 7, Nicholas Barner, tavernkeeper - 3, Elias Barnaby, shoemaker - 2, John Bradenbaugh - 1, John Brown, tanner - 3, William Baker - 1. *Martin Beadle, *Arnold Bambarger, *Stephen Bahon, *George Borfort, *John Butler, *John Bost, *John

89

TAXABLES IN ST. PAUL'S PARISH, BALTIMORE COUNTY, IN 1774

Bather, *Doctor William Beard, *Michael Brown, *Lewis Busson, *Philip Bear,
*George Buchanan, *Clement Brooks, *Andrew Boyd, *Joseph Baxter, *Daniel
Bowley, *Andrew Buchanan, *Henry Brown, *John Bandell, *David Brown, *Charles
Barback, *William Bolster, *Thomas Barling, *Archibald Buchanan.

Sarah Chelton - 4, Robert Christie, Jr.- 5, James Carey, merchant - 1,
Christie & Boyd, acct.- 0, John Craig - 4, Charles Curline - 1, James Carson,
tavernkeeper - 1, Doctor John Clegg - 1, James Cox, taylor - 7, Stephen
Clement - 1, Walter Calquhoun, carpenter - 1, Rudolph Crower - 1, Richard
Curtis, twice taken - 2, Robert Christie, Sr. - 1, Daniel Chamier, Esq.- 3,
James & Robert Christie, acct.- 0, Robert Curtis, shoemaker - 2, Frances
Curtis, Esq., acct.- 0, James Christie, Jr., 6 + 2, Daniel Coffee - 1, James
Calhoun - 3, John Clements, barber - 6, Jeremiah Townley Chase, Esq.- 1, John
Cornthwaite - 3, John Cannon, shoemaker - 3, William Clows, baker - 3, John
Caldwell, wheelwright - 2.   *Henry Conrod, *Edward Carrigan, *John Clark,
*William Clark, *Robert Casey, *John Casey (Carey?), *William Clemm, *Edward
Cole, *Verlinda Clements, *William Cosgrove, *Adam Cramer, *Richard Coughlen,
*John Clark, *Clement Cannon, *Mary Cox, *Joseph Collins, *Thomas Cleef,
*Rosanna Clifton, *Hans Creary, *Richard Carlton, *Richard Culverwell, *John
Cain, *Benjamin Crocket, *John Crocket.

William Douglas - 1, Dalgleish & Amos - 2, George Sewel Douglas - 1,
Pat. Thos. Stranger Duke - 1, William Dickenson - 1, Edward Davis, cooper -
1, Thomas Dewitt, woodcarver - 2, Daniel Diffendaffer - 2, George Devilbis -
2, William Duncan, cooper - 4, Valerius Dukehart - 3, John Dalrymple, joiner
- 2, *William Davis, *Andrew Davidson, *George Donohue, *Michael
Drovebaugh(?), *Alexander Davey, *Henrietta Davey, *Robert Davey, *Robert
Desebra(?), *George Daffen, *Robert Dawson, *Michael Diffendaffer, *William
Danzer, *Sarah Davis, *Alexander Donaldson.

Capt. James Edwards - 3, James Eagan - 1, Frederick Eichelberger - 1,
Barnett Eichelberger - 3, Jacob Eichelberger - 3, Nicholas Eagan - 1, David
Evans - 1, Thomas Ewing, merchant - 4. *David Emmet, *Mary Emmet.

John File, taylor - 1, Alexander Furnival - 1, Abraham Fernandez - 3,
Joseph Ferguson, saddlemaker - 1, Adam Fonarden, blacksmith - 2, James
French, acct.- 0, Firbes & Pratton, acct.- 0, Benjamin Fowler, waterman - 1,
John Forvell, carpenter - 1.   *Henry Fras, *Eliza Ferguson, *Peter Frick,
*Laybolt Frick, *George Fransciscus, *Ormsby French, *Elizabeth Frazier,
*Philip Furguson, *Alexander Finlater, *William Forepaugh, *Furnival &
Garrock.

James Green - 1, William Geathen - 1, Samuel Gerock, shopkeeper - 1,
Jacob Greather, shoemaker - 1, Isaac Mount Gorden - 2, Doctor James Gray - 1,
William Goddard - 1, Mordecai Gist, merchant - 1, John Grosh, carpenter - 1,
Philip Graybill, shopkeeper - 3, Gear Gardner - 1, Charles Garts - 1, John
Gordon, sadler- 11, Cornelius Garrettson- 5. *Catharine Gorden (Gaden?),
*Rev. John Siegfried Gerock, *Andrew Grankel, *James Garrison, *Joseph Green,
*Robert Gilmore, *Benjamin Griffith, *William Graham, *Michael Gordon, *Adam
Gantz, *Robert Gold, *Job Green, *Nathaniel Griffith, *Caleb Gough.

William Hunt, carpenter - 1, Andrew Hoffman - 2, John Hart - 7, Daniel
Hughs - 2, Isaac Hall, bricklayer - 3, Jonathan Hudson - 2, Frederick
Hambreak - 1, Capt. Halbert Hanson - 1, William Hasser, merchant - 7,

BALTIMORE WEST HUNDRED

Christopher Hand - 1, Robert Howard, shoemaker - 1, John Howell, blacksmith-
1,
James Holliday, shoemaker - 3, Christopher Hughes - 4, John Hawkins, tailor -
3, Charles Harris - 1, John Hawkins - 0, Caleb Hall - 1, (illegible) Hopkins,
hatter - 3, Gerrard Hopkins - 8, Thomas Harrison - 8. *William Hollack,
*Andrew Harzog, *Peter Hoopman, *Jacob Heltebrant, *Jacob Hart, *Jesse
Hollingsworth, *James Hawkins, *John Hanson, *Thomas Hamilton, *Maria Hays,
*William Halfs(?), *John Hanright, *William Hawkins, *Jacob Hartman, *William
Harrison, *Philip Hall, *Hoopman & May, *Thomas Hollingsworth, *John Houg(?),
*Jacob Holsinger, *John Holliday, *Charles Harrison.

Samuel Jacobs - 0, Thomas Jebresther(?) - 1, Nicholas Jones - 1, John
Jaffrey - 1, Nicholas Judah - 1, Christopher Johnson - 2, Thomas Jones,
blacksmith - 2, Isaac James, tailor - 1, Thomas Jones, attorney - 0, Wyombest
Judah - 1.

Doctor Patrick Kennedy - 2, Martin Keyser, tailor - 1, David Knox - 1,
John Kennedy, merchant - 2, Mary Kedney - 0, Peter Keenor, sailmakr - 2,
Jacob Keeport, carpenter - 2. *Melchior Keener, *John Keys, *George Keeport.

John Little - 2, Patrick Langan - 1, Abraham Larsh - 1, L. Leatherman -
2, Thomas Lusk - 1, Simon Lindecker - 2, Youngert Lydick - 1, Thomas Lenahan
- 2, Thomas Lansdale - 1, Robert Long - 1, Valentine Lees - 2, Peter
Louderman - 1, Thomas Low - 1, Thomas Logan's assignees - 0, _____ Lloyd - 1
Benjamin Levy - 2, Valentine Larsh - 1, George Lindenberger, Esq. - 2,
William Leavly - 2, Richard Lemmon - 3, Gabriel Lewan (?), silversmith - 2,
Henry Lorah - 4. *Philip Little, *Thomas Lloyd, *Peter Lidding, *Frederick
Lausbaugh, *George Letzinger, *James Long, *Simon Loyadecker, *John Laylost,
*James Lyston, *Elisha Lewis, *John Lorah, *Daniel Lawrence, *Ann Lloyd,
*Aaron Levering, *Joseph Laimane.

William McKnight - 1, John McCabe - 1, Alexander Main, painter - 1,
David McClelland, cooper - 2, Francis Marmell, Thomas Marshall, blacksmith -
1, Alexander McLure - 1, James Musgrove - 1, Joseph McGoffin - 2, Geo.
Martin, silversmith, Thomas Morgan - 3, David McLure - 1, Joseph McCubbin -
1, Ebenezer Mackie - 1, David Moore - 1, John Miller - 1, Conrod Markell - 3,
Alexander McMachan (dead?)- 2, Frederick Mopps, shoemaker - 2, Anthony May
(dead?)-1, James Marshall, drayman - 1, William McCarter, shoemaker - 1, John
McKim - 2, William Moore, Sr. - 1, George McCall - 1, David McHenry and Son -
2, Matthew Maren, castmaker? - 2, William Miller, carpenter - 1, Christian
Myers, sadler - 1, James Moakes, carpenter - 1, William McDowell, pedlar - 1,
Moses M. Mordeca, acct.- 0, John and Daniel More, Frederick County - 0, Peter
Mackenheimer - 4, Robert Moore, cabinetmaker - 3, Joseph Miller, carpenter -
3, Frederick Myer - 2, Richard Moale - twice taken, 9-11, John McFadden - 2,
Phillip Miller - 1, William Moore, Jr. - 1 (or 3?), Aaron Mattison, hatter -
2, George McCandless - 5, James B. S. May, silversmith - 1, John McLure - 3,
Samuel Messersmith - 5, Elizabeth Mohler, David McMechan, Esq. *Mary Marton
(Martin), *John Martin, *Adam McLan, *Samuel Matthews, *Francis Marble,
*Michael Moorehead, *Mary McKight (McKnight), *Jacob Myers, *Phebe McCabe,
*Joseph McFaden, *Robert McKim, *Alexander McKim, *Capt. Thomas Moore,
*Stephen Moore, *Jacob Manwaring, *Michael McCoy, *John McHenry, *Thomas
Moltimore, *Rebecca Mercer, *Charles Mumbro, *James Micajah, *Sylvanis
Merritt, *Thomas Moffet.

TAXABLES IN ST. PAUL'S PARISH, BALTIMORE COUNTY, IN 1774

Septimus Noel - 2, John North - 1, Thomas Niles,sailor, William Neale, merchant - 1. *Mr. Nelson, *Christian Niece, *William Nox, *James Nicholson, *William Newton.

William O'Brian - 1, Esau Oakly - 2, Felix O'Neal - 1, Caroline Orrick - 3, Samuel Owings, of Stephen - 1. *John Omensetter.

Abraham Patton - 3, Matthew Patton - 3, John Phile, merchant - 1, Samuel Purviance - 3, Robert Purviance - 2. *John Proctor, *Mark Pringle, *George Priestman, *Daniel Painter, *Henry Phiherol, *Joseph Plush, *Thos. Pelkington.

Samuel Roddy - 1, Aubrey Richardson - 7, John Rumble - 3, Christian Race - 1, Christian Reems - 1, William Russell - 3, Matthew Ridley - 2, Jacob Ram - 1, Samuel Rubist(?) and Son - 2, John Riddle - 3, Christopher Raeborg - 1, Thomas Russell, tanner - 1, John Ross, jailer - 2, Joseph Roddy - 1 Fidal Rock - 1, Thomas Russell, storekeeper - 1, Ridgely, McClure & Goodwin - 0, John Richardson, carpenter - 2, William Rogers, hatter? - 2, Daniel Richardson, shoemaker - 3, William and Richard Rusk - 2, David Rusk - 6, Walter Roe - 1, Philip Rogers - 6. *Elizabeth Ross, *Christoper Raybarger, *Jonathan Rutter, *James Roney, *John Read, *Christian Ratig, *Charles Reily, *Nancy Russell, *Russell & Gilmore, *Robert Riddle, *William Roe, *Thomas Rusk, *James Ryon, *George Ross, *Henrietta Rogers, *Wm. Rush, butcher.

John Slaymaker, pilot(?) - 2, James Somerville - 3, Charles Swartz - 1, Peter Stribeck - 2, Matthew Scott - 1, Thomas Smith, cooper - 2, Doctor Conrod Small - 2, Francis Smith, tailor - 4, William Shiller, shoemaker - 1, Sarah Stewart - 0, Nicholas Schoopner(?), cutler - 1, Doctor Alexander Stenhouse - 4, Edward Saunders, carpenter - 1, Alexander Saunders, laborer - 1, Richardson Stewart - 1, John Stohler - 1, Capt. William Stone - 1, Enoch Story - 2, Mathew Segapey, butcher - 1, James Smith, cooper - 1, John Seymour - 1, William Skull pedlar - 2, William Sample, shoe- maker - 1, Doctor Swope - 1, William Spencer - 1, James Sterrett - 5, Nathaniel Smith - 3, Michael Shragley - 4, John Skyren - 3, William Spear - 8, Martin Segasser, butcher - 1, Henry Sheaff - 3, John Smith, merchant - 5, John Sterrett - 2, David Shield - 3, William Stenson - 2, Andrew Steigar - 4, John Schley - 2, Robert Slater - 1, Caleb Shields, silversmith - 1, Francis Sanderson - 4. *Lewis Salts, *Susanna Stover, *Peter Swindle, *John Shaw, *Conrad Small, *John Slatter, *George Streback, *Margaret Smith, *Adam Smith, *Michael Schriver, *Francis Smith, *John Sterrett, *George Somerville, *David Stewart, *John Sabader, *George Salmon, *John Schultz, *Joseph Safer, *Jacob Small, *John Somerton, *Stephen Stewart, Jr., *George Slyers(?).

Henry Thompson - 4, John Thompson, cooper - 1, David Thew, painter - 2, Philip Thomas, bricklayer - 1, Richard Tainter(?), shoemaker - 1, Joseph Tomlin - 1, Bartholomew Taylor - 1, Samuel Taylor - 1, Henry Tinsel - 1. *Samuel Turner, *Frederick Teams, *Mary Trapalet, *John Tinges, *David Tarells(?), *George Turnbull, *James Tool.

Charles Vashon - 1, Isaac Vaughan - 1, Thomas Usher - 3 Simon Vashon - 1, Erasmus Uhler - 1.

John Woolfe - 1, James Wilkinson, taylor - 1, James Walker, drayman - 1, William Wilson - 1, Capt. Charles Wells - 1, Thomas Wilkins, bricklayer - 1, Benjamin West - 1, Peter Willevell(?) - 1, Weatherburn & Hethrington - 2,

BALTIMORE WEST HUNDRED

Robert West, Sr. and Robert West, Jr. - 2, Robert Westbay, shoemaker - 1, Christopher Wonder, carpenter - 1, Michael Woolfe, tailor - 1, George Wallarn - 1, George Woolsey - 2, Hugh Westby, tailor - 1, William Wilson, carpenter - 1, William Westby - 3, Jacob Welsh, tanner - 2, Morrice Westlen, organist - 2, Dr. Charles Fredk. Weisenthall - 3. *Frederick Will, *Henry Wannal, *Williamson & Sterling, *Charles Weisenthall, *Henry Weathernton, *Henry Wineman, *Thomas Wellmore, *Henry West, *Isaiah Wagster, *William Wilks, *John Weatherburn, *Henry Wilson, *Robert Welsh, *Cyprian Wells, *James Wilson, *George Willis.

Charles Young - 3, Abraham Youngling (Yingling) - 1, Hugh Young - 1, Englehart Yeiser - 3, Henry Zeigler - 2. *Thomas Yates, *John Yingling, *Philip Yeiser.

BALTIMORE EAST HUNDRED

William Aisquith - 2, George Ackerman, see "Middlesex". *Ann Allender, widow, *Enoch Adams, *James Armstrong, *David Arnold, *William Askew, *John Allison, *Rebecca Arnold.

Robert Bazel, shoemaker - 1, Joseph Baxter - 1, Capt. John Billiard, John Bolton of Kent County, David Brown - 1, Thomas Bailey, mariner - 1, John Barney - 3, Caspar Bevant? - 1, Philip Barnethouse - 1, John Best, drayman - 1, James Brice, Esq, of Annapolis, Paul Balzer? - 1, Peter Baker - 1, John Brown - 2, Francis Bolton - 1, Michael Burn - 2. *James Brown, *George Boyer, *Llewellen Barry, *Richard Bradshaw, *Frances Brown, widow, *James Bryson, *Alice Butler, *Joseph Boone.

Cornelius Clopper - 4, Philip Cromwell, butcher - 1, James Caslin - 1, John Castleran - 1, Thomas Crosden - 1, Thomas Catchly, drayman - 1, Robert Coudon of Annapolis, Henry Clymer, baker - 1, William Clerord(?) - 1, Charles Carroll of Carrollton, John Cockey, mariner - 1, Samuel Cookson of Frederick County, Robert Constable, sailor - 1, Samuel Chase, Esq., attorney, Annapolis, Clapham & Eddes, Frederick Cole - 2, John Constable - 1, Thomas Cromwell - 5, Joseph Cromwell of Elk Ridge, William Coursey - 3. *Philip Crosius, *Chr. Carline, painter, *George Cole, *William Calvin, *William Clower, *John Chunk.

John Day - 2, John Durant - 1, George Daffen - 1; Charles Daffen of Dorset Co. (Dorchester County); Deck and Stewart, Annapolis; Daniel Dulany, Annapolis; Flora Dorsey, Anne Arundel County; Henry Deal, brickmaker - 4, Dr. Moses Darling (Dorling) - 1, John Deaver - 8, John Delkoe - 2, Robert Davidson - 3. *Job Davidson, *James Duesbury, *Francis Dawes.

Hugh Eagon, tavernkeeper - 3, Sampson Eagon - 1. *John Evans, *James Edwards.

Matthew Frenner - 1, William Finn, carpenter - 1, John Frisby, butcher - 1, Nicholas Field, Robert Finley, Hugh Ferral, Thomas Ford, Henry Fulcart, Ann Flannagan.

TAXABLES IN ST. PAUL'S PARISH, BALTIMORE COUNTY, IN 1774

William Gold, Philip Grace, William Gibson, Thomas Glebbs, John Lee Gibson, John Griffith, Benjamin Griffith, Joshua Griffith and Duval Griffith, Henry Gassaway, Edward Gaither, James Galloway. *Christopher Grizler(?).

Justice Hosier?, Jonathan Hanson, Jr., John Haffernan, Richard Hill, Robert Humphreys, William Heller, Thomas Hignutt, Joseph Hayward, John Harbley, Alexander Hannah, Francis Haller, Patrick Hamilton and John Hamilton, John Hannah, Cradle Houser, Samuel Harvey Howard, Catharine Humphrey, Benjamin Howard, Nathan Hammond. *Andrew Hawes, drayman; *Eliza Humphreys; *Sarah Hoseah?, widow; *Jesse Hollingsworth, *David Hellen (Heller), *Rebecca Haywood, *Thomas Hughes, pauper.

Capt. Jarrold, John Jones, Jonathan Jennings, William Jennings, Joseph Joyce.

Charles Augustus Keys, Doctor Patrick Kennedy, James Kelso; Keener and wife; John Keplinger. *Thomas Ketchly, *Ariana Kennedy, *James Keech.

George Leavly - 2, Peter Letzinger - 1, Adam Lukes - 1, James Long - 2, Adam Leonard, shingle drop? - 1, Frank Leeke acct. - 0, William Lloyd, distiller - 3, Moses Lecompte of the Eastern Shore; Jacob Lawrence, tailor - 1. *Cornelius Litery?, *Joseph Lowry, *John Leaver, *Peter Lick, *Nathan Lane.

Nicholas Miller - 1, William McKiver - 1, Malcolm McPherson - 1, John Manning - 1, John Mouldry - 1, Samuel Manahood - 1, Charles Miller - 1, Dennis Murphy - 1, James McGoss - 1, Richard McAllister of Frederick County; Patrick McGott, acct.; Gilbert Middleton, Annapolis; Mary Miller, acct.; David Mitchell, merchant - 1; John Moore, Kent Co.; John Morris - 1; Thomas Murphy - 1; Archibald Monereal act.; Samuel Morris - 3, Matthias Messersmith - 1. *Thomas Moore, *Richard Miller, *John Murray, *Edward McLure, *Michael Moore, *James Marshall.

Michael Neal - 1; Henry Neal, waterman, acct.; William Noon - 1. *Anthony Noble, *David Niece.

Richard Osborne - 3; Benjamin Ogle, Annapolis; Osgood, Hanburg & Co. acct.; John Omansetter - 1.

Jonathan Plowman - 4, John Philpott - 1, John Pearson, bricklayer - 1; William Paca, Annapolis; Joseph Potts - 0, Capt. John Patterson - 1, Joseph Plash - 1, Mary Philpott - 3, Henry Phillips - 1, William Poole - 1, Christian Pooly - 1. *Bryan Philpott, *Edward Paw, *Elizabeth Payne, *Susanna Pearcy.

Thomas Rusk, shoemaker - 1, George Racks - 1, Nicholas Ryland - 1, William Roe - 2, Woolsey Rice - 2, Dennis Risby - 1, Benjamin Robinson - 1; Henry Riston acct.; William Rook of Annapolis; Edward Rose of Frederick County; Samuel Roe of Queen Anne County; Thomas Ritchie, pedlar; Benjamin Rumsey, attorney; William Ryan - 2.

Francis Shoulden - 1, Michael Shriack, sailor - 1, Phillip Sitseller - 0, George Stull - 1, Frederick Shriack - 1, Jacob Sundroak(?) - 1, George Soverbine(?) - 1, Lodwick Sapple - 1, Doctor Henry Stevenson - 4, Lawrence Sullivan - 1, John Shriack - 1, William Stackhouse - 1; Upton Scott of

BALTIMORE EAST HUNDRED

Annapolis; Ignatius Simms of Frederick; John Spear of Cecil County; John Shrink (Shrunk) - 1, John Speck - 1, William Stacey - 1. *William Speck, *John Slaymaker, *John Searles, *Abraham Sedlar.

Thomas Thomkins - 1, William Thornton - 1, Francis Thomas, bricklayer - 1, William Thompson - 1; Mrs. Ann Tasker of Annapolis; Samuel Thomas of Cecil County; John Allen Thomas, St. Mary's County; James Tilghman, Annapolis; Henry Trevine(?), shipper - 1; John Taylor - 1; Geo. Vogan.

Peter Weston - 2, Peter Weaver - 1, Adam Williams - 1, John Welsh - 1, Peter Welsh - 1, Jonathan West - 2, Philip Welsh - 1, George Woniter(?) - 4, Capt. William Waters - 0, Wallace, Davidson & Johnson; John Walker, Anne Arundel Co.; Capt. Zedakiah (Zachariah?) Wythe (Wyllie?); Mrs. Rachel Warfield, Elk Ridge; Welleman (William) Wilkins, Annapolis; Thomas Wilson, attorney; Daniel Weaver - 1, John Wilkinson - 1, L. Wortemberger - 1, Thomas West - 2. *Elizabeth Webster, *William Wilson, *Hezekiah Waters, *Morris Welsh, *George Williams, *James Walker, *Thomas Ware, *Willimon Wilson.

Walter Young - 1.   *Capt. Moses Yell, *Ruth Yates, *Philip Yeiser.

DEPTFORD HUNDRED

James Anderson - 1, John Appleby, bricklayer - 1.

John Beard, barber - 1, Beaumont, wid. Capt. Henderson? - 1, Taylor Brumfield - 2, William Burke - 2, John Burke - 1, Andrew Boyle - 1, Cathamore? Bryan - 1, Henry Bride - 1, Simon Burne (Burns), carpenter - 1, Samuel Bustis, joiner - 2, Capt. Richard Button - 4. *Jane Bennet, *Margaret Brannan, *John Bennet, *John Burns, *Winnifred Brean, *Peter Booze, *William Beachan, *Dixon Brown, *Thomas Bairston, *Stephen Burns, *Henry Brown, *John Boyd, *Joseph Byers.

Alexander Cowan - 1, John Crockett - 1, Hercules Courtney, Esq. - 3, James Cameron - 1, John Coulson - 2, Joseph Crosby - 1, James Coates - 1, Capt. John Cattel - 2, Joseph Chester - 1, Richard Clark - 3. *Thomas Connolly, *James Conner, *Robert Conway, *James Collins, *Doctor John Coulter.

John Deaver - 5, Hamilton Davidson, carpenter - 5, John Dunham, mariner - 1, William Douglass - 1, Dickenson Brittingham - 16, William Davis, blockmaker - 6, Jacob Dawson, cooper - 1. *George Day, *Joseph Dunbar.

John Ewing - 1, Capt. Thomas Elliot - 5, Robert Evans, carpenter - 1, Capt. Robert Forsyth - 1, James Fisher - 2, William Farell, carpenter - 1, Hugh Ferguson - 1.

James Guy, carpenter - 1, James Gaddis - 1, Thomas Gray, tailor - 1, John Givens - 1, Isaac Grist - 1. *John Gibbons, *Abram Gorman, *Edward Gothsar(?).

Jesse Hollingsworth - 5, John Hamilton, laborer - 1, James Hooper, carpenter - 1, William Houlton, bricklayer - 3

William Hammond, shipwright - 2, Anthony Hooke, brickmaker - 7, Isaac Hall, ship carpenter - 1, Elizabeth Hubbard acct., William Hays - 4, John Hall, carpenter - 11, George Helms - 4, Patrick Hanon, carpenter - 1. *John Haymond, *Robert Henderson, *Joseph Hoge, *Mollica Hanley, *Margaret Hall, *Duley Hicks.

Micajah James - 2, Martin Judy - 2, Aquila Johns - 2, Abraham Inloes - 2, William Johnson, sailmaker - 3, George James - 1, Abraham Jackson, blockmaker - 1, William Jacobs - 3. *James(?) Johnson.

Sampson Kirk - 1, Nathaniel Kirk - 1, Edward Kains - 2, Dennis Kelly, taylor - 1. *Gabriel Kingsbury, *James Kings-bury, *Robert Kirkland, *Charles Keys.

Robert Leaves, rigger - 1, Henry Levlin, baker - 2, George Louderman - 1, Basil Lucas - 1, Charles Lovell, soldier, Robert Long - 1, John Lindsey - 1, Catharine Lowry - 1, Philip Liddick - 3, Thomas Long - 1, Alexander Leach - 3. *Adam Lindsey, *Richard Locke, *Margaret Lucas, *Henry Leigh (or G. Henry Leigh).

Alexander McMechan (see Baltimore West), Thomas Mills - 1, Joseph Morris, bricklayer - 1, Hugh Martin, carpenter - 1 Robert Mereton (Martin?) - 1, Anthony McKinley - 1, Ebenezer Mackie - 1, Mackie & Brereton - 1, Fergus Mackelroy, joiner - 1, Mary McLure acct., Malcolm McPherson - 1, Rollan McQuillan, shoemaker - 4, John Morrison, cooper - 2, James Morgan - 12. *Sarah Meeting, *John Mather, *William Morris, *George McClay, *William McClaves, *Benjamin Mason, *John Mitchell.

Samuel Neal - 1, Benjamin Nelson - 17. * William Nicholas, *Daniel O'Brian, *Edward Owings.

George Patten - 2, George Poe, carpenter - 1, Samuel Patten, carpenter - 1, John Pearce, ship carpenter - 1. *William Patterson, *Alice Peterkin, *John Pens.

Henry Reese - 1, Christian Reese, tanner - 1, Samuel Ruckman - 1, Michael Reardon - 2, Jacob Raybolt - 1, Matthew Reany - 1, John Roe, sailmaker - 1, James Rouse - 1. *William Ray, *James Rogers, *David Reese, *John Rogers, *George Reese, *George Robertson, *David Ricketts.

George Shake, ropemaker - 1, John Smith, innkeeper - 2, John Simmonds - 1, William Scarf - 1, John Smith, carpenter - 1, Stephen Sipson, pilot - 1, George Simpes (or Simper), carpenter - 1, William Scott, shipwright - 1, Samuel Scott, shipwright - 1, John Segler - 1, William Smith, shoemaker - 6, Benjamin Sheaver (Shearer), bricklayer - 1, James Stokes, shipwright - 11. *John Stack, *Doctor Small(?), *Job Smith, *Daniel Sturgis, *Philip Smith, *Ralph Story.

Alexander Taylor - 1, Handy Tull, shipwright - 1, George Treakle, sawyer - 1, Francis Tebonses(?), brickmaker - 1, William Trimble, cooper - 1. *James Tibbett, *Littleson Tyler, *Philip Thomas, *William Tinker.

John Vandevort - 3, Abraham Van Bibber - 3, Isaac Van Bibber - 5.

DEPTFORD HUNDRED

Jesse Wilson, shipwright - 1, Samuel Ware - 3, John Ware or Wate - 1, Thomas Wells - 1, John Woods - 1, Levin Wilson - 1, Richard Wooden - 1, Christian Whiskey, shoemaker - 1, George Wells - 10, Jacob Young - 1. *George Wells, Jr., *William Westley, *William Williams, *Henry Webb, *John Winning, *Peter Winkinter.

WESTMINSTER HUNDRED, 1774

William Altimus - 1, Owen Allen - 1, Robert Alexander - 5, Robert Adams' admins., Mark Alexander - 3, Mr. Alcock, schoolmaster - 1, Allburner & Place (?) - 4, William Alderman - 1, John Aldridge - 1. *Rev. Patrick Allison, *Thomas Acton, Jr., *Michael Allen, *Dorsey Altimus.

Balzer Bonsell - 1, John Bowder, tanner - 1, Owen Bryan (dead), Daniel Barnett - 2, Thomas Bell - 1, Joseph Burger - 1, William Bustard - 1, Oliver Button - 1, Thomas Bryan - 1, George Baer - 1, Miss Eleanor Buchanan - 8, Henry Brown - 1 (5 in Gunpowder U.), Andrew Buchanan - 6 (7 in U.B.R.), Caspar Balzer - 2, Anthony Burrise - 2, Archibald Buchanan - 5 (12 in U.B.R.), Buchanan & Cowan, Michael Braughbank - 1, Paul Bisho - 1, David Brown - 1, John Babens, sailor - 1. *Michael Belkey, *Mary Maglin Brackall, *Doctor John Boyd, *Andrew Boyd, *Justice Brown, *Charles Burbank. And, Henry Burkman (Buckman) - 2, Daniel Barnet, William Buchanan of George, Philip Baer, Edward Bennett, Daniel Bowley.

Robert Cummings - 2, William Calvert - 1, Dugan Cravath -5, Erhard Childe - 1, Andrew Citsleman - 2, William Collins plasterer - 3, Samuel Carson - 4, Merryman Cox - 1, John Curtis - 1, Edward Connolly, printer - 0, John Calvert - 1, Daniell Carroll - 3, James Cheston, Esq. - 4, Rev. Thomas Chase - 3, William Creal, casketmaker or basketmaker(?) - 1, James Clark, merchant - 1, James Christie - 1, George Chalmers, Esq. - 2, Peter Celestine - 1, Anthony Celestine, soldier - 1, Sixto Chameau - 1, Peter Cline - 1, Peter Crow - 1, James Caldwell, acct., John Coppersmith - 2, John Cooper, cooper - 1. *James Carson, *Doctor Samuel Cole, *Richard Carson, *Samuel Chester, *Henry Conrod, *Nathaniel Cromwell, *Cornelius Clopper, *Mary Cors, *Charles Carroll, Esq., *William Clower, *Michael Creps, *William Collins.

Lewis Dashain - 1, Patrick Matthew Decour - 2, John Dunn - 1, Michael Diffendaffer - 3, Joseph Dupeau, alias Wells - 1, Peter Dalocer(?) - 1, Joseph Durant - 1, Richard Davis - 3, Bartholomew Dyche - 1, Andrew Davidson - 3, Thomas Dew - 4, Francis Drake - 1, John Dupeau - 1, William Duncan - 1, John Dagon (?) - 2, William Deck, schoolmaster - 3, Thomas Donnelson - 1. *John Dodson, *Col. John Dorsey, *Lewis Dushield, *George Douglass, *Cumberland Dugan, *Isaac Dawson.

John Ewall - 2, Leonard Erback - 5, John Ennace - 1, James Ennace - 1, Andrew Skinner Ennals - 3, Edward Easton - 1. *John Ermine, *Thomas Eavenson, *Modest Mary E. (?) or Mary E. Modest (?).

Thomas Farley - 1, James Frasier, cooper - 2, Jonathan Fossel, drayman - 1, William Forepaugh - 1, John Flannagan - 2, Joseph Frymiller - 1. *Alexander Forsythe, *Henry Fite, *Adam Forney, *Alexander Furnival.

Samuel Goglin, carpenter - 1, John Granger - 1, Martin Garth(?) - 1, William Galvin - 1, Christian Gauge - 1, Mr. Galbreath - 1, William Goddard, printer - 4, Adam Goose - 1, William Goodeven - 1, Doctor John Henry Gilbert - 1, Job Green - 1, Johnson Gildert - 1, Gibson & Donaldson, account in Virginia, Joseph Gotrow - 1, John Gotrow - 1, Paul Gold - 1, Oliver Gold - 1, Caleb Griffin - 1, John German - 1, Daniel Grant - 6, John Gray, hatter - 3, Benjamin Gervis - 1, Andrew Graybill - 1, William Galbreath - 1. *John Gedleman, *John Grove, *James Gordon, *David Gorsuch, *Adam Gerhart, *Charles Gorsuch, *Dr. Lloyd Goodwin, *Catharine Goddard.

Veddus Hartway - 1, William Harris, blacksmith - 2, George Houke, cooper - 1, Walter Hall - 2, Jno. Helstin - 2, Francis Hostater - 1, Habakkuk Holten - 1, Cornelius Howard - 3, John Herman - 1, Jonathan Hendrickson, drayman - 1, Samuel Haslett - 1, Martin Hynes, drayman - 1, Thomas Hynst - 1, William Hannah - 8, Jacob Harryman, tanner - 2, Patrick Higgins - 1, Nicholas Hiner, carpenter - 2, Andrew Hooke, tanner - 3, William Hammond, merchant - 1. *Hannah & King, *Dr. Moses Haslett, *Gualter Hornbay, *Daniel Hart, *Leonard Helm, *Mayberry Helm, *Gerard Hopkins of Richard, *Elizabeth Hart, widow, *Conrod Hush, *Leonard Herbough, *Anthony Hook, *Peter Hoopman, *Jonathan Hudson.

George Isler, cooper - 2, Jno. Leonard Jacobie - 1, Mary James, widow - 3, Samuel Jones, taylor - 1, John Jay or Joy, drayman - 1, Lewis Juns (?), carpenter - 1, *Nicholas Judah, *William Jacobs, *Thomas Jones, black- smith, *Christopher Johnson.

Thomas Knott, dyer? - 1, William King - 1, Daniel Keaf or Keal - 1, Melchior Keener - 3, Murelock Kennedy - 1. *Christian Keener, *Michael Kephart.

William Lux - 25, Christopher Limes - 5, Thomas Lowry - 1, Joseph Lemmon - 1, Jno. Lockerman - 1, Patrick Lansdale - 1, James Lawson - 2, Jno. Lewis, shopkeeper - 2, Thomas Lynton - 2, James Lownes - 3, John Lynch - 1, Cornelius Leary - 1, Francis Lucas - 1, William Lock - 2, George Leavely, watchmaker - 1. *George Lumby, *Hester Linton, *Jno. Lushrow?, *Amos Loney, *Doctor John Labesius, *Robert Lusk, *Abram Larsh, *William Lees, *Captain Richard Lane, *Ann Lux, widow.

William Morris, carpenter - 2, Roderick McKenzie, carpenter - 1, Stephen Moore of William - 1, Thomas Morfoot, drayman - 1, James Mockerbey or Mockorboy, ship carpenter-1, Jno. J. Myers - 5, Jno. McCurdy - 1, James McConkie - 1, William Marys or Morys, staymaker? - 2, Jno. Murphy - 1, Christopher Martin of Annapolis, James McCombs - 1, Francis Manning - 1, John McClellan - 3, William McGatchen - 3, John Moale - 5 (7 in Pat. U., 8 in S. D., 4 in B. R. U.), George Morrison - 1, Jno. Merryman, Jr. - 3 (6 in M. R. U.), James McNeal - 1, Henry Minspeaker, John McGlugry?, stone cutter - 2, Daniel McFelton - 2, Jas. or Jos. Maxfield, drayman - 1, Capt. Jno. McCannon - 1, Jno. McDonagh, carpenter - 1, Samuel Mingay?, pinchman? - 1, Paul Miller, pinchman? - 1, Joseph Murray, pinchman? - 1, Matthew Miller, pinchman? - 1, Thomas Moltimore, skipper - 1, George Matthews, miller - 2, John Myers - 1. *James Manahan, *Elinor Mackabee, *Charles McConnel, *Samiel Morrison, *Elizabeth McCurdy, *William Matthews, *Barbara Myers, *Luther Martin Esq., *Jno. Meakle, *Nicholas Ruxton Moore, *Samuel Miller, *Robert Merick, *John Martin.

David Nece - 1, Edward Norwood's excr.- 0. *William Nelson, *George Niece, *Jno, Nutbrown, *Septimus Noel, *Samuel Owens of Stephen, *William Otterbine or Otterbins.

George Payne, baker - 2, Peter Placent? - 1, Joseph Polonius, bricklayer - 1, Mark Pringle - 2, John Parker, sailor - 1, Frederick Pine - 1, Thomas Pearson - 1, John Proctor, painter - 2, William Phiper - 1, Rosannah Pontenay, acct. - 0, Joseph Prowell - 1, Peter Pereau - 1, George Priestman - 3. *David Poe, A.D.Q.M.Gen., *Robert Pontius, *George Poe, *Jno, Poe, *Matthew Patton, *Michael Profry, *Peter Pearce, *Joseph Prelbotlet, *Mary Philpott, *Rachel Parkers.

Adam Rabe, cooper - 4, John Rupert - 1, Wm. Reynolds, silversmith - 1, Moses Rutter, bricklayer - 1, Joseph Rogers - 1, John Rinea - 1, Edward Read - 1, John Reck, butcher- 1, James Reynolds - 1, Richardson & Howell - 5, James Rant - 1, William Richardson, carpenter, acct., Charles Ridgely, Jr. - 3, Rhema Richards - 1, Ridgely & Nicholson, acct., William Robinson - 0, Hammond Richards - 1, Adam Rothbuck - 1, Nicholas Ridenaur - 2. *Christopher Rheem, *Jno. Rheem, *Sheriff John Ross, *Richard Ridgely, *Aubry Richardson, *George Robinson, *Chs. or Chr. Rogers, *Margaret Renns, *Philip Rogers, *James Rumsey, *George Ray.

Charles Steel - 1, Valentine Snider - 1, William Sinkler, carpenter - 1, Jacob Stephen - 1, Joseph Smith - 1, (illegible) Shanes - 1, Conrod Small or Smalt - 5, John Summers - 1, Andrew Scavong? - 1, David Stewart - 3, Doctor John Stevenson - 5 (6 in Del.), Bartholomew Stapleton - 1, Abraham Shields, overseer for R. Moale - 10, Elizabeth Smith acct., John Stuck, cooper - 1, Jacob Small, carpenter - 2, William Smith, Esq., merchant - 3, Rowland Smith, Sr. - 1, Rowland Smith, Jr., drayman - 1, John Summers - 2. *Peter Smith, *Margaret Sinclair, *James Smith, *Michael Shryock, *Matthias Sittler, *Benedict Swope, *George Salmon, *Peter Shepherd, Esq., *Sixty Shamo, *James Simpson, *George Swope, *Valentine Snyder, *Chs. or Chr. Stewart, *Jacob Summers, *Hannah Stover, *Margaret Smith, *Charles Shields.

Martin Toust? - 1, Robert Thompson - 1, William Tanner - 1, Jacob Taylor - 1. *Catherine Tare, widow, *Henry Thompson, *Samuel Thomas, *Henry Tonstill, *Adam Trompone.

Henry Vider or Victor (unclear) - 1, Thomas Vincy - 1, and Barbara Vibe or Vise (unclear).

Philip Welsh (listed twice), Nicholas Welsh - 1, John Wise - 1, John Williams, carpenter - 1, Thomas Worthington - 2, Robert Welsh - 1, Susannah Wells - 1, Simon Wheeler - 1, John Wilkins - 1, Morgan Williams - 1, Robert Willis, drayman - 1, Thomas Ward, barber - 1, Thomas Wilkins - 1, Henry Weiler - 1, Philip Watters, bricklayer - 4; account of Mary Woodward, Josias Watson, administrator; John Williams, fisherman - 6, Robert Woods - 1, Joseph White, pilot - 1, Simon Wedge - 1, Garrett Williams, drayman - 2, John Wells, bricklayer - 6, Andrew Wilson, tailor - 2, John Winchester - 1. *Robert Williams (poor), *Richard Whalen, *John Wallace, *Thomas Woolhead, *Joseph Wells, *Henry Wider, *Caspar Wart, tanner, *Charles Williams, dyer, *George Warner, *Marshall White, *William Young, *James Young, V.M.

TAXABLES IN ST. PAUL'S PARISH, BALTIMORE COUNTY, IN 1774

Benjamin All - 4, Rachel Annis - 1, Joshua Annis - 1, *George Averhart, *Jno. Asher.

Daniel Biddison - 4, Benjamin Buck - 3, Thomas Burgam (Burgain) - 3, James Buck or Burk - 1, James Boswell - 1, Dixon Brown - 4, William Bond - 1, Thomas Biddison - 3, Greenbury Bartin or Bastin - 1, James Borvins (unclear) - 1. *Buckler Bond, *Jesse Bevans, *Mary Biddison, *Thomas Bond.

William Clark - 1, James Carlisle - 1, Christopher Curry - 1, Nathan Cole, shoemaker - 1, Valentine Carback - 2 Samuel Clark - 5, Richard Carter - 3. *Thomas Carback, *John Carback, *Greenbury Coe, *Joseph Carter, *Duncan Carmichael, *Richard Cole, *William Cole, *Elioner Cabble, *William Coe.

Charles Duke - 2, Thomas Davis - 2, Richard Decks - 1, Henry Decker - 1, Walter Dolles - 1, Joseph Daughaday - 1, Robert Davis - 3, Christopher Duke - 4. *Violet Duke, *James Dahurst, *Thomas Dew.

Chloe Eaglestone - 1. *Abraham Eaglestone.

Henry Frensham - 1, Samuel Francis or Francks (unclear) - 1, William Fowler - 2, Charles Franklin - 1, William Fitz, Sr. - 2, William Fitz, Jr. - 1, Robert Fitz - 1, William Frister (see Mid. Riv. Lower). *Thomas Franklin, *Tamar Fowler, *Thomas Fitz.

Richard Gibbons - 1, William Groves - 1, Captain Job Garretson - 3, Nicholas Grimes - 2, Conduce Gatch - 2, John Gregory - 1, John Graves - 1. *James Gregory, *Vincent Green, *Thomas Graves, *Frederick Gatch, *Thomas Green.

George Harryman - 4, Aquila Hatton (see Mid.Riv.Lower), Charles Harryman - 2, Thomas Harryman - 2, Jacob Hartman - 2, Joseph Hill - 1, James Haines, shoemaker - 1, Michael Headingah - 1, Roger Haile - 1, John Howlett - 2, Solomon Hillen - 8, John Harryman - 2, Josias Harryman - 1. *Thomas Hamm, *William Harryman of George, *Ann Harryman, *Valentine Hiss, *John Harker, *Michael Hittinger, *Lawrence Hickman, *Mary Howlet, *John Hall, *Henry Hendon.

James Isaac - 1, Richard Ireland - 1, Ruth Ingram - 3. Ephraim Johnson - 1, Henry Jackson - 1, Benjamin Jerman - 1, William Johnson - 1, Joseph Johnson - 1. *Thomas Johnson, *Benjamin Johnson, *Sarah Johnson.

John Kitman - 1, Valentine Kittleman - 2. Kingsbury Works - 38.

John Long - 2, Thomas Logan - 1. Lancashire Works - 39.

John Mercer - 11, John Mattox - 3, John Murray - 2, John McCluah - 3, Peter Miles - 1, William McNutt - 2, William Peter May - 1, John McCabe - 1, Thomas Miles - 1, John Marshall - 1, David Mummy - 3, Nathaniel Martin - 12. *William Mattox, *John Minsher, *John Nitzer.

Henry Oram - 2, Charles Partlett - 1, Francis Petty - 1 Orns Petty - 1, Buckler D. Partridge - 3, John Patterson - 2 William Partlett, Sr. *William Partlett, Jr.

BACK RIVER LOWER HUNDRED, 1774

George Riely - 1, Leven Roberts - 2, George Randall - 1 William Rusk -
1. *Rachel Raven, *William Rollings, *Isaac Richards.

Benjamin Sedgwick - 1, William Stansbury, Sr. - 5, Jacob Short - 1,
Joseph Story - 1, John Stansbury - 5, Edmund Stansbury - 5, Richardson
Stansbury - 2, Philip Shields - 1, Samuel Sindell, Sr. - 3, Thomas Simms - 2,
Charles Stansbury - 4, Luke Stansbury - 4, Benjamin Sanders - 1, William
Sanderson - 1. *Joseph Stansbury, *Dickenson Jno. Stansbury, *Benjamin
Stansbury, *Aquila Stinchcome, *Thomas Stansbury, Sr., *Dixon Stansbury,
*Samuel Sindel, Jr., *William Stansbury, *Nathan Shepherd, *Tobias Stansbury,
*Isaac Stansbury.

James Taylor - 2, Joseph Turner - 1, Francis Turner - 1, Richard Taylor
- 2, Samuel Taylor - 1, Joseph Taylor - 15. *John Taylor, *Moses Thompson.

Edward Wigley - 3, Henry Wise - 1, William Warrington - 1, Henry
Warrington - 1, Brown Webb - 1, John Weston - 1, Luke White - 2. *Edward
Wigley, Jr., *Allison Edward Watts or Edward Allison Watts, *John White, Jr.

MIDDLESEX HUNDRED (SO FAR AS IN ST. PAUL'S IN 1774)

George Akerman - 2, Paul Adams - 1, Jacob Andrews - 1, George Ackerhead
- 2, Michael Armstrong. *James Armstrong, *Christian Allen.

James Barclay - 1, Humphrys Brooks ("belongs below in Dr. W's list") -
1, Moses Baney (Barney?)- 1, William Butler - 4, Isaac Brown - 1, Thomas
Beach - 1, Thomas Boon - 7, Andrew Bonnet - 1, Tector Berger - 2, John Bell -
1, Richard Bell - 1, Benjamin Barney - 1. *Frances Bloomer, *Richard Bond,
*Philip Braum, *Mary Brooks, *Sarah Boon, *John Boone, *Thomas Buckingham,
*Frederick Baymer.

Charles Carroll, Esq. - 26, Salathiel Cole (see B.R.U.), Henry Carter -
1, Michael Crainer - 4, Jacob Cromwell, over- seer for Charles R.; Richard
Cromwell - 5, Richard Croxall - 3. *Conrad Cumber, *Andrew Carring(?).

Richard Davis - 1, Robert Dew - 5, William Davis - 1, John Demitt - 1.
*Rachel Demitt.

William Fleming - 4, Robert Fright - 3, James Franklin - 30 (14 in
G.P.U.).

John Grimes - 1, Pleasant Goodwin - 5, Michael Gardiner - 1, John
Gardiner - 1.

Elis Hosler - 1, Edward How, miller - 4, Thomas Holland - 1, Matthias
Hooks - 1, William Hoppum - 2, Mayberry Helm - 6, Leonard Helm - 1, Mayberry
Helm, Jr. - 1, Stephen Haile - 1, Jacob Hewell - 5, Jacob Hooke - 2, Rudolph
Hooke - 5, Edward Hanson - 6. *Christopher Henry, *Christopher Hartman,
*Jacob Hooke, Jr.

Richard Jeffries- 1, Thomas Johnson- 6. *Meade Jarvis, *Michael Kraner,
*Jacob Kerns.

BACK RIVER LOWER HUNDRED, 1774

Edward Lowry, tailor - 2, David Linn - 1, Alexander Lawson - 8, Benjamin
Longley - 1, Jacob Leaf - 1. *George Lux, *Christopher Little, *Jno. Arnold
Loush.

Robert McKim - 2, Robert McGrew - 2, William Miller - 1, Jacob Myers -
5, Michael Moore - 1, Joseph McGrew - 1, William Murphy - 1, Joseph
McAllister - 1, Samuel Merryman, Sr. - 4, John Meals - 1. *Mary Moore,
*Robert McAllister, *Charles Meriken, Christopher Nice - 2, Samuel Oram - 1.

Edward Puntany - 1, William Pullen - 1, Henry Penny - 1, Richard Parken
- 4, John and Joseph Pearce - 2, Robert P. Parish - 1, Amon Price - 2, John
Pluck - 1, Absalom Price - 5. *Jacob Peters.

Thomas Rite - 1, William Richardson - 1, Mary Rutter - 3, Thomas Rutter
- 5, Robert Ricks - 1, Henry Reston - 1, John Reat - 1, Anthony Rutter - 2,
Charles Ridgely of John - 9, Henry Rutter - 4.

Joseph Smith - 1, John Smith - 1, Thomas Shadwick - 1, Joseph Stoakes -
1, Jacob Semanus - 1, Nicholas Smith - 1, John Smith - 1, John Spicer - 3.
*Michael Steitz, *John Stevenson.

John Taylor - 1, Philip Thatcher - 1, Frederick Teams - 1, Ezekiel
Towson - 2. *Henry Vite, *Henry Vite, Jr.

Jacob Warren - 1, Edward Ware - 1, Stephen Wooden - 1, John Wooden - 3,
Solomon Wooden - 1, James Welsh - 3. *Jonathan Webb, *Michael Wolf,
*Christian Weltshom, *Jacob Welsh.

Thomas Yarum - 1, John Young - 1, Jacob Young, Sr. - 5, Jacob Young, Jr.
- 1.

PATAPSCO UPPER HUNDRED IN 1774

Richard Acton - 3. *Andrew Appenheimer.

John Bradding - 1, Matthias Britchtell - 1, Moses Black - 2, Joseph
Burgess - 1, James Butler, joiner - 1, James Brady - 1, Joseph Browning - 1,
James Barton - 1, Matthew Boys or Boyd - 1, Elam Baker - 1, Joseph Burgess,
acct. - 0, Ezekiel Basil - 1, Luke Brown - 2, John Bailey - 7, Sarah Bailey -
1, David Black - 1, Chs. Barton - 1, Nicholas Baker - 1, Benjamin Banniker -
1, William Black - 1, Baltimore Furnace - 76. *John Burns, *Isaac
Blatchford, *Jacob Black, *Capt. Elam Baily, *Clement Brooke, *Andrew Barnet,
*Ephraim Bailey, *Matthias Berkley, *Elizabeth Black, *John Belson, *Josephus
Bailey, *Richard Brass, *Catharine Barton, *Joshua Black.

William Creswell - 1, Joseph Cunningham - 1, Bank Cole - 1, John
Cornelius - 2, Joseph Cornelius - 1, William Cornelius - 1, Thomas Clarke -
1, Samuel Cooper - 1, Joshua Carey - 1, Charles Croxall - 12, James Croxall -
1, Jno. Connoway - 2, Daniel Carroll, merchant (see Westminster H.), Henry
Crooks - 2, Oliver Cromwell - 5. *John Coale, *Thomas Curtis, *George
Cimmerman, *James Cromwell, *John Cromwell, *Edward Cook.

Thomas Down - 1, Hezekiah Dean - 1, William Dignen - 1, John Dollenson - 1, Dorsey's Forge - 25, Daniel Dulany, Esq. (Hunting Ridge) - 6, William Delworth - 1. *Edward Dorsey.

George English - 1, Robert English - 1, Joseph Evans - 1, John Ellicott - 7. *Andrew Ellicott, *Jonathan Ellicott.

William Flood - 1. *Andrew Fite, *J. Howard Ford, *John Ford, Sr.

John Grundy - 5, Jacob Greer, Sr. - 2, Thomas Griffith - 2. *Thomas Goldsmith, *Richard Gibbs, *Thomas Greenwood, *John Gardiner.

Lawrence Henly - 1, Andrew Hoppenheimer - 2, Abraham Henderson - 1, William Ham - 1, Jonathan Hibbs - 1, Timothy Hunter - 1, Isaac Henry - 1, Henry Hissey - 2, Charles Hissey - 1, Valentine Husk - 3. *Francis Hardesty.

William Jarvis - 1, Shadrach Jackson - 1, Meshach Jackson (no number given). *William Jessup, *Martin Judy.

John Kennedy - 1, Samuel Kensey - 1. *Jacob Kearns, *George Kerr.

Charles Lewis - 1, Nicholas Lewis - 1, Samuel Lett - 1, Thomas Lloyd - 8, Morris Lane - 1, Edward Lewis - 1, Henry Lewis - 1, George Lighthiser - 1, Andrew Lineberger - 2. *Robert Long, *Samuel Long, *John Lewis, *Ann and Clement Lloyd.

John Man - 2, John Moale (unclear) - 7, John Miller - 1, John Murray - 1, Samuel Moreton - 2, William Matthias - 1, James Murphy - 1, Greenbury Moreton - 1, Edward Morris - 2, Joseph Miller - 1, Zachariah McCubbin - 10, Henry Mock - 1. *William Miller, *David Morgan, *William Miller, *William Mowrik (unclear).

Patrick Nowland - 1, Mary Norwood - 3, Samuel Norwood - 10. *Edward Norwood, *John Night.

John O'Bryan - 1; Asenath Owings, acct.; Elizabeth Owings - 1, Henry Owings ("taken before") - 2, Meshack Owings - 5, Caleb Owings - 3, John Oram - 2. *Zacheus Onion, *Joshua Owings of John.

William Payne - 1, Joseph Partridge - 2, John Penn (taken before ... illegible...), Nathan Penn - 1, John Penn, Sr. - 2, Charles Pierpoint - 2. *Richard Patton, *Samuel Penn.

John Read - 2, John Ryan - 1, Joseph Robinson - 1, Henry Runnicks (unclear) - 1, John Ross - 5, James Rowe - 1, Charles Ridgely of William - 10, George Read - 1, Thomas Robinson - 1, Robert Rix - 1, Michael Richards - 1, Roger Robinson - 1, John Read - 1. *George and Beale Randolph.

George Simmerman - 2, John Shekell - 5, Aquilla Stinchcomb - 1, Adam Smith, ship carpenter - 1, Charles Stomper - 1, John Sank - 1, Robert Steward - 1, John S----, (illegible) - 2, Godlip Sheromelter (unclear) - 1, *John Stinchcomb, Sr., *McLane Stinchcomb.

PATAPSCO UPPER HUNDRED IN 1774

Taylor's bank - 27, John Teal - 1, Emanuel Teal - 2, Edward Teal - 3, George Teal - 5. *Thomas Evans, *Taylor and Thornton, *William Tidy, *George T-----, (illegible). *Abram Vandegrift.

Richard Whitman - 1, William Wood - 1, Benjamin Wells, Jr. - 3, William Weston, Jr. - 1, James Winkpold - 1, William Williams - 3, Elisha White - 2, William Wright - 1, George Wharton - 1, Jno. Wilson - 1, John White - 1, Jacob Wilderman - 2, Abram Walker - 2. *Philip Walker, *John Wells, *Mary Williams, *Richard Walls, *Captain Charles Wells, *Walter Young, *John Young.

PATAPSCO LOWER HUNDRED IN 1774

Joshua Arnold - 1, Nicholas Ammice - 1, William Armstrong - 1, Samuel Arrowsmith - 1, Peter Arnold - 1.

Jno. Blanshield or Blunshield - 1, Jno. Baker - 1, Absalom Bowen - 1, Samuel Bowen - 1, Edmund Baxter - 1, Richard Burke - 1, Robert Brown - 14, Ferdinand Battee - 4, Josias Bowen - 4, James Bryant - 3, Rachel Brock - 1, Edward Bowen - 1. *Martin Bullear, *John Bowen, *Sarah Bowen.

James Cunningham - 1, Thomas Chapman - 1, William Chapman - 1, William Cockan - 1, Thomas Coldskill - 2, Duncan Carmichael - 2, Thomas Colegate - 2, John Clarke - 1, George Childs - 1. *John Chappel, *Thomas Cole.

Ann Davis - 1, Richard Dicks - 1, Daniel Davis - 1, Christian Davis - 2. *Samuel Dunn, *Henry Diehl.

(Illegible) Eaglestone - 2, William Edwards - 1, Job Evans, Sr. - 1, Job Evans, Jr. (dead), Abraham Eaglestone - 5, Daniel Evans - 2, Jonathan Eagleston - 1, Abraham Ensor - 7. *Dinah Eaglestone, *Eliza Edwards, *Abraham Enloes.

Michael Fowler - 1, Lloyd Ford, Sr. - 1, Lloyd Ford, Jr. - 1. *John Foreman, *Zechariah Fowler.

Aquila Gorsuch - 1, Lynch Gray - 1, Zechariah Gray - 1, James Grimes - 2, John German - 1, Mary Green - 1, Vincent Green - 2, James Grimes - 1, John George - 1, John Grimes - 1, Ephraim Gray - 1, David Gorsuch - 7, John Gorsuch - 2, Charles Gorsuch - 2, Solomon Green - 1, Moses Green - 1, Josias Green - 1, Thomas Gatch - 5. *Benjamin Griffith.

John Haile - 1, Joel Higginbotham - 1, Fetter Hisey - 1, Samuel Hardesty - 1, William Holmes - 1, Jonathan Hanson, Sr. - 6. *Margaret Hurner, *William Howard, *Amon Hanson.

William Joyce - 1, Thomas Jones - 10. Joseph Keys - 1, Capt. Thomas Kells - 1, Darby Kelly - 1.

Nathan Linnix - 1, Christopher Lowry - 1, Darby Lux - 2 (B.R.U.), Edmund Logan - 1, Wiliam Lynch - 1, Richardson Linnix (dead), William Lynch - 9, John Leach, blacksmith - 1, Roebuck Lynch - 9, Patrick Lynch - 1, Miles Love - 3.

Dennis McCarty - 1, Avarilla Merryman - 6, George Moore - 1, James McKelley - 1, Paston Monk - 1, Joseph Merryman - 2, James Madewell - 4, William McCubbin - 6, Moses McCubbin - 8, James McKinley - 1. *William Moody, *Luke Merryman, *Samuel Merryman, *Joseph Merryman, *Alexander Madewell.

John Neale - 1, Arthur Neale - 1, Nicholas Norwood - 6. John Oram (dead) - 1, John Oak - 1, Gabriel Oysten - 1, Charles Orrick - 2, Lawrence Oyston - 3, John Oyston - 1. *Margaret Orrick.

Ann Partridge - 5, Anthony Pringle - 1, Nathan Perigo - 2, John Perigo - 2, William Partridge - 2. *George Parker, *John Partrel, *John Pearce, *Josiah Pennington.

Thomas Rooke - 1, James Rodgers, shipwright - 1, Richard Rowles - 1, Charles Rogers - 6, Benjamin Rogers - 2 (at his quarters), Capt, Charles Ridgely - 13, John Ready - 1. *Joseph Rutter, *Joseph Right.

Robert Sweeting - 1, Nathan Shaw - 1, John Addison Smith - 9, Richard King Stevenson - 2, John Stevenson - 5, Hithe Sollers - 5, William Slater - 1, John Sargeant - 1, Edmund Smith - 1, Joseph Stansbury - 1, Darby Sullivan - 1, Samuel Smith - 2, Thomas Knight Smith Shaw - 3, Edward Sweeting - 5, Richard Sprigg - 11, Thomas Shaw - 3, Daniel Stansbury - 3, John Smith - 1, Sater Stevenson - 3, Sabrit Sollers - 12, Thomas Sollers - 9, Joseph Sollers - 2, Tobias Stansbury - 4, Jacob Snydell - 3, Richard Stansbury - 2, Philip Sindall - 1, George Stansbury - 3. *Doctor Henry Stevenson, *Rachel Stevenson, *John Stevenson, *Mordecai Stevenson, *Abraham Shiels, *Job Smith.

Charles Taylor - 3, Cornelius Trimble - 1, Luke Trotten - 9, Rebecca Talbot - 1, Lancelott Todd, Sr. - 1, Lancelott Todd, Jr. - 1, William Thackham - 1, Thomas Todd - 10, William Thornton - 1, Thomas Todd, carpenter - 1. *John Toon, *Benjamin Talbott, *Susanna Trotten, *Francis Turner.

Lewis Wise - 1, Robinson Wood - 1, Mary Worthington - 7, William Wilkinson - 9, Joseph Wells - 1, Edward Watts - 1, David Walker - 2, John Wheeler - 2, Michael Woolfe - 1, William Wallace - 1, Peter Woolrich - 1, John White - 1, Elijah West - 2, William Withe - 1, John Watts - 1, John Woodward - 4, Philip Woolrich - 1, Sarah Watts - 3. *Eliza Wise, *Aberilla Wheeler, *Brown Webb, *James Woodward.

RECAPITULATION OF TAXABLES:

Baltimore West...	666	Back River Lower.	323
Baltimore East...	221	Middlesex........	279
Deptford........	256	Patapsco Upper ..	404
Westminster......	466	Patapsco Lower ..	410

Total: 3,025

APPENDIX

The following lists were not included in "Inhabitants of Baltimore County, 1692-1763," published by FAMILY LINE PUBLICATIONS in 1987:

SPESUTIE HUNDRED RESIDENTS AS OF 1693

"This list is taken from a map which shows the Spesutia Hundred as of 1693. The listing of names with dates are those who were residents within the present boundary of that portion of Harford County which is now Aberdeen Proving Ground. While the list is not complete, it does give a fair account of who the early settlers were." Harford was part of Baltimore County until 1773. (Source: The 1953 Harford County Directory, page 7)

Spesutie Island
  Nathanuel Utie, 1658
Bush River Neck
  Sam. Goldsmith, 1658
  Jno. Collett, 1658
  Abe Holdman, 1659
  Thomas Sampson, 1659
  Jno. Rigby, 1659
  -----Shocken, 1662
  John Collier, 1662-1663
  Thomas Overton, 1660-1662-1663
  -----Collier, 1665

  Oliver Shea, 1668
  Miles Gibson, 1671
  John Digger, 1672
  Jos. James, 1672-1673
  William Palmer, 1673
  Joseph Philips, 1673
  Jno. Cook, 1678
  Col. Geo. Wells, 1678
  Rev. Jno. Yeo, 1681
  -----Barry, 1683
  Geo, Utie, 1687

ASSOCIATION ADDRESS OF 1696

This is an account in 1696 "of the persons in Maryland who signed the association address to His Sacred Majesty upon the news of the horrible conspiracy against His Royall Person. Signed by the Justices, Grand Jury and Clerk of the Provincial Court and by the Military and Civil Officers of the several counties." (Source: 1953 Harford County Directory, page 29)

Signed by these Baltimore County military officers:

Col. John Thomas
LtCol. Thomas Richardson
Capt. John Oldton
Capt. Charles Merriman
Major James Maxwell
Capt. John Ferry
Capt. John Hall
Capt. Thomas Preston
Ensign Richardson Thompson

Lt. William Levyson
Lt. Roger Mathews
Ensign Daniel Scott
Ensign Daniel Parmer
Lt. Saml. Sycklemon
Lt. Thomas Roberts
Capt. Thomas Hammond
Lt. William Slade
Ensign James Jackson

ASSOCIATION ADDRESS OF 1696

Signed by these Civil Officers and Magistrates:

John Thomas
Mark Richardson
Thomas Richardson
John Hall
James Phillips
Richard Adams
Thomas Hedjo
James Maxwell
Francis Robertson
Israell Skelton
Nieha. Simons
Ionas Bowen
John Hayes
Thomas Brooke
Thomas Roberts

Josiah Bridge
Seallah Dorman
Gene Samson
Francis Smith
John Boone
Francis Whithead
Joseph Peake
William Wilkinson
Luke Raven
William Barker
James Todd
John Harryman
Thomas Grenfield
Nathl. Anderson
Robuck Lynch

PETITION IN 1746

"We, the Subscribers Inhabitants of Baltimore County and Town, and many of Us Members of a Club kept in said Town, having understood that an Information hath been made to this Government, that Mr. James Richards, high Sheriff of Our said County, and a Member of Our Club, hath spoken Words reflecting on his present Majesty King George his Person and Government. We therefore in Justice to the Character of the said James Richards do certify that He at all times and on all Occasions, when in Our Company, expressed the Greatest Loyalty and Zeal for his present Majesty and the happy Establishment both in Church and State, and frequently declared his utter Abhorrence of the present unnatural Rebellion; and always was One of the most Active and forward in expressing his Joy, on making any Conquest or gaining any Victory over the French, the Pretender, or any of his Majestys Enemies, and particularly distinguished himself on the Days We celebrated the taking Capt Breton, The Victory obtained over the Rebells at Culloden, under his Royal Highness the Duke, and on his Majesty's late Birthday. And further We believe the said Information to be malicious, spiteful and without Foundation."
(Source: _Archives of Maryland_, Vol. XXVIII, page 375)

Darby Lux	William Fell	Nicholas Rogers	T. Sheredine
William Hammond	Thomas Franklyn	William Bond	Henry Morgan
George Buchanan	Thomas Sligh	T. Stansbury	William Titfin
Richard Croxall	Edward Tulley	William Dallam	Sab: Sollers
Walter Tolley	Thomas Cradock	Thomas Gough	Alexander Lawson
James Slemaker	Charles Ridgely	William Payne	William Lyon
Edward Dogan	William Rogers	Thomas Harrison	James Walker
Lyde Goodwin	Robert North		

RESIDENTS OF BALTIMORE IN 1752

"The following list of families, and others persons residing in the town of Baltimore, was taken in the year 1752, by a lady of respectability, who was well acquainted with the place at the time, and is believed to be correct." (Source: Maryland Historical Society Library, Filing Case A)

The article (typed and unsigned) was apparently prepared by a member of the Lyon family because it states, in part, that "my grandfather was Dr. William Lyon, and he emigrated to this country about the year 1751 or 1752; my grandfather, Robert Lyon, was born in the year 1754."

It goes on to say that the Governor and Council lived east of Jones Falls on Jones Street, the General Assembly sat in William Rogers house (Innkeeper), the first child (a female) was born in Baltimore Town in 1741, the number of persons in the Town of Baltimore in 1756 was supposed not to exeed 300, and John Eager Howard was born 4th June 1752.

The list of Baltimore families in 1752 were:

Captain Lucas	Mr. Pain
William Rogers	Christopher Carnan
Nicholas Rogers	Mrs. Hughes (midwife)
Dr. William Lyon	Charles Constable
Thomas Harrison	Mr. Fergueson
Alexander Lawson	Mr. Goldsmith
Bryan Philpot	John Moore
Nicholas Ruxton Gay	Mr. Sheppard (tailor)
James Caray (innkeeper)	Bill Adams (barber)
Parson Chase	George Stieback (drove a
Jacob Keeports (carpenter)	single team--only wagon)
Conrad Smith	Captain Dunlap
John Crosly (carpenter)	Philip Littig & his wife
Robert Lance (cooper)	(was a German midwife)
Kilt Stranwick (laborer)	John Ward
Mr. Gwinn	Nancy Low

PETITION IN 1761

The following is a petition circa May 6, 1761, from the Freemen of Maryland to Governor Horatio Sharpe and the Upper and Lower Houses of the Assembly, in which they are against the proposed bill "to prevent the making or repairing of any fish dams & pots on the River Susquehannah;" it is contrary to the natural rights of the fisherman; they suggest other means of preserving the young fish. They appear to be the residents of that part of Baltimore County which today is Harford and Cecil Counties, along the Susquehanna River. (Source: Calendar of Maryland State Papers, No. 1, The Black Books, p. 165; also see Maryland Archives, Vol. LVI, p. 432)

John Litten	Robert Conn
Richard Wells, Jr.	Samuel Fulton
Stephen Fisher	Richard Gay
Joseph Morgan	Thomas Love
Joseph Husband	Willm. Ewing

PETITION IN 1761

Thomas Andrews
Charles Orrick
John Laughlin
John Worthington
Joseph Hopkins, Jr.
John Neeper
William Neeper
Stephen Jay
Edward Lewis, Jr.
Thomas Husband
E. Andrews
Nathan Rigbie, Jr.
Aquila Hall
William Wells
Samuel Morgan
Francis Downing
Jonathan West
Richard Wells, Jr.
John Stepelton
Joseph Morgan
Fred. Fullton
John Smith
John Ewing

John Waller
William Husband, Jr.
William Ewing
Samuel Gillespie
Robert Gillespie
Elihu Haller
Robert Walter
Charles Worthington, Jr.
Joseph Hopkins, Sr.
Joseph Neeper
James Neeper
Joseph Hayward
Ephraim Gover
William Collins
Gerrard Hopkins, Jr.
William Cox
Leven Mathews
Nathan Horton
Edward Morgan
James Lee
John Short
John Ross

INDEX

INDEX

145

INDEX

161

Other books by the author:

Made in the USA
Las Vegas, NV
11 November 2021